# INDOMITABLE

## Advance Praise for *Indomitable*

Arundhati Bhattacharya was the first woman to head India's largest bank, the State Bank of India. *Indomitable* is the engrossing story of her journey from modest beginnings, the challenges she faced, especially as a woman, and her grit and inventiveness in overcoming them. This book is about more than a CEO's management lessons or a banker's war stories, though it has those, of course, all recounted with self-deprecating humour. It is also importantly about how women can, and will, succeed in modern India.

**Dr Raghuram G. Rajan, former governor,**
**Reserve Bank of India**

'Arundhati is ... one who is unstoppable,' told her mother in her childhood, pointing at a star in the sky. Living up to the name, Mrs Arundhati Bhattacharya has carved a life path as impressive as it can be interesting. 'Indomitable' aptly defines her spirit in this gripping narrative, sprinkled with humour, that vividly picturizes a fulfilling journey.

The reader will bump into sober advice like 'Books are our best friends' from her mother or the experience during induction at SBI that remained valid for a lifetime or her husband's wise counsel in times of distress. The intricately woven account of her tenure at SBI in all its vicissitudes – not to forget the challenges impeccably handled during demonetization – makes it an inimitable read. Needless to say that through her impactful work, Mrs. Arundhati Bhattacharya is bound to inspire a generation of women to scale greater heights in their professional pursuits.

**Dr Devi Shetty, chairman, Narayana Health**

*Indomitable* is one of the 'unputdownable' reads of recent times. It is a remarkable story of a great professional who has risen to lead one of the largest banks in the World. But that doesn't do justice to the narrative, woven lattice-like with a rare feel for words. I think, in becoming a career banker, Arundhati has denied us a great fiction writer. *Indomitable* raises non-fiction to the level of fine storytelling that we expect from some of the great names in contemporary Indo-Anglican writing. In this book, she is unreserved, sometimes vulnerable and comes across as an authentic human being and a professional par excellence. And along the way, very reassuring to all those people who believe ordinary people can achieve extraordinary things. This book is not one little girl's journey to the pinnacle of success. It is many-layered. It presents a country in the making in post-Nehruvian India at a social level. It will inspire many people across the spectrum. I hope she will write more in the years to come.

**Subroto Bagchi, co-founder, Mindtree**

*Indomitable* shares the incredible journey of one of the world's most remarkable business leaders. Her life is a story of courage, determination and resilience that will inspire and empower others to follow in her trailblazing footsteps.

**Marc Benioff, chair and CEO, Salesforce**

Arundhati Bhattacharya has earned her credentials as one of the most respected bankers in modern India. This autobiography is a testimony to her indomitable conviction that has broken societal and gender barriers to [help her] rise through the ranks and head the largest bank in the country. Her legacy is her bold and transformational modernization of banking practices driven by her strong belief in a digital future to usher in universal and inclusive banking. It is an inspiring read for young people to pursue their ambition with purpose and perseverance.

**Kiran Mazumder-Shaw, chairperson, Biocon**

Arundhati remains one of the most charismatic leaders I have met. She wanted to and succeeded in being a banker to every Indian. By the very force of her personality, we know what she has done to make diversity much more a part of SBI than it ever was before. This book serves as a fascinating journey of one who will and can achieve.

**Zia Mody, managing partner, Azb & Partners**

# INDOMITABLE

## A WORKING WOMAN'S NOTES ON LIFE, WORK AND LEADERSHIP

ARUNDHATI BHATTACHARYA

HARPER
BUSINESS
*An Imprint of* HarperCollins *Publishers*

First published in India by Harper Business 2022
An imprint of HarperCollins *Publishers*
4th Floor, Tower A, Building No. 10, Phase II, DLF Cyber City,
Gurugram, Haryana – 122002
www.harpercollins.co.in

2 4 6 8 10 9 7 5 3 1



P-ISBN: 978-93-5489-450-3
E-ISBN: 978-93-5489-454-1



Cover design: HarperCollins *Publishers* India
Front cover photo/Back cover photo: Sanjay Borade

Typeset in 11.5/15.4 Bell MT
Manipal Technologies Limited, Manipal

Printed and bound at
Thomson Press (India) Ltd

HarperCollinsIn

This book is produced from independently certified FSC® paper to ensure responsible forest management.

*To my husband Pritimoy and daughter Sukrita, for their constant encouragement and support; my parents Prodyut and Kalyani, for allowing me to bloom; and to all the millions of young Indians who hail from the small towns and villages of India, with stars in their eyes, hope in their hearts and the grit, determination and belief that they can excel and contribute to building this nation.*

# Contents


| | | |
|---|---|---|
| | *Foreword* | xi |
| | *Preface* | xv |
| 1 | Bhilai: The Best Time of My Life | 1 |
| 2 | Bokaro: Growing Up Pangs | 36 |
| 3 | Kolkata: The Feeling of Independence | 56 |
| 4 | SBI: The Journey Begins | 76 |
| 5 | Kharagpur: Of Friendships and Finding a Partner | 98 |
| 6 | When Challenges Lead to Opportunities | 131 |
| 7 | New York: Discovering a New World | 144 |
| 8 | Walking the Tightrope: Achieving Work–Life Balance | 170 |
| 9 | Bengaluru: The Return of Harmony | 196 |
| 10 | The Eighteenth Floor | 218 |
| 11 | *Sabka Saath*: The Key is Collaboration | 225 |
| 12 | The Future Is Digital | 236 |

13 Risks and Rewards 245

14 The Banker to Every Indian 268

15 Employees First: Managing a Diverse Workforce 284

16 Leading a Banking Behemoth 304

*Acknowledgements* 317

*About the Author* 319

# Foreword

September 2021: It was a rainy, three-day weekend. I got a call from the usual effervescent Arundhati, requesting me if I would be inclined to read her book and write the foreword. Before I had even made up my mind, her unedited manuscript was in my inbox. As I began to scroll my iPad, I soon realized I just wanted to keep reading more.

I cannot claim to have known Arundhati for years. I first met her in 2013 when she was heading SBI Capital Markets, a subsidiary of the State Bank of India (SBI). I had been asked to chair a committee set up by the Central Electricity Regulatory Commission, and Arundhati was the lone member. Over the many years of my working life, I have met several people from the banking and financial cadre. I instinctively knew Arundhati was a cut above the rest.

As a public person, Arundhati made her mark in history as the first woman to lead SBI. Yet, those who followed her story more closely will always remember her for graciously embracing her title as 'chairman', as the SBI Act could not legally permit the change to chairperson. Admirably, the title never frazzled her. She knew she had to get on with the task, tackling challenge after challenge that confronted her as she helmed the country's largest bank.

As an SBI lifer, she remained driven by a simple mantra which was to leave the bank better and stronger than when she joined it. And clearly, she did. Much credit goes to her for the bank's changes in human resource management, effecting the mega-merger of six banks into SBI in record time, driving the financial inclusion agenda and spearheading the bank's digital transformation amongst several other milestones.

This book is an endearing read with a narrative of her personal life interspersed with her work life. She is brutally honest with work–life struggles, but it never weighs her down. She steers away from aspiring to be a 'superwoman', nor does she wallow in guilt for being away from home when work demands it. To her credit, she seized every opportunity to help other colleagues facing similar issues.

Few know that she was instrumental in getting the Indian banking system to shift to having two Saturdays off in a month rather than a six-day working week. Drawing from her own experience, she knew how exhausted she used to be each Monday morning at work, especially in her early days of motherhood. I am sure generations in the Indian banking sector will remain grateful to Arundhati, perhaps silently chanting, *Thank God it's Saturday*! Thanks to Arundhati's efforts, SBI now allows a two-year sabbatical, initially intended only for women but later extended to all single male employees. Her 'people-first' leadership trait has always held her in good stead.

For career women, Arundhati is iconic. She reasons that the advantage of female leaders is 'their ability to be less territorial and far more collaborative'. The only instance where Arundhati humourously admitted to asserting herself on gender issues was on behalf of women in the boardroom. She believed, for far too long, women in saris froze in the boardrooms as the air-conditioning temperature was always suited for men wearing coats and ties. So off went the coats of her male board members, allowing the 'chairman' to carry on with business without freezing in the boardroom!

Besides being revered for her competence, she attributes her success to a simple plan – get the right people, in the right place, obtain their buy-in, empower them and back them up to take courageous calls with the right intent. She demonstrates that the qualifications for the top job do not come from the degree one holds but from dogged determination, keeping the learning curve steep, carrying people along with one's successes and reaching out for help when needed.

Few can imagine this powerful lady struggled initially to balance ledgers or count cash correctly. She acknowledges the opportunity of standing on the shoulders of giants – from her mentors and supportive colleagues to her family and friends who always rallied around her whenever she needed it (which was more often than not). In equal measure, she shares multiple instances of tackling roadblocks and naysayers at work.

While frequent transfers are par for the course for SBI officials, she amusingly reveals the unwritten law of SBI, which is that one always gets transferred the moment one discovers a good tailor for sari blouses and a good hairdresser! Yet, with each transfer that strengthened her career path, she remained sensitive to the disruptions it caused the family and the strains of recreating support systems in new locations.

Staying grounded whilst in a position of power is always a tricky test of character. That is why family and friends are so important. Her anchor remains her spouse. One does recall her self-deprecating comment of excitedly telling her husband that she and the Queen of England were on the list of the most powerful women in the world, only to have her husband text back saying the Queen would be on that list for life, while she would be off it as soon as she retired! Ultimately, no accolade or award matches up to her true joy of milestones achieved by her daughter, who has learning disabilities. For the ever-humble Arundhati, she knows life's true triumphs.

She leaves the reader with a thought-provoking conclusion. Work is transitory, family and friends are not, and the balance must be found. As for Arundhati, she continues to live up to the meaning of her name – one who is unstoppable.

*Indomitable* is one of the best memoirs I have ever read, though Arundhati is already trailblazing in a new avatar as chairperson and CEO of Salesforce, India.

**Deepak Parekh**
Chairman – Housing Development
Finance Corporation

# Preface

'You're always reading! Isn't it time you started writing?' My mother's remonstration still rings in my ears as though I heard it just yesterday. Well, Ma, the time seems to have finally arrived, and I hope you enjoy this book (wherever you are) as much as I have enjoyed writing it.

However, it almost felt as though the book wrote itself.

I belong to that generation that went from the single Doordarshan channel to the hundreds we now get on television – not to mention YouTube and streaming platforms like Netflix. We went from walking to school, our bags loaded with books, to learning from home on iPads; from train rides that left us exhilarated – if grimy from the coal dust streaming behind the engine – to pest-infected, air-conditioned coaches to state-of-the-art bullet trains.

In this book, by tracing my journey, I attempt to record the growth of India as seen through my eyes – from an innocent child to a callow teenager to being a woman in the country's banking sector.

When I started my career forty-five years ago, opportunities were limited – more so for women. One needed connections, as well as sheer grit and determination to land a job. There were barriers erected within and outside the home. Society was far less forgiving back then. The choice of careers for women too was very limited.

While the women of my generation dared to set out to chart a course and tread untrodden paths, we must also acknowledge that we needed help from a lot of people at work, at home, and from friends and acquaintances. Without the generosity of my support system, I for one would not have progressed as far as I did. They are the ones who helped me cross the many hurdles I faced and they enabled all the highs in my career in myriad ways.

Through it all, I have enjoyed every bit of my journey in the State Bank of India and hope you will too through this book. If I can bring back the stars in one pair of despairing eyes, a smile on one tired face or rekindle a fire to challenge and conquer in one heart, I will consider the time I put in writing it well spent. Remember, as Audrey Hepburn said, 'Nothing is impossible, the word itself says "I'm possible!"'

# 1

# Bhilai: The Best Time of My Life

'I may never have been born at all!'

Every time I say this, my husband, Pritimoy, looks at me as though I am being melodramatic.

But no, I am not being overly dramatic here. To understand why I say this, one needs to travel back to the time of my birth.

I am the youngest of three siblings – I was born after my elder sister and brother. My father, an electrical engineer, was a very upright man with a great sense of humour. But he was also of a very sensitive temperament.

My parents got married the year India gained her independence. It was an unlikely match. My father was a Brahmin, my mother a Kayastha. She was a college friend of my father's younger sister. The fact that they had a 'love' marriage back then was only because both of them had lost their parents early – so they had no guardians who could stop them from being together.

Both of them came from families who could trace their lineage back over a hundred years. My grandfather's grandfather was Jagadananda Mukerjee, a leading figure in Bengali society in the mid-1800s. He is best remembered for an incident that caused him to go into self-exile. The Prince of Wales – later King Edward VII – during his visit to India in 1875, had expressed interest in visiting a Bengali babu's residence. Jagadananda's house in Bokul Bagan, in south Kolkata (it was earlier known as Calcutta, but the name was officially changed in 1996), was famed for its grandeur, for its décor consisting of Belgian mirrors and chandeliers, as well as the crystal balustrades along the stairs. He volunteered to host the prince. However, Bengali society erupted in indignation, not because he had invited the prince home, but because he had the temerity to introduce the womenfolk of the household to the visiting royal. The outrage was such that when his friend, the Maharajah of Bettiah, now in Bihar's Champaran district, invited him to come and stay with him, he left the city, never to return. I, however, credit him with having contributed to women's equality as there were very few in Bengal in those days who would have done what he did.

The famed house in Bokul Bagan was eventually sold to the family of C.K. Sen, one of the first entrepreneurs in Bengal, and incidentally the ancestor of one of my closest friends and ex-colleague, Manjira. With her help, I visited the house, which still exists, to check out the family lore. Yes, I saw the famed drawing room where the prince was received. The room was still adorned with the Belgian mirrors and the crystal balustrades still exist, as does the palm print of the prince taken on the walls of a room. The walls of the room were decorated with beautiful flowers, painted using ground semi-precious stones, which had been left untouched all these years.

My mother's family, on the other hand, belonged to the Dutt family of Ram Bagan – a noted locality in north Kolkata. Her grandfather was the younger brother of Romesh Chandra Dutt, one of the first Indian Civil Service (ICS) officers from India and the first Indian to be appointed as District Magistrate. He retired early from the service, and is remembered as an economic historian, and for his translations of the Ramayana and the Mahabharata. Another scion of my mother's family was the poetess Toru Dutt, who also wrote in French and whose works are still read in France. My mother's grandfather passed his law exams in England and, on his return to India, was given an assignment in Kashmir. Unfortunately, on the way to his posting he fell sick and passed away. Family legend has it that he was poisoned, though I prefer to think that it was probably cholera, which was quite prevalent in those days.

My father – after obtaining his engineering degree from Jadavpur University in 1942 – took up employment as the state engineer of Bettiah where his family had migrated. My sister was born two years after my parents' marriage. She was a cosseted first child, and had her very own nanny as well as a pony! My brother was born three years later, but my family's luck took a downturn around this time.

My brother was born with a deformity of his foot but doctors reassured my parents that with early treatment it could be corrected.

Just about then, my father was superseded at his workplace by a junior, who, my father felt, was far inferior in his abilities. In a huff, he gave up his job without really taking into consideration his young family and the looming cost of my brother's treatment.

The next two years were a period of real hardship for my family. My parents gave up their quarters in Bettiah and migrated to Kolkata. My father had no relatives to help him in times of difficulty. In fact, as the eldest son, he was expected to fulfil his dead father's obligations when it came to his three married sisters – such as sending their in-laws gifts during festivals and various other occasions.

My mother had an elder brother and a younger sister, both unmarried. Her brother had a job in a printing press and it paid him just enough to cover his needs – but not beyond. Her younger sister was a school teacher, and was putting herself through college.

Money was scarce and so were jobs. One of my mother's school friends magnanimously took us in and allowed my family to stay in the ground floor of her house at a nominal rent.

My brother's treatment had to start soon. The family Morris car – a prized possession of my father's – had to be sold to cover the costs, which he never got over. It added one more layer of sorrow to his sensitive soul. His mother had passed away when he was just twelve years old, and it was something that affected him deeply. He considered it a betrayal of the highest order, an abandonment that he could never rationalize, and it created a core of sadness within him that we could feel during his vulnerable moments.

Family lore has it that my grandmother died during the childbirth of her sixth child. My grandfather apparently blamed himself for her passing and took to alcohol to escape his misery. Seven years later, he too died of complications arising out of some ordinary illness.

Anyway, to return to my story, while my father looked for a job, my mother took my brother to the orthopaedist to get his foot treated. The treatment in those days consisted of anaesthetizing the child, twisting the foot a few millimetres in the right direction and then plastering it. Obviously, as the anaesthesia wore off the child would find himself in immense pain. For almost a week after the procedure, my brother would cry every waking moment of the day. Neighbours started calling my mother a witch – for torturing her young son so. But she stuck to her guns. Her brother and sister took turns carrying him through the night to provide him some degree of comfort. My aunt, ten years my mother's junior, became extraordinarily attached to the doe-eyed, curly haired, roly-poly boy, though she herself was a waif of a woman and my brother was by no means easy to carry.

He was indeed a lovely child. He weighed five kilos when he was born – one of the doctor's believed that the womb carrying him was too small, and therefore, he developed the deformity of his foot. My mother's life revolved around him, but then she suddenly felt the stirring of new life within her.

It was totally unplanned. They could hardly afford another child. When she told my father, his world stopped for a moment. Another mouth to feed was unthinkable.

Probably as a result, a few weeks later my father asked my mother to accompany him for a check-up.

Trusting him, she got into a rickshaw. But when the rickshaw stopped in front of a ramshackle building, she took one look and understood why she had been brought there. She simply refused to get out of the rickshaw. My father pleaded, but she would have none of it. So he got back in again, and asked the rickshaw to take them home.

On their way back, my mother told my father that she firmly believed that the newborn would come with its own destiny. If he or she was meant to grow up in poverty, so be it. But she would be the last person to stand in its way, and he must have faith that all things happen for a reason.

And so I was born. A scrawny little child. My father's younger sister (the one whom my mother had studied with) took one look at me and told my father that she had no doubt that bad times were his lot.

My father, however, fell utterly in love with the thin little baby. He probably felt a twinge of guilt for having considered an option that would have prevented my entry into the world. As long as he lived, he loved me the most. He came to believe that I was a reincarnation of his dead mother, and called me Majononi (mother) for the rest of his life. Indeed, my siblings were miffed that he loved me so unabashedly and was always my greatest support.

The next three months were extremely difficult for my family. My mother fell grievously ill – the tensions of my brother's treatment and childbirth proved too much for her.

My mother's friend, who had rented out the house to us, took over as my caregiver. Coincidentally, her husband and son both served as clerks in the bank of which one day I would become chairman. Even in my earliest hours, the bank contributed to my upkeep. I was allowed to visit my mother once a day. Maybe I never got over the lack of motherly contact in my earliest days. Till I grew up, whenever I was upset or unable to sleep, I would get into her bed, and snuggle up to her. She always used satin quilts or the softest sheets to cover herself. It was one of her few indulgences. She couldn't stand rough cloth against her skin (a trait that both my daughter, Sukrita, and I have inherited). As I wormed under her quilt, the satiny-velvet softness coupled with the heat of her body spread a warm glow of security around me and my eyes would automatically close.

Three months after my birth, our luck turned a corner. My father landed a decent job through the Union Public Service Commission, as an engineer in one of the 'temples of modern India' – a steel plant under the Steel Authority of India Ltd, being built with Russian collaboration. He left for his work place at Bhilai, and a few months later – my mother having recovered by then – we joined him in what was to be our home for the next ten years.

The next few years, as far as memory serves, were quite idyllic. The township of Bhilai was getting constructed alongside the steel plant. Facilities back then were few and far between. For the first year or so, even items of daily consumption such as eggs had to be bought from the weekly haat – impromptu markets where locals brought their produce – or from the nearest town of Raipur, about 80 kms away. The place was a flat wasteland, covered by red gravel, indicating the presence of iron ore in the ground. Even trees were scant.

The township grew rapidly. Our streets were initially mud tracks – but soon, there were mounds of sand stacked on both sides as the road-building operations picked up pace. The mounds of sand were our favourite play areas – sliding down their sides, scrounging around in them for shells. A favourite game of ours was to collect these shells or pebbles polished smooth by the waters of whichever river the sand came from and then see who had the most at the end of the day. Hectic bartering for the shells was the order of the day, as we exchanged duplicates to collect ones we didn't have. But soon, the giant road-carpeting machines arrived, and over the week the mud roads turned into black metalled ones and our favourite play spots disappeared.

Most of the families in the vicinity were young. For many of the engineers, this was their first job. My parents were among the older ones. Most of our neighbours had children our age. The Roys lived opposite us. They had a son, Manas, who was my brother's age, and a daughter, Rupa, a year younger to me. My best friend was Smita. She was exactly my age and lived one house down from ours. The other two in our friend group were Ashok, again my brother's age, and Ranju, a year younger. They lived on the next street. The seven of us were really close and, oh, what grand times we had!

Manas was the naughtiest of the lot, and though I was a timid soul, I often followed his lead in his various escapades. We decided one day while playing doctor that we needed to give a blood transfusion to the one rag doll that I owned. 'Mini, your mother's rouge box! Quick, go fetch that and a cup of water. We will soon have blood to save this doll.'

My mother used no makeup other than face powder. But on her spotless dressing table was a little golden box. When you flicked it open, there was a rose-pink disc of rouge in it and a tiny mirror on the lid. It was something I loved looking at. Mother had told me that it was a gift from my father from before they got married. She never used it, but it held pride of place on her dressing table.

I dashed inside to pick it up, and soon we had a beautiful pink-coloured liquid, which we struggled to fill in the plastic syringe of our playset. By the time my mother discovered our misdeed, her rouge was all but gone. What I remember clearly though was the pain in her eyes when she realized what we had done. She seemed to be at the point of losing her cool and then I could almost see her shaking herself inside. *They are kids,* I am sure she thought, *and I don't use this stuff anyway.*

'Both of you have been very bad children,' she said instead, 'but I won't punish you. However, because you took something without asking, you won't get your share of the coconut laddoos I just made. I hope you will remember to ask the next time.' She walked off, but left me feeling really small. I somehow knew that I had destroyed something for her forever and it was not a nice feeling.

Manas too was feeling guilty. Plus, he was worried about how his father would react if he got to know what we did. He was punished often for horsing around, but that never dampened his enthusiasm. He liked being locked in the bathroom as a punishment, he explained, because he could draw on the mirror with toothpaste, or see how high a mountain of bubbles he could make with the bath soap. When he was about ten years old, he broke his leg while jumping off the top of the slide in a park. When his cast was cut open, he was so excited that as soon as he came out of the doctor's chamber he let out a whoop and jumped in the air. But as luck would have it, there was a puddle of water on the floor, and as he landed he slipped and fell, breaking his other leg! He is the only person I know who went to get a cast removed and retuned with a new one on another limb. His sister Rupa, on the other hand, was a quiet child, and the only sad memories I have of our times in Bhilai pertain to her.

I suffered benign neglect at home, for much of my mother's time was taken up managing the house and organizing the other women in the township for undertaking social work at nearby villages. She was also an avid gardener, but more on that later. The menfolk had no time for housework, nor were they expected to do any. In fact, it was customary to wait on them hand and foot once they returned from work. Sometimes, they would not return home for seventy-two hours at a stretch, as the gigantic structures of the steel mill took shape and there was continuous casting that required constant supervision.

On top of handling all the housework, my mother also had to care for my brother. His foot had straightened, but he was yet to walk properly. His leg needed massaging and he had to be coaxed to walk. Amidst all this, I ran wild with my friends. There were no playschools back then – we all gathered outside after breakfast till our mothers called us in for lunch. Afternoons were hot and we were required to stay indoors. During summer, the floors of the house would be covered with thick wet sheets, which we would remove in the afternoon, so that we could sleep on the cool floors. The windows would be covered with mats made from a sweet-smelling grass called khus. Water would be piped on to the mats, and the dry, hot winds blowing on them would evaporate the water and cool the rooms within. My favourite game was to sneak out of the house with a fistful of tamarind pickle and sit beneath the grass mats, where the water dripped to the ground. There I would dig a shallow hole and watch it fill up to become my 'pond'. I would then float tiny leaves in the water and pretend they were fish.

For the menfolk, summer was a trying time, given the temperatures in Bhilai and the fact that most of them had to supervise activities at the open construction site. My father would leave for office around 9 a.m. He would return for lunch at 1.30 p.m. He would carefully hang up his work clothes, have lunch and then lie down for a quick twenty-minute nap, before leaving for office again. I remember when I was two or three, I would pretend to make Horlicks for him, and he would have to pretend to drink the same before I let him sleep. But he never grumbled, no matter how tired he was. In fact, he used to joke that I had to look after him as I had been irresponsible enough to have abandoned him early in my last birth!

But I digress. When he would leave for office in the afternoon, he would tie a thick, wet towel around his face and neck so that only his eyes showed. Mother would give him a tall glass of cold water from the earthen pitcher and an onion to carry in his pocket. It seems the onion prevented heatstroke.

On summer nights we would sleep on charpoys outside the house. It was a great ritual with all the cots getting laid out in a row. Mattresses, sheets and pillows had to be lugged out and then spread out to cool as they would be warm from the day's heat. Table fans would be placed strategically to provide some breeze should the wind falter. As I lay on the cots and stared at the night sky twinkling overhead, a sense of wonder would overwhelm me. On clear days I could even make out the hazy swathe of the Milky Way.

'There, look up. Can you see those seven stars shaped like a kite with a tail? That is the Great Bear. In India we call this constellation Saptarishi, after the seven famous sages,' my father would point out. 'Look at the second star in the tail. Can you see a star faintly twinkling next to it?' I would nod, even though I had no idea where he wanted me to look. 'Well, that is Arundhati, the wife of Vashistha, and your namesake. She was also a great sage.'

This was how I found out more about my name. As I screwed up my eyes and peered harder to make out the tiny dot of light that I was named after in the never-ending darkness of the sky, it felt as though the stars had begun moving and I felt like a speck hurtling through space. The vastness of the heavens overwhelmed me. This feeling of wonder is something that infuses my very being even today.

What called me back to reality that night was my mother speaking. 'Mini, just as you have been named after a great sage, you must also know what your name means. The word 'arundhati' comes from the Sanskrit root 'rundh'- which means to stop or obstruct. So, A-rundhati is one who cannot be stopped or one who is unstoppable. Remember that whenever obstacles come your way.' I have not forgotten, Ma. Though I sometimes joke that during my years in New York I spent at least a quarter of my time spelling out my name. But I would not change it for the world.

My mother was an avid gardener. But the soil in our yard was hard and unyielding. She coaxed my father to allow her to hire a labourer for a few days. His name was Bhageloo, and he became an expert gardener under my mother's tutelage. First, the front yard was marked out in rectangles with a circle in the centre. Then, bricks were laid to mark out the borders of the flower beds. Bhageloo dug out the soil of the beds about three-feet-deep. The soil was then mixed with sand and manure in equal proportions, and left to air for a few weeks. Thereafter, the soil was sieved and put back into the beds. The garden that grew became a sight for sore eyes. It taught me at an early age that one can turn wasteland into islands of beauty, but one needed to address the origin of the problem and there was no alternative to hard work.

I can still picture the garden in winter in my mind, covered in a riot of colours. The central flower bed would be filled with delicate red poppies, their heavy heads drooping as they danced lazily in the breeze. The outer border would be lined with yellow calendula, their flat green leaves forming a beautiful counterpoint to the striking yellow of the flowers nestled in between. Then there were beds of yellow and violet pansies – I especially loved these, as the black markings on each flower made me feel like I was looking at a sea of tiny faces. The stalks of the blue larkspur were interspersed by the vivid red salvia. And the road leading to the door from the gate was bordered on both sides with delicate white bunches of candy tops, outlined by the multicoloured hues of phlox. Besides the flowers, there were fruit trees planted behind our house. We had three prolific guava trees, quite a few papaya and banana plants and a custard apple tree. My mother tried desperately to raise grape vines, but they only yielded the tiniest and the sourest grapes I have ever tasted. But she had a never-say-die attitude, and there were times when she raised beautiful ears of corn bursting with juicy kernels or even onions and peanuts. The pride of place was a mango tree raised from a seed planted by my sister. When the sapling sprouted, wiser voices, including my father's, had counselled that she uproot it and throw it away. Trees from seeds rarely bore fruit was what the experienced voices told her.

My mother, however, continued to nurture it with the help of my sister, and by the time the tree was four years old it had started yielding fruit. It was a short tree and the fruit-laden bows had to be propped up so they wouldn't droop. Year after year, it repaid my mother and sister for their care and belief that it was a sapling worth protecting. Fifty years later, when I visited my childhood home, I was amazed to discover the mango tree still standing, and I learnt it fruited prolifically. The mangoes were as I remembered them, hanging low on the branches, and as I pulled one close to my cheek to have a picture taken, it almost felt like my mother's caress.

Every year my mother won several prizes for her garden; the high point was when she received a prize from Premier Nikita Khrushchev when he visited Bhilai for its formal inauguration (the town was built with Russian collaboration). When she grew much older, I would sometimes catch her looking at the black-and-white photograph of the event and know that she was reliving that glorious day.

There was a pair of hibiscus trees that grew luxuriantly just beside the front gate. The leaves were dark green and the flowers blood red. As summer peaked, we looked out each day for the dark monsoon clouds on the horizon. Soon, the wind picked up and black clouds rolled, the dark-green leaves of the hibiscus and its striking red flowers swaying crazily against the thunder grey of the oncoming storm. The temperature would suddenly drop and the next moment fat drops of water would hit the parched land. One could hear the hiss of the water as the dry land greedily sucked up the moisture, our nostrils assailed with the mesmerizing smell of the rain falling on the dry dusty earth.

The smell of the first showers still transport me instantly to those days of my childhood. A long time later, when I was working in Uttar Pradesh, I discovered that attar manufacturers sold an attar which bottled the smell of moist earth. I bought it, and sometimes I would open the bottle, sniff it and be transported back to my childhood. Even today, it remains my favourite fragrance and has a place far above any French perfume.

As the monsoons gathered speed, all of us neighbourhood children would rush out and dance wildly in the rain. Our mothers made half-hearted attempts to herd us back inside and then they too joined in the fun. It rained heavily, almost as though the heavens had opened up, and soon, the nullahs on either side of the road were filled with water. We often went to the junction where the water emptied into a bigger nullah. The day after the rains, there was knee-high water in these nullahs, and we splashed around in them with empty Horlicks bottles, trying to capture the tiny tadpoles and fish that magically appeared from God knows where!

Winter in Bhilai too brought in its share of fun activities. Early in the morning, we were expected to lug a small bucket of water outside and leave it in the sun to be warmed. There were no geysers or immersion heaters back then in the township, and the sun-warmed water was our best bet for a quick bath. There was one other way to beat the cold. We would leave a small bowl of mustard oil to warm in the sun. Before we went in to bathe, Ma would massage us with the oil. I especially liked the massage she gave. No spa has ever been able to replicate that fantastic back rub with sun-warmed mustard oil. Coconut oil too would turn solid inside its green tin. That needed to be set out in the sun if we wanted to oil our hair, which we were required to do. Winter was also when we got to roast seekh kebabs over an open charcoal-filled pit in the garden. Many years later, when I was staying in Lucknow, I would frequent a restaurant that smelt exactly like those kebabs cooked over an open pit, immediately taking me back to my Bhilai home.

All was well in this little world of ours, but illness of any kind was a massive challenge. We still had no full-fledged hospital in the vicinity. Once in a while, the sirens of the plant would start blaring, and women and children across the township would freeze. The sirens indicated a major accident – and there were quite a few back then – and no one knew whose life had just got snuffed out or who was to struggle for days between life and death in their journey to recovery.

Every time I heard the siren, I would rush to the garden gate. I would climb on to the lowest rung of the gate, and swing back and forth awaiting the arrival of my father's Jeep. The familiar toot of the horn just before it turned the corner of our road put me out of my misery for the day.

My mother believed that self-help was the only way one could alleviate the troubles that came our way. Because of the paucity of medical care, she took to using homeopathy. Her father was a homeopath, but his early demise had prevented her learning much from him. Still, she clearly remembered how grateful the people he helped were. So, she began using homeopathy to treat us at home when we got colds, coughs or stomach upsets.

Rupa – Manas's sister – fell sick. She had a low-grade fever regularly, and she began coming out to play less and less. She was taken to the local health centre and, after some fruitless attempts, doctors suggested she be taken to Kolkata, the closest metro. Rupa's mother often came to our house to get my mother's advice. Her husband had applied for leave, but it had not yet been sanctioned. The whole neighbourhood was on tenterhooks at that time.

Then, one day, she came home to tell us that the leave had been granted and they were to leave for Kolkata in two days. We all heaved a sigh of relief. But fate had other plans. That very afternoon, we all saw our mothers frantically running in and out of Rupa's house. By the evening, Rupa had passed away. She breathed her last on my mother's lap.

My mother was distraught for days. She refused to come to bed with us and I could see the light on in the house till very late at night. One day, I gathered the courage and crept out of bed to see what was happening. It was 2 a.m. My mother was sitting at the dining table, surrounded by her homeopathy books, making notes. On seeing me, she looked up and called me over. As I tried to clamber on to her lap (I was getting too big for that by then) she said, 'You know what happened to Rupa, don't you?'

I nodded miserably. 'She's gone forever, isn't she? Roy auntie told me she has gone away forever and we can never play with her again.

It's really not fair and I miss her! Why couldn't you make her better, as you do for us?'

For a moment, I could feel her breath on my hair.

'That's exactly the reason I am studying so hard,' she said then. 'I didn't know enough to make out what was wrong with her. She had tuberculosis and I couldn't recognize it. I didn't try hard enough. But I won't let that happen again. Remember, books are our best friends. They have within them many answers, but we must seek them out. Make them your best friends and you will never be disappointed. I want to become a certified homeopath so that I can help all of you ... And now, off to bed. I will go to bed shortly.'

With that, she gave me a gentle push towards the bedroom and as I walked away, I knew that she was already lost in her books and had forgotten about sleep totally.

My mother did go on to become a homeopathic doctor, and a very good one at that. Through my school years, I took allopathic medicines only once – when I had paratyphoid (diagnosed by her) – and went to hospital only once – to set a broken collarbone.

I learnt a valuable lesson that day from her – it's easy to give in to helplessness. But it is so much better to stand and fight. She had also told me the truth about books. They have remained my best friends – in good times and bad, never once failing to get me through whatever situation I was faced with.

Indian parents, especially in my generation, rarely displayed affection. My parents were no exception, but through their little gestures we understood how deep their bond was. My mother's given name was Gauri. In those days, after marriage, women were expected to change their first names and take their spouse's last name. My mother took the name 'Kalyani', but I never heard my father call her that ever. For him, she was Rani – the queen. In fact, their friend circle used to tease them about it and called my father Raja. And, in turn, my parents' closest friends – the Boses – came to be called Nawab and Begum.

My father liked to have two fried eggs with two slices of toast every morning. He would cut up the eggs into little pieces, liberally douse them with salt and freshly ground pepper, and ladle it on to the toast. To me, it looked like the most desirable delicacy. The children got eggs once in a while – but mostly our breakfast was a glass of milk and two slices of toast with guava jelly made at home by my mother from the guavas we grew in the garden. In fact, I got so sick and tired of guavas, guava jelly and guava jam that I gave up eating all three as soon as I left home, and it was only in my late fifties that I started having them again.

To return to my father – every morning, he would eat one slice of bread with an egg and leave the other one for my mother. She never sat down with us for breakfast and my father, quite correctly, surmised that she mostly skipped breakfast or had the end slices of the loaf that none of us wanted – most probably with the guava jelly. This was my father's way of making sure she ate something nutritious in the morning. But that slice of bread was terribly tempting. Though I never remember having asked for it, my mother understood how much I wanted it and she would quietly pass it on to me. And I was more than happy to gobble it up. Looking back, I now realize the sacrifices she made for her kids.

When food was concerned, my mother had one other strange practice. She always cooked for one extra person each day. This meant that on most days she ate the previous day's leftovers. Father remonstrated against this practice often, but she would turn a deaf ear. I once asked her the reason. 'Mini, what will we do if we get a sudden guest at lunchtime? If I don't make a little extra, one of us will have to go without food that day. Vasudhaiva Kutumbakam,' she explained. 'The world is your family. You must treat every guest as though they are your own people and look after them well.' I understood what she meant. Nobody ever came to our house and left without being fed, and given the fact that in those days one cooked on earthen fireplaces, she would never have been able to extend that hospitality if she didn't have a little extra food on hand.

Around this time, my parents decided to send my elder sister to Kolkata. She was four years my senior, but was almost a mother figure to me. Because of my brother's health issues, which kept my mother occupied right from my birth, my sister had been the one to take care of me. As I was a very thin child, she carried me around on her hip, and I turned to her often for things like tying my shoe laces and finding my clothes. Bhilai at that time had only a rudimentary Hindi-medium school. My mother decided that she would be better off in an well-established Bengali-medium high school in Kolkata and so a reputed school with a hostel was chosen for her.

It was probably one of the biggest mistakes my mother ever made. My sister felt convinced that she wasn't loved or wanted by our parents any more and, hence, she was being banished. I found her crying secretly into her pillow at night. My heart ached, but I was too young to understand fully what was going on or know how to prevent it. Soon, my sister left for her school hostel in Kolkata and my aunt had promised to oversee her stay.

I too joined school shortly after. There was a mandatory written test for entry to class one, where we were expected to know the English and Hindi alphabets and numerals from 1 to 100. I remember I struggled with the letter 'झ' in Hindi and had to erase so many times that the answer sheet tore. Horrified by what I had done, I started crying uncontrollably, and the teachers had a hard time consoling me. I envisaged a life of staying at home and not making any new friends at school for not knowing how to write one letter. I turned in a torn answer paper, soggy with tears and snot.

However, I need not have worried. The steel plant had a policy of only having schools run by the project. And every child – be it the child of a sweeper or the managing director (MD) – was required to attend the same school. It was a really good practice – a leveller of sorts – though I do remember the son of a particular MD, who was in our class, being a bit of a bully, empowered no doubt by his father's position.

Our school was co-educational and, in those days, some amount of corporal punishment was accepted. My first brush came within the first week of school, when Smita and I were made to stand outside our classroom (the 'room' was actually in a verandah of the school and 'outside the classroom' meant standing beyond the columns!), because we had not brought our maths books as our fathers had not yet had the time to go pick them up. I sometimes wonder whether my love/hate relationship with numbers began at that time.

When summer vacation came around that year, we were ecstatic. After the kind of unbridled freedom we had enjoyed for the first five years of our lives, school was a regimentation we all disliked, if not actively hated. The vacation came with its share of homework, though. I remember one such piece of homework vividly. We were required to complete one page of cursive handwriting every day. Whoever was the teacher who set this task had little idea how much of a burden this could be when the child realized three days before school reopened that she had not yet started!

Of course, I was that child who remembered my pending homework at the very last minute. In desperation, I turned to my mother. 'There are still three days left. So if you do twenty pages a day, you should be able to finish,' she reasoned. That was no help at all! Twenty pages in a day – that was impossible. I wondered how my friends were managing. They were in the same straits as me, but everyone was tight-lipped about their predicament. I longed for my sister. Had she been there, she would have surely helped me out. In the end, I started myself. But twenty pages was really no joke. I kept at it till it was bedtime. But I was still not nearly done. My mother arranged for a small table and a stool next to her bed, as I was unwilling to work in the study room alone. My father consoled me by saying that he would stay awake no matter how long it took but soon, I could hear his gentle snore.

The stillness of the night magnified all the sounds – a dog barking somewhere, a scratching noise, maybe a mouse, the far off vroom of a motorcycle. My ears seemed to have grown longer and bigger, picking up every tiny noise.

Suddenly, I heard a creaking sound close at hand. I got up and crept to my father, and pulled up his eyelids to check whether he was asleep. No one could possibly sleep after such torture. Neither could he. But, over the next two days, he got quite adept; whenever I pulled up his eyelids, he would reassure me in a groggy voice that he was very much awake. But I did complete my sixty pages of handwriting with no help at all. The signals given were clear – your work is to be done by you and no one else so you better get used to it.

I was a rather sickly child. I had been so since birth, and I was also prone to breathing distress, diagnosed in those days as childhood bronchitis. There were no inhalers back then, and when the attacks came on I had to sit leaning forward with a pillow on my lap, and I had to do this for two or three days until the wheezing eased. My mother's homeopathy helped, but her hand on my brow, massaging my back helped more. As a result of this sickness, I was irregular at school. Maybe stress too brought on the attacks. I came tenth in the class that year, but was upset that I hadn't done better.

But class two was a real challenge. First of all, we had a teacher who frightened the life out of me. Actually, she never even punished me, but for the naughty ones she had some real nasty punishments. One was putting a pencil between the child's fingers, and squeezing and rolling them – and oh boy! Did that hurt. The other was pinching the offending child's cheeks with her long red-painted nails. We also had, at the same time, a burly boy in our class named Simon, whose sole joy in life was to pick on the weaker kids. I remember him running after me with the scissors we carried for our craft lessons. He would threaten to cut me up with one of them, and though I knew that was impossible, its pointed ends and sharp blades still made it a fearful weapon. My wheezing attacks became more frequent and I ended the year with a rank of twenty-six out of thirty-two students. I felt devastated looking at the result, more so when I saw my father's sorrowful face. I could never ever disappoint him, and it grieved me enormously that I had done so.

Class three started in much the same manner. But I knew I needed to do something to lessen the tremendous weight I felt every morning while walking to school. School was about three kilometres away, and children from the same neighbourhood walked to and back from the school together. Except for summer (schools were closed in peak summer), when we would arrive sweaty and dusty, walking to school during the rest of the seasons was actually fun. Especially the rainy season – we jumped into every puddle we could find. We lost umbrellas regularly (as also sweaters in the winter and water bottles year round) and so often had to go without them. All that was great fun, but the moment I entered class my heart would sink.

After a few weeks of this, I resolved to do something about it. I asked my father to request a change of section. I knew all my friends in section B would consider it a betrayal. I knew my class teacher would be aggrieved as well. I also knew making friends in section A would be tough – by then they all had their special friends, having studied together for the last two years. But still I thought it worth a try.

My parents backed me up. It was a strange request for the school, because they hadn't been presented with anything like this until then. But after some internal deliberations, they agreed to give it a try.

And so it was that I transferred to section A and lost the fealty of Smita, my first best friend, though outside the school our friendship continued. All that I had anticipated about making new friends at school came true. Simon stopped scaring me and, in fact, looked at me with something akin to respect for having escaped his clutches!

Strangely, he also became quite friendly. One day, while standing in line at the assembly, I got a nosebleed. I kept wiping my nose on my dark-blue skirt as there was nothing else at hand. But every time

I lowered my head, more blood flowed out. The children around me looked the other way, probably horrified at what was happening. The news was whispered down the line. When it reached Simon, he took one look at me and rushed to the teachers standing at the head of the line to inform them. I was whisked away to the school infirmary, where I lay with my head thrown back and an ice pack on my forehead, while a worried Simon hovered nearby till the nurse shooed him away. 'I told teacher quickly so that nobody would think I had punched you in the face,' he said when we caught up later, but I could feel that he was a little embarrassed for having displayed a softer side, which otherwise I may have never seen. Did I have the ability to bring out the best in people? If that is the case, I am grateful for this gift.

By now, as a family, we were able to afford small luxuries. For instance, I remember, when I was in class two, we bought a refrigerator. It was a lovely white, shining box with rounded top corners. It had pride of place in the covered veranda, which we called our dining room. But there was little money to waste. Each of us siblings wore hand-me-downs – especially shoes and sweaters. However, the only things I refused to accept second-hand were my brother's school books. By this time, he had joined regular school and was just two years ahead of me. Most of his books would be the ones I too would need in a couple of years. But he was never good at keeping his books neatly. The brown-paper covers would come off in about a month's time. There would be scribbles and lunch stains and ink blotches. Sometimes, pages would be torn. I told my father that I could accept hand-me-downs of clothes and shoes, but not books. My mother railed at the waste of money. But my father stood firm: 'She will have a new set of books; it is her right!' And so it came to be that I got to bury my nose in a spanking-new set of books every year. How I loved the heady smell of new books! It remains one of my favourite smells to date. But, most of all, it made me feel as prized and precious as my brother. My parents', and specially my father's, insistence on treating my sister and me in the same manner as my brother laid the foundations for the confidence that seemed a natural part of me as I grew up. In hindsight, I now understand how important that was.

Every alternate year, we went to Kolkata for our summer break. It was a big event, akin to the manoeuvring of a large regiment of troops. We had to take the train from Durg, where Bombay Mail stopped for a princely two minutes. Within that time, we had to board along with the trunks that contained our clothes, the holdalls that held our bedding, the many bags and baskets of food, and a wooden frame on which was fixed an earthen long-necked pitcher filled with drinking water. All of these were essentials.

But what a grand adventure it was. Kolkata was about twenty-four hours away by train. So a whole day's provisions had to be taken along. There were stacks of *luchi* (puris made with white flour) and a dry dish of potatoes to have it with. Then there were boiled eggs that would be delicately shelled before being cut lengthwise into four, and sprinkled with salt and fresh-ground pepper. For the evening, there were braised mutton cutlets on the bone (I learnt this recipe from my mother, and still make it well). There were also 'chops' with a filling of fish mixed with fried onions, ginger-garlic paste and raisins, covered with a layer of mashed potatoes and bread crumbs and then deep fried. Pickles and bananas were not allowed as they were considered bad omens for a journey. But bananas could be bought on the train. There were biscuits and little savoury treats called 'nimki', made of flour, cut in diamond shapes and deep-fried in ghee for the in-between times when one felt peckish, and we were permanently peckish on the train. Then, of course, there was the earthen pitcher that had to be refilled with drinking water at ever major station where the train would halt for more than five minutes. I was mortally scared that my father would get left behind whenever he stepped off, either for water or to buy something. I would press my nose to the train window and the tension would mount as the minutes slipped by. Once in a while, he was not back even as the train started off with a jerk. But then he would appear, swaying with the train, holding on to the pot of water for dear life.

Of course, great fights would erupt between my brother and me if we had access to only one window seat. But normally, as there were four of us, we would have two. However, when I was little, there was no separate berth for me. At night, the trunks were pulled out from under the seat and placed in the space between the berths to serve as my bed. The holdalls would be opened and the beds made. We carried thin cotton mattresses, as the seats were not cushioned in those days. Then crisp white sheets were spread out on top and another to use as a coverlet. Pillows were pulled out and, lo and behold, we had a bed that was fit for a king.

We usually stayed at my aunt and uncle's place in Kolkata, and my sister would come from her hostel and join us. Both my uncle and aunt were unmarried, and would remain so for life. My uncle liked to tell us stories. One of them was about a pair of birds who lived in a hole in the ground. A flat stone that they pulled to cover the hole served as their door. They would emerge from the ground the day we reached, and every day they would have an adventure. The day we left, they would return to their burrow and pull the stone in place after them and await our return.

Every evening, my uncle took us for a stroll to a swimming club nearby. He had been a champion swimmer in his youth and had a box full of medals with which we often played. The place had a large pool with diving boards at both ends. Around it was a walking track, with benches and a grass verge. I loved the smell of water and watched in awe as people gracefully dove off the boards. But the biggest attraction was the *phuchka* – a spherical pastry made of dough that is punctured on top and stuffed with a mixture of mashed potato and gram, and then dipped in a vessel of tamarind water. With each phuchka we got a small taste of heaven. I think in those days we could get three for a *naya* paise. The paisa was still new back then, hence, the term. We would gorge on phuchkas until we couldn't eat another. With no parents around to stop us, we could eat as much as we wanted. The next stop on the way home was the *churan wallah.* He used to sell balls of tamarind and other exotic stuff, such as dried berries, raw mango slices and the like. We were allowed one ball of tamarind, which he would put in a square bit of paper, liberally add various condiments such as salt, chilli powder, garam masala powder, and then twist the paper into a tiny parcel. We had to wait till we got home to mash the tamarind with the masala and savour it over the day.

The house in Kolkata was in a narrow lane. Through the baking hot afternoons there would be street vendors who passed by, calling out their wares. There were people selling balloons and toys, and others selling cosmetics and items such as ribbons and pins. There were a great number of people selling various eatables. My favourite was the fellow who sold *golas.* This was a small earthen pot filled with ice shavings, doused with a brightly coloured syrup, and a hollow stick stuck into it, which served as a straw. The gola-seller's cart had bottles of syrups in hues of the rainbow lining the sides. In the middle would be a big block of ice and a wooden shaver with a sharp blade. My aim was to always be the first one to get served. That way, I could quickly suck the brightly coloured syrup off the ice shavings and show it to the vendor, telling him he had probably handed me the shaved ice without adequate syrup, and go for a second round. The vendor, aware of the tricks children played, was quite tolerant and would wait to see if I came back for another helping.

There were various others – the fellow who sold *jhalmuri,* puffed rice mixed with roasted peanuts and slivers of onions; the person who sold *telebhaja,* various vegetables dipped in a batter of gram flour and deep-fried; and the ones who sold mutton cutlets and chops. The moment we heard a vendor's cry, we would rush out. Sometimes, we were sorely disappointed, like the time my brother called someone to stop by, only to discover that the man polished shoes! The high points of the trip were visits to the zoo and the Indian Museum, where the two things that entranced me were the lower jaw of an enormous whale that set off my imagination as to how big the animal was; and the 4,000-year-old Egyptian mummy and the realization that this was an actual living person at some point of time. The idyllic six weeks would pass by in a whirl, and soon, the holdalls were packed again and it was time to go home. The only consolation for the end of holidays was the train journey back to Bhilai, but leaving my sister and the pleasures of Kolkata behind was never easy. That year was otherwise uneventful; I finished class three somewhere in the middle of the class, but at least, I was off the bottom.

The next year is stuck in my memory for a few notable incidents. The year was 1964, and I was in class four. Every morning my mother would get up at 5.30 a.m. and switch on the radio at 6 a.m. and as the familiar tunes of Akashvani rang out, we scrambled out of bed. Ma would be sweeping the floors, and we would go about our morning ablutions to the accompaniment of the melodious tunes and soulful lyrics of Rabindra Sangeet. This was the way most Bengalis began their day. All was the same that day when I woke up, except that my mother was crying and wiping her tears on her sari pallu. I was terribly concerned. That's when I came to know that Independent India's first prime minister, Jawaharlal Nehru, had breathed his last. The cynicism of the present generation towards politicians contrasts sharply with the feelings our parents seemed to bear towards the leaders of yore. Many a time in their evening addas, I had heard them passionately arguing about the role of the Indian government in Partition, or the occupation of Kashmir, or the Sino-Indian war. But they were never disrespectful of our leaders or what they stood for.

The next memory of that particular school year is not pleasant either. It was the one and only time in my life that I got slapped – I was a timid child at best, and being of weak disposition, I didn't really need to be disciplined much. My father was against corporal punishment and he never raised his hand at any of us through our childhood. Our mother too was hardly the kind to discipline us by hitting and, therefore, being slapped was like being hit by a bolt of lightning. It happened when my maths teacher in fourth standard, Mrs Raman, lost her patience with me. We were doing arithmetic problems – of trains going at various speeds, and water tanks filling and emptying at different rates. I had always hated these problems – maths became much more palatable once we started algebra in class five. Mrs Raman came around my desk to check on how I was getting on with the classwork. If memory serves me right, she caught me doodling flowers in the workbook. The next moment, I was startled out of my wits as a resounding smack landed on my cheek. I was stunned. Tears pricked my eyes – from the pain, but just as much from the humiliation – for I had never known that a slap could hurt so much.

I don't know whether Mrs Raman is alive any more. But I am sure if she were asked today if she remembers slapping a small waif of a girl in maths class, she wouldn't be able to recall it. It was just a slap – something meted out freely by a teacher impatient to see her charges improve. Looking back, I realize there was no malice, no premeditated effort to undermine confidence, but that's what it ended up doing. The net result was that for the first time in my life I flunked in a subject in the quarterly exams. I might have come twenty-sixth in a class of thirty-two, but I had never ever failed in a subject until then.

My parents were shocked. My father especially took it hard, but he sat me down and extracted from me my fears, anxieties and worries. Also, for the first time, he promised to really help me with my maths. For the record, I never flunked the subject again, but my ambivalent attitude towards numbers – they excite me with the challenge they present, but scare me a little as well – remains.

I understand now that it also taught me a valuable lesson: one needs to mete out different rewards and punishments for different people. I know that the slap was too much for me. So also I know that a smile and a word of appreciation is something I treasure. Even today when I feel out of sorts, I close my eyes and go back to the moments when someone smiled to encourage me, and such memories are enough to turn my mood around. The idea of cash incentives has taken the world by storm. Yes, they are the easiest ones to give – but I think there are lots of people out there who will work just as hard if they see and feel the appreciation of their managers. We need to customize appreciation and punishment. By following the one-size-fits-all model, we lose, to a great degree, our ability to truly inspire people. At the same time, a heavy-handed application of punitive action brings on total paralysis and inaction, as I know from personal experience.

But now to return to the other major life-changing experience from that year. I contracted paratyphoid and spent twenty-three days in bed. It was also the first time I had allopathic medicine; I couldn't swallow the tablets – so I had the foulest-tasting liquids poured down my throat. It was also the first time I had doctors coming and checking me out. I didn't mind the injections, but what I really hated was the tongue depressor that made me gag and choke and want to throw up. I had till that age not learnt to read Bengali – my mother tongue. Though we never seemed to have enough money to buy toys, my father religiously bought books. He bought us graphic novels based on all the classics, such as *Oliver Twist, The Red Badge of Courage, The Strange Case of Dr Jekyll and Mr Hyde, The Invisible Man, The Call of the Wild, A Tale of Two Cities* and numerous others. When I read these books in their original forms much later, the pictures in my memory made them come alive. Neighbours would sometimes tell my father that he was spoiling our reading habits by allowing us to read comics, but he had his own logic. He felt, and time proved him right, that he was whetting our curiosity and igniting in us an appreciation for literature. He also regularly subscribed to a Bengali children's magazine in the hopes that we would learn the language. Every month, the magazine was eagerly awaited by my brother, who, because he started school two years after me, had been taught to read Bengali at home. After he had completed reading the magazine from cover to cover, he would disdainfully hand it over to me, but I would only look at the pictures.

Those twenty-three days I was bedridden I was bored beyond belief. My mother would load my bedside with books as she had little time to give me company. The hours stretched on before me, bleak and boring, but soon enough, I would pick up a book. It was during this time I somehow began reading Bengali. I don't know how the letters suddenly ceased to be a jumble and became decipherable, but there I was, fluently reading the script.

My brother was just two years older and we were, in hindsight, highly competitive. My childhood is strewn with his pranks, our fist fights and each of us loudly complaining about the other to whoever would listen. I remember being late for school once when he had tucked away one of my shoes behind the cistern in the toilet. Luckily, it fell out when someone pulled the chain (in those days, cisterns had chains) to flush the toilet. That night, an essay he had written for a class assignment the next day, disappeared.

But my illness brought his brotherly love to the fore. He would take me for a spin on his bicycle. It is a cherished memory, because it had always been a give-no-quarter engagement until then.

I have forgotten the travails of my illness, but the good things that happened remain bright in my memory. We all need to develop this ability to remember the good and edit out the bad – unless it is as bad as a tongue depressor!

Some of my fondest memories of those years in Bhilai are to do with Durga Puja. It's a five-day festival celebrated in autumn when Goddess Durga visits her maternal home on Earth, along with her four children. The triumph of good over evil is also celebrated in this festival.

About six weeks before the puja, the idol-makers would arrive. The puja was held in a large field which was soon covered with canopies. The idol-making would start almost a month ahead of time and, for us youngsters at least, it signalled the fact that holidays were around the corner. It also signalled my sister's return from the city. Kolkata schools had a month-long holiday, so my sister and aunt would come over to celebrate with us. As the idols took shape, our happiness only increased. In those days, there was no TV and very little Bollywood. So a community like ours entertained itself by putting together small plays, dance dramas, and other song-and-dance programmes that were performed every evening for the five days of the puja. The kids were a big part of these, as we regularly attended dancing and drawing classes and found the perfect platform to showcase our dancing on stage. The dance and art classes were organized by my mother, more in order to provide financial support to those with talent rather than to ensure we learnt the arts well. In an upcoming steel city, where there were no great facilities yet, we still picked up the rudiments of art. I remember how the drawing teacher would make us endlessly draw straight lines that never came out straight. When I rebelled after an afternoon of drawing straight lines that always came out crooked, he convinced me that it was the ABC of drawing and that without this ability nobody could become an artist.

What really used to appeal to me were the plays we put up, but I was still too young to be a part of these. The rehearsals, however, used to take place at our house. I memorized entire plays just by listening to the rehearsals and would rattle off the entire play, even changing my voice as I changed roles. It was a game that I played only with myself, to the thorough amusement of my family members. When the puja finally arrived, there would be new clothes and no cooking at home for the five days.

The mothers were busy putting together the various items required to conduct the rituals flawlessly. The children were responsible for collecting and plucking flowers, and then stringing them together with a needle and thick thread into garlands. We would be up at four in the morning as we were expected to bathe and dress in new clothes before venturing out with our friends. The deity had to be given a garland of 108 lotuses on the third, and main, day of the festival. Lotuses were hard to come by in Bhilai, so, instead, we used another large flower called 'land' lotus. We had to get up really early and go around more than twenty gardens before we could get the required 108. But the flowers I liked collecting the best were called 'sheoli', a white bloom with an orange centre and stem, and a heady smell. The flowers would carpet the ground below the trees by the time we landed up. The fallen flowers would be collected and put in trays of water in our rooms, so that the scent would perfume the houses. But these were not to be used for the deity. So we jumped around to pluck the flowers off the boughs before sitting down to string the garlands.

The high point in the day for us was the '*anjali*', when we handed over our flower offerings to the goddess. The priest intoned mantras that we would repeat. It was all about asking the goddess for various boons and supplications to her to grant us health, wealth and fame. I remember a particular invocation that went like this – 'Hara klesha, hara shoka, hara roga, hara priye'. The word 'hara' means to take away; 'klesha' is suffering; 'shoka' is grief and 'roga' is illness, while 'priya' means dear one. So I interpreted the mantra to mean that we are asking the deity to take away our suffering, grief and illness, and also our dear ones! I was very puzzled and asked my mother why we asked God to take away our dear ones. Ma couldn't understand what I was saying, but when she did she couldn't stop laughing. After she managed to control her laughter, she explained that she had never heard such a weird interpretation because 'hara priye' was another name for Durga, as she is the beloved of Shiva, who is also known as 'Hara'. So, basically, it was an invocation to Durga to take away our suffering, grief and sickness. I felt a little deflated at the explanation, as I had begun to feel that we were so virtuous and spiritually evolved that we were asking God to even take away our loved ones.

Puja in Bhilai was a time of unbridled joy. We rarely went home, other than to change our clothes. Most clothes were sewn at home;

those who could afford it got them tailored. The age of the ready-mades had not yet arrived and this was certainly not the age of branded clothing.

Our breakfast always comprised the fruits and sweets of prasad, while we had khichdi for lunch. This too would be first offered to the deity before being distributed amongst us, and to our hungry mouths it tasted like ambrosia. At night food stalls were set up and we gorged on parathas and mutton, cutlets and chops, and the numerous sweets available. Though the puja was a Bengali festival, all communities participated – that was the best thing about these 'temples' of modern India: its cosmopolitan nature. It was a melting pot of cultures, religions and languages, and we wallowed in it to our heart's content.

My sojourn in class five was unremarkable, except for the fact that we had a teacher called Mrs Henry. Her beauty could not be defined by regular standards, but I found her calm exterior and sensitive way of handling kids beautiful. I never got around to telling her this (and I wish I had), but she did much to restore my self-confidence. She encouraged and appreciated us, challenged us without making it apparent and patiently listened to our stumbling stories of failed attempts. But mostly, it was her acceptance of who we were, warts and all, which went a long way in restoring my confidence in myself. My ranking in class rose. I felt more confident that I could do better, and with that my aspiration rose as well. I also made a new friend called Sati.

Since the change of sections, I had been struggling to find a good friend. The girls in my class were led by a good-looking and confident youngster. She had lovely skin and hair, and sturdy health to boot. But being the ornery person I was, I thought her to be too domineering. Maybe it was jealousy or pure contrariness that made me remain on the fringes of the gang. The only other girl who resembled me in the class was Sati. She was thin, with enormous eyes, and we struck up a friendship in defiance to the gang's diktats.

As my confidence grew, I started doing better in school. Perhaps, the typhoid attack had opened up a few more cells in my brain. I was healthier than before, and was able to attend classes more. My handwriting improved, as did my understanding of subjects.

The next year saw me breaking into the top ten in my class. We had now migrated from primary to middle school. We took a bus because the school was further away. While waiting at the bus stop, one game was to rush across the road when you spotted an oncoming vehicle – though, today I can't even imagine how we could have been that stupid. However, I got the fright of my life when I did this with an oncoming truck and felt the whoosh of air raise the hair on the back of my neck as I crossed over in the nick of time. I never tried anything so idiotic ever again. But we had the freedom to make our own mistakes. Our guardian angels must have worked overtime to keep us safe, but by God's grace, we managed to stay alive without any big injuries.

But by the end of the year my world came crashing down. My father, along with eleven other engineers, were laid off.

In India, in the public sector, one could lose ones' job only if a mala fide intent or activity was established. However, it seemed that, in this case, the steel plant was making losses. The managing director wanted to cut costs, and decided to lay off some middle-level employees, so that substantial savings could be made. The reason given was that the construction phase of the plant was over and so these officers could be let go.

My father was shattered. There were dark talks back then as to how only honest people had been targeted, and that those who looked the other way when questionable deals were made were spared. In hindsight, my father's mental state probably was compounded by those earlier years when he had given up a job and couldn't find another one immediately. I could sense his fear, and my heart broke as the lines on his forehead got deeper and deeper. People who remember the India of those days would understand the acute lack of opportunities for employment or the near impossibility of becoming an entrepreneur if one didn't come from a moneyed family.

There were frenzied consultations at home. I was hanging on to the back of his chair when the termination notice was delivered by hand, as the affected engineers had gone on leave. The sight remains etched in my mind – especially the sad smile that played on my father's face as he signed the notice.

I was still wondering why he had been picked specifically. It was true that he was scrupulously honest – never even bringing home writing pads, pencils and office supplies from work (something which I saw in many other houses). But what if it was on account of him not being good enough at his work? It was a thought I could not even bear to think about.

The dismissed band of engineers decided to approach the court. My father visited Delhi a few times, approaching ministries and other powers that be, for justice. Luckily, he found a few sympathetic listeners. They helped my father and his friends get the right legal help, so as to enable the case to come up quickly for hearing.

Those were difficult, stressful days. The get-togethers that my parents held on weekends ended abruptly. My family became a bit of a social pariah. Those who still had jobs were unsure how the powers that be would like them fraternizing with us. They didn't want to fall foul of their seniors. They also didn't know how to show their sympathy without being awkward about it. It was as though we were in quarantine for a fatal disease that could be contagious.

Meanwhile, my studies at school were going well. Though, there were some dark clouds gathering there as well. My earlier best friend and neighbour, my partner from infancy, Smita, suddenly started spreading stories about me. It was to do with my supposed 'love' for a boy in a senior class. Again, I felt totally embarrassed and humiliated. I had probably mentioned at some gathering that he seemed to be a nice fellow, but to treat it as a declaration of 'love' was preposterous. I thought Smita was setting me up to become some kind of laughing stock – for here I was, a nondescript girl talking about one of the most popular seniors. I cringed at what I thought were pitying looks as the rumour did the rounds.

Smita and I had a big fight one day, and we stopped talking. I never spoke to her again till I found her on Facebook forty-seven years later and made peace. When I did meet her again, what a great meeting it was – the outpouring of love nurtured in our hearts washed away all the petty misunderstandings of our childish selves. We remain fast friends to date.

Around this time, the court decision also came, instructing the management that such arbitrary dismissal of employees needed to be reversed. The management was told that if it was a matter of saving money – the LIFO principle (last in, first out) should be followed. I felt quite grown-up finding out what LIFO meant. The court also said that if it was a performance issue, then evidence for that needed to be presented, which was not done. The court directed that if the work of these engineers had been completed (as construction of the plant was over), the services of these engineers should be transferred to a new plant that was coming up at Bokaro then. And so it was that my father got reinstated and received transfer orders to Bokaro Steel City.

While there was great joy at the outcome, there was an overlay of sadness as well. All the affected engineers realized that their careers would always bear a question mark – why were they the ones targeted and laid off. That question would remain unanswered.

The MD too didn't last long after the incident. In any case, he did not enjoy a stellar reputation. The scandal created by this incident, and the ignominy of being rapped by the court, didn't go down too well with the central government and he too was transferred soon after.

We left Bhilai shortly afterwards. My father preceded us. I was excited to go to a missionary school – 'Senjeveurs', as per my understanding, till my father corrected my spelling to read St Xavier's!

As I trod the streets of Bhilai one last time, Tagore's song came to mind: 'Jakhon porbe na mor payer chinha ei bate' – when my footprints will no longer adorn these paths. I was to return to Bhilai fifty years later, as the chairman of SBI.

# 2

# Bokaro: Growing Up Pangs

St Xavier's School, Bokaro Steel City. It sounded quite grand. Having studied in a project school until then, I was excited. I may have been a little apprehensive about the new school, but I was not really sad as Bhilai now held too many painful memories, including my fight with Smita. We were a few months apart in age and had literally grown up together. There was not a day in all our years together when we had not talked or shared our joys and sorrows. Not talking to her for the last two months of our stay had been heartbreaking and I was glad to get away.

Our school was held in temporary quarters, in rooms that had tin sheets for roofs. There were just twelve of us in class seven. There was only one class ahead of us with eight students. The principal was an Australian, Rev. Fr John Moore SJ. He was a noted educationist, having established St Xavier's Hazaribagh as well. Whenever he walked around the school, there would be a group of tiny tots following him around, hoping for a smile or a few words from him.

He was like a Santa Claus whose bag of goodies was in his mind rather than over his shoulder.

Our vice principal was a New Zealander, Fr Tom Keogh. He was a young, extremely energetic man with twinkling blue eyes and a dazzling smile. There was no job he was not good at. From swabbing the floors when the sweeper was away to driving the school bus when the driver fell sick, he was everywhere doing everything. His lunch often consisted of two rotis and dal, which he had standing up as he didn't have the time to sit down to eat. I still treasure one of my interactions with him. When I was in ninth standard, I was the editor of the school magazine. This was also Fr Keogh's responsibility. The publication had gotten delayed and he had called me to talk it over. I became very serious during the conversation, as I realized that I had not done enough to follow up on its timely execution. Seeing me in that sombre mood, Fr Keogh said, 'Arundhati, you know the value of exercise, don't you?' Not quite understanding what this sudden turn in our conversation was leading to, I nodded. 'Well then, you don't seem to be doing enough of it!' he said. I looked at him uncomprehendingly, so he continued, 'The best exercise is the one that exercises the maximum number of muscles, isn't it?' I nodded again. 'Well then, please smile because that exercises twenty-six muscles of your face. It costs you nothing, and it will not only help you but also its recipient.' The comment was so unexpected that I spontaneously broke into a smile. It's one of those life lessons that I have not only tried to assimilate but also pass on to as many people as possible.

Our class teacher, Ms Noonan, was an Australian as well. The school was run by the Australian Society of Jesus and we would frequently have exchange teachers from Australia.

It was the first time I had interacted with people from Australia. I found their accents slightly difficult to follow, but other than that, this school was where I really found my feet. The teachers were 'different' – maybe because they were all quite young and readily approachable. Maybe because the school was still in its infancy, both teachers and students found it easier to communicate for no system had been hard-coded yet. Students were considered stakeholders of the enterprise, and our voices and opinions mattered. My experience as a member, and then subsequently as the head, of the students' council made me feel important, but also taught me a lot about being responsible.

From the beginning, in this school, I was determined to do better in my studies. The nurturing atmosphere probably provided the right trigger. Plus, truth be told, there was less competition here. The two together gave me the right impetus and, within the first three months, I topped my class. I never slipped below second rank after that, so at least one of the things I had wanted to achieve came to pass. From my own experience, I feel cut-throat competition can sometimes be debilitating. Especially if the person is physically weak and of a reticent temperament. To improve performance, especially in those who are well-intentioned and motivated, it is better to foster a supportive environment. Results of this are often quite striking and certainly sustainable. On the other hand, excessive competition can cause quick burnouts.

At home, too, the situation was changing. My parents missed their friends sorely. My father also seemed to have withdrawn more. The ready jokes were few and far between. He had frequent headaches, and when those happened we tiptoed around the house. It was later diagnosed as high blood pressure, probably brought on by stress, but his easy humour seemed to have deserted him entirely.

Amidst this, my sister fell sick in Kolkata with typhoid and jaundice at the same time. She was brought back post-haste to Bokaro. In the few years that she had been away, we seemed to have grown apart as a family, but, for me, she had the same protective feelings. I too felt deeply for her and wished with all my heart that she could stay back with us.

My aunt had come back with my sister. It appeared that the landlord of the house they lived in wanted it vacated. After a lot of negotiating, my uncle decided to give up one room for the landlord's use. As such, unless they found another place to live in, it would be difficult for my aunt to continue living in Kolkata. We were all eager to have her stay with us – she was a caring and capable person, and so it was decided that my sister would not return to the hostel and my aunt would find a job in Bokaro.

My sister's hostel stories were enough to give me nightmares. Starting from the state of the toilets. Indians seem to have an ambivalent attitude towards toilets: we want them clean, but most times, won't leave behind a clean one! The students in the hostel were supposed to be given a fruit every day. What they were actually given was a green tomato. Such stories were enough to understand what she must have been through.

When she returned, she was in her final year of school. But Bokaro, being a new township back then, had no schools with classes at her level, other than the local Hindi-medium school. It seemed like a cruel joke – that she had to stay away from home at a hostel she hated in order to go to a reputed school, only to be forced back into a mediocre Hindi-medium school. This change of schools impacted her studies badly and she never really recovered from it. I think my mother too realized the mistake she had made. It was the one thing that used to haunt her till the end of her days.

Parents, in spite of their best intentions, sometimes do make erroneous decisions, and sending my sister off, because of an inherent prejudice about the quality of the school, was one of them. In my mother's defence, all that can be said is that Hindi was not so commonly spoken at that time and the teaching materials at such schools were of questionable quality, and she did genuinely believe she was doing the best for her child by sending her to a leading school in Kolkata. My brother and I were very lucky; being the younger siblings we got access to the better schools that were subsequently set up. Even then, in Bokaro, while I went to St Xavier's, my brother had to go to Kendriya Vidyalaya because he was two years ahead of me, and my school at that time had classes only one level higher than mine. These were the common problems of developing cities, and the sacrifices made by the people who founded and built them. The lack of such facilities affected many lives, which we rarely remember or acknowledge.

With my aunt and sister back home, my mother decided that the time had come to open up a dispensary and start practising homeopathy regularly. She rented a room near the marketplace and set up her dispensary. She took to leaving at 6 p.m. after giving us our evening tea. My father would return at 7 p.m. and then go pick her up at 9.30 p.m. Around this time, my father bought his next car, an Ambassador. He allowed me to pick the colour and I chose thunder grey because it reminded me of the welcome clouds that heralded the end of the burning summer in Bhilai.

My mother also managed to build up a solid practice and, in Bokaro, I was known more as her daughter because of her wide circle of acquaintances. Many more people knew her than they did my father.

Because of her popularity as a homeopath, our circle of acquaintances grew rapidly, but as she was away in the evenings, the addas my parents regularly hosted in Bhilai were done away with. I think, in a way, this contributed to my father becoming even more reclusive. My mother, meanwhile, became one of the founding members of a local Bengali club. She continued her social work through the club, which included teaching the village women stitching and handicrafts, masala-making and various other income-generating activities. When the club members wanted to stage a play, to my delight, I was offered a role.

On the first day of rehearsals the gentleman directing the play, Chatterjee uncle, pulled me aside. He asked me quite seriously whether I could devote the time required for rehearsals and ensure my studies didn't suffer. I was eager to be a part of the production, so I said yes. But the test of my commitment came soon enough.

We had our summer vacation at that time. A telegram arrived bearing the news that my uncle in Kolkata was unwell. Both my mother and aunt wanted to go and, as the holidays were on, it was decided that the children too would go with them. But I had given my word to not miss the rehearsals. So I dug in my heels and refused to leave. Ma tried to reason with me and then told me that I would need to cook for both my father and myself if I decided to stay. She thought that would scare me, but I was adamant. So there it was – while the rest of the family went to Kolkata, I stayed back with my father. When we went to see them off at the station, I felt a serious twinge of remorse. I was giving up a train journey and a sojourn at Kolkata – but then it was only a temporary regret. I was more upset, I suspect, as I had never been away from my mother. I steeled myself and waved them goodbye, though when the train pulled out it took considerable self-control not to burst into tears.

The tears would come later, not from my missing my mother but from the smoke of the *chullah.* I faced epic struggles as I tried to light it every day to cook lunch. Father gave me detailed instructions on how to boil rice and make an egg curry. As soon as he left, I started my preparations. Washing the rice and grinding the ginger and garlic were easy enough. Slicing the onions was another matter altogether, but I valiantly completed the task. After all the preparations were done, I tried lighting the *chullah.*

I had seen my mother do it many times. Pieces of dung cake went at the bottom, just above a grate. This was topped by pieces of coal and then she would light a newspaper and push it below the grate, through an opening at the bottom, and the *chullah* would start smoking till the pieces of coal glowed red. The *chullah* was ready to use in about fifteen to twenty minutes. I did all of the above, but pages and pages of newsprint turned to ashes with nary a piece of coal catching fire. The *chullah* emitted plumes of smoke, the ashes of the newspaper floated around, I fanned the flames for all I was worth even as I choked and coughed pitifully. After I had burnt up something like ten days' worth of newspapers, I managed to light the *chullah* on one side (though I don't know how I managed even that!). I finally got the rice done and then the egg curry. When my father came home in the afternoon, I proudly served him lunch. He could make out my struggles from my dishevelled look and the state of the kitchen. But he ignored it and concentrated on his food. 'You have done really, really well, do you realize? Your mother is in for tough competition when she returns!' Those words were reward enough.

My struggles would also have another reward. When my father narrated my labours to Chatterjee uncle, and told him the reason I didn't go to Kolkata, he was visibly moved. As a reward, he took me under his wing and taught me the secrets of acting, gleaned from his own experiences.

'From where does your voice come, Arundhati?'

'From my throat, of course.'

'No, it should come from the pit of your stomach. You need to learn to throw your voice.'

In those days there were no cordless microphones. On the best of stages, there would be mics hanging at fixed spots. Therefore, if you could not throw your voice, you would not be heard. He next taught me to enunciate: how to speak so that each word is distinct and yet the whole effect remains one of normal speech. He also taught me voice modulation and how to emote. I never went to an acting class, but over the next few years I went on to win many prizes in dramatics – all learnt from one person who was generous enough to teach me because he said he felt in me the same passion he himself had for acting.

Those lessons in communication have served me in good stead many times as I pursued my career. Be it in a group discussion, or while making a presentation, or while appearing in an interview, the ability to communicate clearly has always given me a distinct advantage. I do not know how much people around me realize this, but I do, and I thank my lucky stars for that summer when I learnt to cook and to speak.

These lessons in communication were improved when I began taking part in activities like debating, elocution and extempore speaking at school. As in our school in Bhilai, this one too had a strong programme of extracurricular activities. I started debating when one of the regulars on the Hindi debating team fell sick. Our Hindi teacher was in a quandary as an important inter-school debate was coming up. Sensing an opportunity, I volunteered. Mrs Bishnoi, our Hindi teacher, was a little doubtful. She knew that for the life of me I couldn't determine what should be the gender of Hindi words, where even inanimate things were classified as male or female. Most people who are not native speakers of the language have this problem while speaking Hindi. For instance, a dhoti, worn by men, is a feminine noun, whereas a blouse that women wear is is a masculine noun. The word for home – *ghar* – masculine, but the word for shop – *dukaan* – is feminine. But she had little choice. So she accepted me into the team. The results, however, were beyond her expectation. We floored the opposition and lifted the trophy. Thereafter, I became a regular on the Hindi debating team, as well as a regular actor in the year-end Hindi drama at school. My ungrammatical Hindi came to be accepted because, as she said, it didn't matter as long as I could make myself understood.

By the time we got into class eight, the new school building had come up and we moved into the spanking new campus. Our playgrounds had also come up and I learnt to play many new games such as softball, netball, throwball, hockey and quoits. I was never very good at games as I was still physically rather weak. It didn't help that when teams were being formed I was almost always the last one picked. The school placed enormous importance on sports. During the peak of summer, our classes would be held between 6.30

a.m. and noon. But the school bus would come around again at 4.30 p.m. to take us back to school for an hour of games from 5 p.m. to 6 p.m. So there was no way I would be allowed to slide out of physical training. I tried hard, but my physique and breathing troubles made it difficult to excel. I pushed myself to keep up and, on one such day, while playing netball I was trying to get hold of the ball when two of the other girls lost their balance and fell on top of me. It wasn't their fault. They had jumped higher and when we fell down, I was at the bottom of the pile. I could feel the breath getting knocked out of me, followed by a sharp pain near my shoulder. I couldn't stand up. The girls scrambled off me and tried to pull me up, at which I let out a blood-curdling yell. They backed off, wondering what had gone wrong. Nothing much, except that I had broken my collarbone. On being taken to the hospital, the doctor, looking at the X-ray, commented that my bones looked too thin for my age. My father dutifully reported this to Fr Moore when he came calling. He immediately decided that the only way to take care of this issue was to get me to do more physical stuff, to 'toughen me up', so to say. In fact, he was medically correct. Unless there is sufficient physical activity in the growing years, calcium absorption by the body becomes insufficient. Which is why sports or physical training must be mandatory in schools – something many schools in our cities prefer to pay lip service to on account of lack of space, thereby endangering the health of their students in later years.

I realized that I had to find a game in which I could do well, or else I would have to live in ignominy through school. I took up something which few girls played, quoits – played with a thick rubber ring, in teams of two. Somehow I was able to catch and throw the quoits well. I even made it to the quoits team on merit. It strengthened my belief that even in a discipline where one may have little natural inclination, one can still find a niche to excel in.

At this time, I also learnt to swim. That first year of swimming was like an addiction. We couldn't wait to get into the water and had to be literally dragged out of the pool. I had never enjoyed anything as much since my days of playing in the sand dunes by the side of the road in our house in Bhilai. Unfortunately, we didn't have trainers, but we made do splashing around. It did do wonders to my frequent bouts of cold and bronchitis, which receded to a great extent. It also left me with a voracious appetite. So, at long last, I began to look healthier and lost my two-dimensional look (had I known the appreciation for size zero in the future, I may have felt less pleased with my progress). Even with this exertion, when I left school I weighed all of 32 kgs.

I remember class eight for one other incident. Fr Moore would often be visited by many of his ex-students from St Xavier's, Hazaribagh. He would ask them to address us and mostly this was something we enjoyed. One such gentleman was in Delhi School of Economics back then. Father Moore introduced him with pride, narrating his many achievements and then left us to interact.

The gentleman started by asking us what we wanted to become. 'A biochemist,' I said when my turn came. 'You're sure? Not a kitchen chemist?' he asked, a palpable sneer in his voice. It's a small incident, but I still remember it clearly, including his slightly superior look and smile. It was my first brush with gender stereotyping that, at various times since, has reared its ugly head.

This was also the time when we were introduced to social service. Our school conducted coaching classes in the evening for children from disadvantaged backgrounds. The idea was to help integrate them into the school, and if they improved after a year of coaching they would be absorbed into a class as per their abilities. Moreover, they could study free of charge if they were admitted to the school. For these evening classes, we were encouraged to give two hours once a week. I realized that I enjoyed teaching, especially as the class was a medley of children at various stages, and they needed individual attention and coaching. The amazing pace at which some of them improved brought me face to face with the curse of poverty that denied children the opportunities that surely everyone deserves.

At least two of the children I helped coach were integrated into the school and passed with flying colours.

The school also awakened in me an abiding love for reading. As I had mentioned earlier, my father always found money to buy us books. This also extended to board games, but rarely to other toys. The first English books I read were Enid Blyton's Noddy series. Our school in Bhilai issued us storybooks every week, and so I had never known the joys of browsing. At St Xavier's, one of the first rooms to be set up was the library. It was a large room with a high ceiling. There were tall bookshelves inside stacked with books. On one side was a staircase leading up to a wide gallery filled with more bookshelves. We had permission to take up to four books a week. What joy it was to browse through this forest of books! The gems that I found there were unparalleled. Many a time when I started a book, I couldn't put it down and often I would be reading even after everyone else at home had gone to bed. I read voraciously – be it Dickens or Billy Bunter books, I devoured them all. Till date, if I don't have a book with me – though I do read on my Kindle specially while travelling – I feel as if an essential part of me is missing.

As I moved to senior school, classes became more engaging. I chose to study both maths and biology, though as a favourite subject the latter won hands down. My brush with chemistry made me realize that my dream of becoming a biochemist was probably just that – a dream. I disliked the subject, especially organic chemistry. At the time, I blamed the teacher for making the subject so unattractive, but in hindsight, I realize that I must have been to blame as well. One really can't clap with one hand!

Physics, on the other hand, I liked. As for the language courses, they came to me easily. The recommended books were ones I loved, so studying them was never a chore. I loved school so much that I hated missing even one day, and I remember sneaking off to class even with high temperature, only to be sent home promptly.

Though the memories of those years often bring a smile to my lips, it was not all rosy. I had my share of ups and downs.

While I was in class nine, the school decided to have its first fete. The money raised through the fete would be contributed to the evening school. I was given the responsibility of organizing it and felt immensely proud at the honour. I worked feverishly at conceiving the various attractions, listing out who would man the stalls, what would be the prizes, as well as the entry fee and so on. It felt great, allocating students and teachers to various committees, ordering people around and generally behaving as though a job of national importance was getting executed.

The day dawned bright and clear, and the gala got off to a great start. The hordes of people expected to attend arrived and everything appeared to be working as per plan. The shock came later. After the fete, when the accounts were tallied I realized that in spite of the apparent success, we had made a loss! It was a shattering realization. What was I to tell the teachers? And what about the contribution we were to make to the evening school? I realized my mistake in not having sought wiser counsel in the matter of pricing the various tickets or the other expenses we made. I sneaked off on my own to a deserted classroom, closed the door and had a good cry. It was a lesson learnt the hard way, but one I never forgot – that, at the end, the books must show a profit, and while doing something new, one needs to not only work hard but also work smart. Had I sought more guidance and collaboration, I may have avoided the ignominy, but at that point, I had to face up to the fact that the first venture organized by me had been a failure.

There is one other regret I still have, which appears petty in hindsight but bothered me for days on end. Our school had a system of three major exams, the quarterly, half-yearly and the final exams. Besides these, there were five monthly tests we had to take up. If anyone scored five A's (80 per cent and above) in all five monthly tests, they got a silver medal at the end of the term. If someone got three silver medals in three successive years, they would be awarded a gold medal. As can be expected, there was enormous competition for the medals. It was a good way of keeping us on our toes and ensuring that we studied through the year. I got silver medals in classes eight and nine. The first four monthly tests in class ten also went well, with me receiving the requisite number of A's. In the last of the tests, however, disaster struck. I got four A's, but in my favourite subject of biology I scored an A- for want of half a mark. I was absolutely gutted. Having coveted the medal for so long, to fall short at the very end for half a mark was simply too much to bear.

Sadly, our biology teacher and her husband were close friends of my parents. I beseeched my parents to talk to her and reason with her. I felt that she was being extra hard on me as she wanted to prove that friendship with our family was not influencing her treatment of students. But my parents refused to interfere. But my distress was so real that my father ultimately requested Fr Moore to counsel me.

Fr Moore was patient. He said a few things that struck a chord and have stayed with me through the years. 'Arundhati, when something like this happens, you have to learn to accept it. Life is rarely fair and some situations cannot be cured. In such cases, acceptance is the only way forward. Today you are hurting, but time will heal the pain. The scar will remain. Use that as a reminder to prepare better, try harder. Try to find the lesson hidden in this failure – did you become too complacent and sure of success? Did you try hard enough? Did you plan to get just the required five A's, and should you have planned to do better in all seven subjects, so that if you missed the grade in one of them, you could make up for it in another? Also, it is easy to externalize blame. Your father tells me you feel that one of the teachers has been unfair to you. But before externalizing the blame, assess your own performance. It is comforting to blame someone else for your failures, but then you lose the opportunity to learn from it. I hope you will not do that.'

At the time of the conversation, I came away saddened and disappointed. It was only as time went by that I could appreciate the truth in what he was saying. But talking about it to him did seem to lift the gloom then. It was also with great effort that I continued to behave normally whenever the biology teacher visited my family, and though no mention of the matter was ever made to her, I know my parents greatly appreciated the effort I made to ensure that this incident did not show up in my social interactions. I did get a third silver medal at school, but this was for being the head girl. The coveted gold medal, however, remained elusive.

A similar incident happened in class eleven. The school had instituted a system of having two wooden plaques on which names were recorded of the final year student who headed the students' council and is considered the Head girl/boy, and the second plaque would record the name of the student who stood first in the final school 'send-up' test. In the final test, I missed the first rank by a few marks, again courtesy of the biology paper. This time, however, I decided that there was no point in getting upset. Instead, I concentrated on the board exam and was cheered when in those results I scored above the rest of the class. That was reward enough for me.

The other incident that marked the year 1971 was the India-Pakistan war. I had been in class two when the Sino-Indian war was fought. I had caught a sense of the deep anguish that our elders seemed to feel at the end of that war. There was a lot of talk about the naivety of our leaders and how they had misled the nation and themselves with the slogan of 'Hindi-Chini bhai bhai'. The 1965 Indo-Pakistani conflict had seemed to restore the confidence of the nation in its leadership. Even then, I was too young to understand the true import of war. There seemed to be a lot of disdain that the government hadn't struck while the iron was hot and pursued the enemy deep into its territory. The 1971 war, rooted as it was in the Bangladesh conflict, was in a separate category. There seemed to be a righteousness about the whole endeavour, a feeling of service beyond self as the horrific events in erstwhile East Pakistan made the press. There was a huge upswelling of patriotic fervour, and the wave of nationalistic feelings seemed to carry all ahead of it. We used to hang on to our radio sets for the news bulletins, and, every morning, the newspaper was read from top to bottom. It was at that time that I got into my habit of reading the morning newspaper – a habit that has remained till the Covid-19 pandemic struck. No amount of electronic media can make up for that simple act of opening the day's newspaper first thing in the morning. The end of the war brought huge cheer and joy, and as people went back to their daily jobs, the feeling of having accomplished something remained.

We were heading towards the end of school and there was a lot of talk on what we should do next. My father was due to retire in four years. There was no pension in his service. I did realize that supporting my brother and me after retirement would be difficult for my parents. I very much wanted to study medicine, but this was a five-year course. The closest centre for higher studies was Kolkata. In those days, however, the Naxal movement had Bengal in its grip. It was for the first time after Independence that a social agitation of this dimension had affected the youth. It had communist ideology as its base and started on account of tenant farmers being denied their basic rights in a place called Naxalbari. It quickly gained traction amongst the student intelligentsia in Kolkata, getting buttressed by the lack of employment opportunities. It remains an example of what can happen if the aspiration for a more equal society is ignored. The movement perpetrated violence against authority figures at a scale not seen in India since Independence. However, the state machinery moved swiftly. The movement was ruthlessly stamped out. As Bokaro was close to Kolkata, a few of our cousins from other parts of the country studying there would often flee the hostel and land up at our place to stay for a week or two till normalcy was restored.

As a result of these troubles, my brother signed up to study at St Xavier's College in Ranchi as my parents refused to send him to Kolkata in the midst of turmoil. But by the time I was to graduate from school, the movement was on its last legs. However, the academic sessions were all badly delayed. The five-year medical course that I was interested in was taking as long as eight years now. With father's retirement due in four years, I was in a deep quandary as to what I should do next.

Going to study at a place other than Kolkata would have been the right solution. I had, however, never travelled to any place other than Kolkata. In those days there were no provisions for 'leave fare concession' – an allowance that most jobs give once in three or four years for taking a vacation with one's family. Besides, my father hated being away from home and its associated comforts, and so throughout my childhood, all my travels were through the books I read and my imagination. Apart from the towns of Bhilai and Bokaro, the only city we knew was Kolkata, and so it was a default choice.

The days of the final exams arrived. Our school promised to take us for a Hindi movie called *Aradhana* the day the exams ended. The movie had been released a few years ago but in those days re-runs were common as movie releases were not so frequent. It was to be my first Hindi movie and I was hugely excited. The restrictions of those days would appear ridiculous to today's children, who, thanks to TV and streaming platforms, can probably watch three movies a day if they wanted to. When we were young, though, we had no TV. On top of that, Hindi movies were considered a corrupting influence, and many families would not allow children to watch these. As for my parents, they not only didn't allow us this liberty but in their favour it must be said that they didn't go to the movies themselves.

However, when the school suggested taking us for the movie, my parents agreed – probably as a concession to the fact that we would soon leave our homes for further studies. The movie starred the reigning Bollywood heartthrobs of the times – Rajesh Khanna and Sharmila Tagore – and I could hardly wait to watch it.

Our last exam was the third paper of advanced maths and only four of us in the class had taken up the subject. As the final minutes neared, I could see the rest of our classmates peeking from the door to see how much longer we would be. I could sit still no longer. I was struggling with one particular problem in solid geometry and had decided to leave it till the end. It carried sixteen marks. I was in a real quandary, longing to leave and torn by remorse that I would throw away sixteen marks. I finally gave up. The sum remained half done as I packed up and left for what would be my first step into adulthood – watching a Hindi movie with friends. I had arrived! Of that experience, I can only say that the movie didn't disappoint, though those sixteen marks still bother me to date.

The debate for future studies resumed at home. It was also the first year of the joint entrance exams, which have since become ubiquitous for entry into engineering and medical schools. Our batch was the first to take it up and to my absolute delight I was offered a place in one of the medical colleges in Kolkata. The problem arose when we realized that the college had no hostels for women. The whole narrative changed after that. We quickly understood the paucity of private women's hostels in the city (something which I feel has still not been addressed properly). In those days, there were no paying guest accommodations available either. People stayed with relatives, and the only one with whom I could stay with was my uncle, but he too had a paucity of space. We had to turn our gaze to those colleges that had hostels for women to begin with and then identify which course I'd like to study.

With medical school ruled out, I tried to discover a college that taught zoology. In a way, I felt that this would help me study a subject I liked and also address the problem of not completing my course before my father's retirement. But as luck would have it, the only college offering zoology was Presidency, which too didn't have a hostel for women.

It was around this time that my father had a chance meeting with Fr Moore. On being asked what I should pursue, Fr Moore suggested I study English. I had scored very good marks in the subject at the board exams and he felt I would have enough job opportunities in fields such as journalism or teaching.

My father knew my reservations on taking up teaching, especially in schools, and I must narrate the incidents which led to it.

Our final board exams had taken place in December. Most college sessions started in July. In Kolkata, on account of sessions running late, classes were expected to start by November. That meant that we had almost a year between school and college. Our school was still expanding. The building didn't have enough rooms, so sufficient number of sections for each grade were not available. In some of the lower grades, there were as many as sixty students in a class. This made it difficult for teachers to give adequate attention to all the students. Fr Moore came up with the idea of employing us as teacher's assistants during this gap. Our job was to stand at the rear of the class and ensure that the students sitting at the back were paying attention. We also helped with classwork wherever a student got stuck, as well as help with homework correction. Being at a loose end, I jumped at the chance. The salary was a princely amount of ₹150. But being employed had its own charm and I became a teacher's helper for class two students.

I had never known until then that children in a group could be so difficult to manage. One day, in the middle of a maths class, I was startled by the sound of screaming. There was a girl standing by the window, crying with all her might. After a lot of effort, I could extract the reason for her tears. It appeared that the boy next to her had thrown her notebook out of the window. I boxed his ears (in those days, this was allowed) and sent him off to fetch the notebook. After about fifteen minutes, I realized that the boy hadn't returned. I looked out of the window to see what was keeping him. There he stood, bawling away as a large cow munched at the notebook. The boundary walls of the school had not yet been built, and the cow had wandered in to graze and probably found the notebook. The next day, the mother of the little girl was in school with a lengthy complaint and I spent that entire evening copying all the previous work for the girl to take home!

I had a great collection of answers given by these children. But my favourites were the responses provided by a child to questions in the environmental science paper. The first question was, 'What are clouds made of?' The answer: 'Clouds are made of I scream.' The next question was, 'What is a spring?' and the answer to this was, 'Springs are nuts and bolts.' For pure entertainment, the fellow should have got a passing grade!

Some experiences, however, were not so pleasant and in fact downright disturbing. A sharp unnatural scream interrupted our class one day. It came from the rear of the class and as I reached the little boy who was still screaming, I could see a thin line of blood spurting from his knee. I was puzzled as to what had happened till I realized that the boy sitting next to him had slashed him with a blade held between two fingers! This was in class two and I was shocked beyond belief. We summoned the boy's father who was a doctor, but he flatly refused to believe that his son would do such a thing. On the other hand, the injured boy's father threatened to sue the school for having failed to protect his son. It was around this time that I realized that teaching was not for me as the daily duties, especially of homework correction, left me drained. I truly admire members of this profession, as their hard work is vastly underappreciated. Managing a class full of rambunctious kids for five to six hours, on their feet throughout the day, followed by loads of corrections to be done at home – the life of a teacher is indeed difficult. However, had I known then of the many hours I would spend disposing files at home after dinner, I may have been less unwilling to take up this profession.

To return to my struggle of understanding what I would like to do next, my father came away from the meeting with Fr Moore convinced that studying English was a good suggestion. Though I may not want to teach, journalism was still a viable alternative. We ended up looking for colleges that offered English and had a good hostel, and that's how I entered Lady Brabourne College.

These days, I often wonder whether Fr Moore – a well-noted educationist and a great inspiration in my life – would have suggested English had I been a boy. After having studied both maths and biology, and having done quite well in both, it seemed strange to take up English. To tell the truth, I too am a little at fault for not having fought harder to study some other subject. The prospect of having to stay in a private hostel was something that didn't appeal to me then. I had visited a few of them. Most had dormitory accommodations, where one had space for a single bed and a desk. The biggest problem were the toilets. The stench was overpowering even as one passed them, and there I rest my case.

The apprehension of having to stay at such a place dampened my ambitions considerably. Today, I chide myself for having been faint-hearted, but at the time it seemed an insurmountable problem in studying a subject of my choice. I remembered my sister's horror stories, and could not bring myself to stay at any of these establishments. I rationalized my capitulation by telling myself that this way, I would surely complete my studies before my father's retirement. Also, Lady Brabourne was a government-run college and the fees for the hostel was only ₹25 (it was increased to ₹40 during my stay). The college tuition fee was ₹12, and so I reasoned that the burden on the family would be low if I agreed to attend this college. Further, it had an excellent reputation in respect of its teaching standards – and so the die was cast.

# 3

# Kolkata: The Feeling of Independence

I was at last going to college! The butterflies in my stomach wouldn't stop fluttering. It was my first experience of staying away from home, and I was raring to go. My parents accompanied me to the college. I liked the look of the building, situated as it was in a large campus surrounded by gardens and leafy trees. The building had a certain grandeur, having been built in the British times, though the classrooms were not too spacious. After completing all the formalities we were directed to the hostel, which was separated from the college by just a lane.

The junior matron received us and showed us the dormitory in which we would stay. She reassured us that should we perform well, we would be eligible for a single room in our second year. We could choose our beds. I found that the first three beds were already made, indicating they already had occupants, so I chose the fourth. My trunk containing my clothes went under the bed. I would live out of it for the next year. At the head of the bed was a desk with an attached chair. The desk had enough space for all my books. There was also a chest of drawers beyond the desk, and we were told that we could use one of the drawers each. This would hold our foodstuff and toiletries. The hostel had no fans. We enquired whether we could hire one, but received an unequivocal no in response. It seems there were many students from underprivileged backgrounds who would find it difficult to hire a fan, and so none of us was allowed the privilege. Besides, who would foot the electricity bill? An offer to do the same or allow the girls to contribute to it was also met with dogged resistance. There was 'no provision for such an arrangement' and there ended the matter.

It was November then, therefore bearable without a fan. I decided we would have to shelve that battle for another day. Suffice to say, we never won that battle during our time. The net result was that whenever I went home and sat under the fan, I would promptly catch a cold. During the worst of the summer nights, after endless tossing and turning in the humid heat, we would stumble to the bathrooms, sit under the tap in our night dresses, and stumble back to bed fully drenched and finally fall asleep.

My parents saw me settled in and bade me goodbye. I started by making friends with the girl in the next bed. Her name was Mukta and she was from Asansol, a mining town close to Bokaro. She was from Loreto Convent, a school we had visited for various inter-school activities such as debates and sports. As luck would have it, she also turned out to be a student of English. Our friendship got off to a great start that very night. At home we were not used to mosquito nets and I had not brought one with me, even though the list of items to be brought had specified one. I felt hemmed in whenever I had used a net earlier and, therefore, had left it out as something I would, in any case, never use. At bedtime I found that everyone else had nets, which they put up. As the lights went out, the song of the mosquitoes began. All of the pesky brutes must have realized there was only one body to feast upon. Soon, I was sitting up in bed, swatting away. There was no way I could sleep. Mukta woke up in the middle of the night and, seeing my plight, offered to share her net. We pushed the two beds together, but her net wasn't large enough to cover both beds. As a compromise, I stuck my head under her net, but this only allowed some of the mosquitoes to find their way into the net. Ultimately, in sheer desperation, we both crawled into her bed and spent the night lying on our sides, as there wasn't enough space for two people to lie flat. It was a solid foundation to what would be the friendship of a lifetime. Mukta insists that I was kept awake not by the mosquitoes, but the fact that I was homesick and was having a quiet cry – though I continue to claim that was not the case. However, the first job I did the next morning was to arrange for a net. I had learnt that one ignores instructions at one's own peril.

In those days, young girls were just about beginning to wear salwar–kameez and the really modern ones were adopting pants. My father's ideas were, however, different. He felt that girls should wear frocks and skirts, especially for important or formal occasions. I rebelled hugely, but was unable to get him to understand that frocks were now worn by babies only. However, I was okay with skirts, and I had some really smart skirt suits. I had worn one of these – a green one – on my first day. I should actually have taken a little more care to find out what college-going girls were wearing in the city. Anyway, I was the only one in a skirt that day and the seniors lounging on the steps of the building immediately latched on to me: 'You there, in the green skirt!' I had heard of ragging, but had little idea what it entailed. Once I got called upon, the seniors wanted to know my name. I gave my name in the way I had always heard it, only to realize that the Bengali pronunciation was different, with rounded O's as opposed to the A's.

I spent the next hour repeating my name ad infinitum, the Bengali way. After an hour, they lost interest in me and latched on to the next girl. The next day, all the freshers were shaken awake at three in the morning. We were told to oil our hair well, put on a sari and present ourselves on the grounds in an hour sharp. Never having worn a sari by myself before, I was in a quandary, till another fresher came to my rescue. Her name was Sushmita, and she taught me well. Many people have over the years complimented me on my ability to keep my sari draped in such a manner that it still looks fresh at the end of the day. Well, the art was learnt at 3 a.m. in a hostel room, with oil dripping from my hair. The ragging itself wasn't too bad. We were marched around, singing a parody of the college song and swearing lifelong fealty to the seniors, before being let off. Many of these seniors became good friends of mine with time. When I consider the innocence in our ragging, I feel blessed because there were institutions where ragging had robbed freshers of their life or limb, and caused untold mental trauma.

By the end of the first few days, groups had begun to form. My group consisted of Mukta and two girls from St Joseph's in Chandannagar. One was Indrani, a beautiful, large-eyed girl with lots of energy and an infectious smile. She seemed to draw followers naturally. I was at best a reluctant follower, but her compelling energy still drew me to her. Her friend and the fourth in our group was Sayeeda, better known as Jessie, after her 'home name' of Jasmin. (Everyone in Bengal has a 'home name', or pet name. We have a grand-sounding name that we use in public and – in most cases – a ridiculous one that friends and family use to address you.)

But let me first describe the hostel so that one may better visualize our lives therein. The main gate was in a 20-foot-high wall. The gate led into a quadrangle at the centre of which was a flagstaff with circular steps surrounding it. On the far side was a garden consisting mainly of trees and shrubs – not very well kept, but green. As you walked into the gate, to the right was the hostel building. On one side of the building was a long room with a table down the centre and chairs on both sides. This was the visitor's room. Boarders were allowed to receive visitors, pre-approved by parents, twice a week. As a result, boyfriends often presented themselves as uncles and even grandpas, if that was what was on the list! Luckily, there was no photo ID required. Visitors would walk in, sign their names and convey whom they wanted to meet to the female attendant. She would then go next door to the hostel – go up the stairwell (the building was three-storeys high) and then shout the name out: 'Rita didi, vijitaaaaaaar.' The girls who expected visitors would already be sitting around on the flagstaff steps or on the steps leading to the hostel itself. Those who would be lounging inside would often drape a sari over a nightdress and rush down to see who the visitor could be. It was quite primitive, but it worked! Boarders were also allowed to go shopping twice a week. Girls were herded together under the care of one of the male watchmen, who would take us to the corner of the road and tell us to get going after warning us to get back by 8 p.m. so that he could escort us back.

Attendance was taken in a simple way. The dining room consisted of fifteen tables, each seating ten girls. We were required to sit at fixed tables, and everyone dined at the same time – a gong would sound indicating it was mealtime. Any gaps at the tables were investigated by the junior warden, a mountain of a woman, who would lumber up the stairs to personally check whether the missing boarder was in her room and why she didn't want dinner. The result of this system was that all the rotis were required to be prepared in advance, before the dinner bell rang, so that everyone could be served simultaneously. Unfortunate were those who got the rotis made at the very beginning – they were so stiff and cold, we could have easily used them as weapons. One needed to be in the good books of the wardens to ensure that one got the warm rotis or the small extras, like slices of lemon and green chillies, to help the tasteless food go down easily.

Such small favours, that meant a lot and went a long way, were not given or received by being reticent. One needed to extract them through a covert show of strength. Early on, the group at our table realized this. All four of us were at this table, and after a few days of deliberations, we decided something needed to be done quickly to show that we were no pushovers. The junior warden was universally disliked for the expletives she liberally showered on us boarders. Of course, we were not all blameless souls and could often get up to antics, enough to drive one up the wall. But that lady generally displayed extreme amounts of disdain for all the souls under her care, and this didn't go down too well. From the loud and continuous snoring emanating from her room each night, it was surmised that she was a sound sleeper. She would wake up at 5 a.m. in order to complete her daily ablutions, about which she was very particular. Her room was at the head of Indrani's dormitory, which was in a corridor to the right as one walked into ours. It was decided that past midnight, we would latch her door from the outside, so that she would not be able to get out in the morning. The plan needed adjusting several times before it could be executed.

The first hurdle was that the latch outside her door made a hideous sound when being opened or closed. We got past that by oiling the latch and the hinges for a few days. It had to be done carefully so that she didn't get suspicious. We were cautious and used a drop or two of oil each day so it wouldn't drip and alarm her. On the appointed date, after she had gone to bed, one of the girls in Indrani's dormitory crept out and quietly slid the latch shut. The whole matter was kept a secret and, except for very few of us, no one knew who had done the deed. That night none of us slept, waiting for the sun to rise. As expected, around five in the morning, there was a string of loud curses from the warden's room, followed by the sound of her thumping the door. The noise grew progressively louder and those closest to her room rushed to find out what the matter was. On realizing that her door was latched from the outside, they unlatched it to confront a raging tornado inside, spewing out the choicest verbal abuses. But these girls were innocent and knew nothing about the plan and so no matter how much the warden shouted at them, they could throw no light on who the culprit was.

An enquiry took place, but all the girls held together and as nothing could be proved, no action could be taken. During the enquiry, many girls complained instead about the treatment they received from the warden, and as a fallout, her usage of expletives decreased. Somehow, though nothing was proved, the warden understood that such a plan could not have been executed without the knowledge or consent of our group. And so our place in the pecking order was established and would remain so for our three-year sojourn in the hostel. Of course, she had another latch installed, which could only be locked by her so that there were no repetitions of the incident.

Hostel food taught us the real meaning of hunger and the value of food. I think during our three years there all of us remained constantly hungry. We had to arrange our own breakfast, and would only be served a cup of tea. Normally, we would all keep a bottle of jam or jelly and buy a small loaf of bread from a shop next to the gate. If you went around the corner, there was a small shop serving hot kachoris with a potato curry. This was a treat we indulged in only once in a while, as the guard would have to be cajoled to let us go out – he had strict instructions not to let us step beyond his line of sight. As most of us went downstairs with saris draped over our night dresses, we argued that he ran little risk. During our last year, however, we did once walk off to the Maidan for a morning stroll followed by a proper breakfast at Flury's, consisting of delicate chicken sandwiches, baked beans and pastries. We found this was what most of the overweight ladies huffing and puffing during their morning walk at the Maidan did, and we found it a splendid way to celebrate the calories lost. (Little did we realize that we would become those huffing and puffing ladies in another thirty years – we may have laughed a little less at them.) Afterwards, we went off straight to college and returned with the rest of the girls when classes for the day got over.

Lunch was between 9 and 9.45 a.m. as our classes started at 10. One could eat whenever during that time. The tables would have containers of coarse parboiled rice (I found a leg of a cockroach in the rice once; another time, a broken piece of a green glass bangle). Once, at home during vacation, I found our domestic help having his lunch. Quite innocently, I commented on how white and fragrant the rice looked and smelt, causing my mother some consternation as to where she had sent her daughter for her studies.

There would be a bowl of dal, which I always felt was three-layered. The topmost layer was thin yellow water. The middle layer was slightly thicker, and tasted of the starchy water one decanted while boiling rice. The last layer had a few grains of dal of some indeterminate variety. There would be a vegetable – normally either potato or eggplant. And a two-inch-long piece of fish, as thin as a bay leaf. Dinner was the same, except that there was no fish. Instead, we were served two pieces of mutton on Tuesday and egg curry on Friday. Tea was at 4.30 p.m. and consisted of two thin slices of bread smeared with margarine in the middle (never covering the entire slice!), two sour rasgullas the size of large marbles and a cup of tea. I don't know to date how they managed to get sour rasgullas day after day, but somehow they did! There was a lady, however, who came with aluminium containers filled with dal puri and aloo dum, fish chop and mutton cutlets to sell. The moment she arrived, it was as though a swarm of locusts had landed in a wheat field, especially if it was the beginning of a month, when all our pockets had just been replenished by remittances from home. Those blessed with generous pocket money could have a good meal that day and many survived on this fare alone. We never found out her name. We all called her 'bhadra mahila', which meant lady in Bengali, and an unnamed lady she remained – a saviour to many generations of girls as they passed through the portals of the hostel.

Hot water was a prized commodity. Of course, there was no running hot water in the toilets. In winter, one would need to lug a bucket to the kitchen and lug back the half bucket that was each girl's quota – filled from an enormous black kettle of constantly boiling water, billowing white clouds of steam. In the night, should one feel hungry or peckish, the option was to have a hot drink like Complan or Horlicks. For the purpose, one could get a thermos flask of hot water, which again we would need to go to the kitchen to fill. Heaving the heavy kettle back and forth and filling the flask without spilling a drop needed a certain kind of dexterity. Those girls unable to do it would be yelled at for wasting a precious commodity both by the students waiting in the queue as well as the staff. Often during exams, this was a lifesaver. Many of us would fall asleep after a busy day, only to wake up an hour or two later, refresh ourselves with a hot drink, and commence our studies. On one such occasion, a number of us woke up to find that our flasks were empty. A quick look around revealed that one of the girls, who had a steady boyfriend, had 'borrowed' the hot water from a few of us to do a DIY pedicure as she had a special date on the morrow. She came very close to getting lynched that day. To our delight, though, a few days later, fate intervened to teach her a lesson. This time, she 'borrowed' a tin of condensed milk from another girl, as she was very hungry and a search of all our drawers had yielded no other food. As she held it over her mouth to pour the thick liquid down her throat, she felt something solid fall into her mouth. To the delight of those watching, it turned out to be a cockroach that had crept into the tin and drowned. But that one incident was all that was needed to put an end to her 'borrowing' our stuff.

At a pinch, if we were famished, especially on Sundays, we could also boil an egg in the hot water. The result was a quarter of a quarter boil, but to us hungry youngsters, the runny egg liberally seasoned with salt and pepper and soaked up with squares of stale bread, tasted wonderful. On weekdays, it was a different matter. There was the ubiquitous phuchka wallah in front of the college. Each college had its own, and there was a huge debate as to which college had the better one. Each college claimed superiority and students proclaimed undying loyalty to their own. There was also the seller of 'vitamin'.

This was a fellow who sold sprouts with chopped onion, tomatoes and coriander leaves, topped with a dash of lemon and chaat masala. To a hungry horde of girls, it tasted better than the five-star food I eat these days. The fellow would keep his wares in a rectangular glass box perched on a stand made out of bamboo sticks. I loved watching him prepare the dish. It was the work of an expert. Five large spoonful of sprouts would be ladled on to a cone made of sal leaves. A handful of finely chopped onions and tomatoes would then be tossed in, followed by a squeeze of lemon and a sprinkle of coriander leaves. I never could figure out how he managed to squeeze so much juice out of one half of a lemon. He would then shake a tin container with a few holes on top containing the chaat masala. Next, he would cup the cone with both hands and expertly toss the contents with a few flicks of his wrist, stick in a wooden spoon and a mouth-watering concoction would be in your hands. Before going to the hostel there were numerous things I didn't eat – all types of gourds, papayas (I disliked their smell), apples (I hated the crunching sound they made when bitten into – it gave me goosebumps like the scratching of chalk on a blackboard), to name just a few. By the time I left the hostel, I ate everything gratefully and genuinely appreciated them as well. People say I am quite adventurous with food, and it all started at the hostel.

My father, was averse to us watching movies. Probably as a reaction to that, in the first month of college, I watched eleven movies by bunking classes. I used every strategy you could think of – sitting at the back of the room and creeping out when the teacher's back was turned, asking friends to provide proxy attendance, feigning sickness within minutes of the class starting, and so on. In two weeks, I watched *Ben-Hur* six times. The next month, cutting classes became a little more difficult as teachers became familiar with us, but I still managed to watch six movies. It was then that the senior matron asked me to see her. I went in confidently, never expecting to be confronted for my movie-watching spree. But instead of reprimanding me, she asked if I had looked at the weekly test grades. Of course they were bad, but I was still adjusting to a new life. 'Well, it's your funeral,' she said. 'I have seen your grades in school and they were good. The result of your low grades now will be that you will not be eligible for a single-seater room at the end of the year, but will have to stay on in a dormitory. It is a choice you must make.' This brought me to my senses quickly, and my movie-going exploits ceased.

In those days, law and order were not matters of concern for ordinary people. Bokaro Steel City, where my parents lived, was five hours by train, from Kolkata to Dhanbad, and then another ninety minutes by bus. There was a train for Kolkata starting at six in the morning from Dhanbad. I would leave home at 3 a.m. to get a bus that would take me to the station at that hour. Back then, it was never unsafe to make this journey alone. There were a number of my friends who lived quite far away, and during short vacations they would come over to my place. And during longer vacations, I would go to theirs. I discovered that I loved travelling. I planned these longer trips with great enthusiasm, but little wisdom. On one such occasion, I was to go to Meerut to visit a friend whose father was a brigadier stationed at the cantonment there. Anju, my friend, gave me directions as to how to get there: 'Take a train to New Delhi station. Then take a bus to Meerut. I will be at the bus station with my mother.'

It seemed simple enough. I bought a ticket in the AC deluxe express – a prestigious train in those days, but one that had only chair cars for an overnight journey. On alighting at New Delhi, I discovered to my horror that the bus departed from a place quite far away and I would need to take yet another bus to get there. In those days, suitcases didn't have wheels, and I was still painfully thin. Still, I managed to lug my heavy bag to where minibuses departed for the main bus terminal. As I got off the minibus at the terminus, a young boy came running up. 'Didi, where are you going?' he demanded. 'Meerut,' I said. 'Then hurry up! That bus is just departing.' He deftly picked up my bag, heaved it on to his shoulder and started running. I ran after him, relieved that I didn't have to carry the heavy bag myself but apprehensive he would run off with it. The boy ran towards a bus that was just nosing out. We ran towards the rear exit and he banged on the back of the bus to make it stop. As it slowed down, he handed my bag to the conductor, pushed me through the door, snatched the five rupees I offered him and ran off to look for his next customer.

I found an empty window seat at the back of the bus. Soon, the conductor came around and I bought my ticket. The bus continued meandering its way through the dusty roads. It would enter a bus station, some people would get down, others would get on and after a halt of about ten minutes the bus would be on its way again. The bus stations were busy, bustling places. I loved the colours and sounds. In those days, there were no air-conditioned buses and, given that we didn't even have fans in the hostel, I didn't even feel the need for such comforts. There were all manner of peddlers selling their wares at these stops. There were coconut sellers with wedges of coconut lining a steel plate, like the petals of a giant white flower calling out the merits of the fruit. There were people selling freshly roasted peanuts in their shells, in cones made of newspaper containing salt ground with green chillies. There was the ubiquitous chai vendor doling out tea, thick and milky, served in little clay pots, from a shiny kettle. The heat and dust made me very drowsy and my eyes closed of their own accord.

I was jolted awake as the bus screeched to a halt at its fifth or sixth stop. I was wondering how much longer it would take when suddenly my eyes fell on Anju and her mother standing in the shade of a tree next to the stand. Panic-stricken, I jumped up, grabbed my bag and hurtled off the bus. But even before I greeted them, I ran to the front of the bus to see its destination. 'Hardwar' it read. I had been extremely lucky! Had I not noticed Anju I might have landed up in Haridwar, having never considered that I had got on to a bus whose final stop wasn't Meerut. My guardian angels certainly had their work cut out.

College was good in respect of the friends I made. Even today, when I see them after long periods of virtually no contact, we easily pick up from where we left off. But my studies didn't excite me, nor did they challenge. I knew in my heart that I would never be able teach literature. I loved reading and I loved poetry. But I had no interest in analysing what, if anything, the author meant. I would rather enjoy their writing with my heart than analyse them with my mind. I 'felt' literature, I 'felt' poetry and what I 'felt' was a personal experience, not meant for sharing with one and all. I did well enough in my exams – enough to qualify for the single rooms – but I was far from brilliant.

The college union elections came up. I wanted to fight for the general secretary's position. But my father's admonition as I left home came in the way: 'I am sending you to Kolkata to study, and not to take part in politics. Several of our friends' children have suffered in the recent past by getting swept up in ideologies. But life is tough, and I will retire shortly. This is the time for you to prepare yourself for the future. It is essential you find your feet as quickly as possible.' I decided to not be on the front lines, and instead to stand for the position of assistant general secretary. In view of the enormous problems created by the Naxal movement, the college insisted on a strictly apolitical agenda. We therefore fought for better facilities, more disciplines of study, etc. We once marched for blood donation, except that when it was my turn to donate and I stepped on the scale, the intern collecting blood asked me in a loud voice whether I had come to donate or to receive blood (I weighed a respectable 35 kgs at that time).

It was time to actually start thinking what I would do once I completed my degree. We didn't have counsellors back then, and parents were not too aware of opportunities either. In any case, the only way to communicate was through letters that were infrequently written. Letter writing, however, taught me to write in Bengali as my mother had made it clear she would not respond to letters written in any other language. As a result, my written Bengali looks like the printed script rather than the cursive hand one would develop if taught the subject formally. Of course, in emergencies one could use the telephone, but it was horrendously expensive and one had to book calls and then wait for them to materialize. Friends remained our biggest source of information (as they are even today).

The Indian Administrative Service provided great career opportunities. But to my dismay, I found that I needed knowledge in a subject up to postgraduate level, and that subject could not be a language. Had I chosen something other than English, I would have a better chance at that exam, or else I needed to study a subject on my own time. It was at this time that we discovered the entrance exams for the probationary officers at banks. The matter was brought to my notice by a friend, who dared me to take up the exam as I was so concerned about a career. I knew that the competition would be intense, but as it cost little and our whole group was planning to appear together, I went along with it. It seemed a good bet as the papers were in the areas of English, general knowledge and logic, which we felt were manageable. And that's how another journey began.

Life in college had its ups and downs. Hostel life had its challenges, but it was a great way of learning the art of survival. You learnt to tolerate cramped and shared living spaces, hunger, heat, bad food, dirty toilets, quarrels, delayed remittances, weekly exams (for which one had only a night to prepare), break-ups and making up with boyfriends, heartbreak, fevers and stomach upsets, smuggled cigarettes and wine – sometimes even mild drugs taken by the really adventurous ones, willing to experiment with anything – and we learnt to overcome any pitfall that came our way. Staying in dormitories taught us many skills, even changing clothes without letting any part of the body to be seen. My mother used to call it the 'Houdini trick'. We arrived as sixteen-year-old kids, mostly from small towns, and left as fully grown responsible women, raring to take on the world.

Soon, our graduation exams were over. As the session was delayed by a few months, those wanting to do post-graduation degrees started classes straightaway. Having selected English for my graduate studies, I continued with the same discipline. In those days, changing subjects at the postgraduate level wasn't allowed. I shifted to Jadavpur University for my post-graduation and found accommodation at its women's hostel, as did a number of other girls from Brabourne. Indrani's parents were insisting on her marriage and so she didn't join post-graduate studies.

This was a hostel which didn't have the restrictions of Brabourne. The quality of food too, though not great, was better. Here we needed to share a room with two others, and I found a room with two of my old friends from Brabourne – one was from geography and the other from history. Next door, Mukta too was sharing a room with two other girls from Brabourne. One of the girls, Swarupa, was also a student of English, and both Mukta and Swarupa became good study partners.

In the meantime, I started looking for work as I was determined to stop being dependent on my father at age twenty-one. As luck would have it, one of our married classmates who tutored two Marwari girls wanted some time off. One of the girls was in class five, the other in class seven. She offered to arrange for me to tutor these kids for the next few months. Though the work was hard – five days a week and two hours per day – the salary of ₹200 a month was quite grand in those days. At that point, I was getting a remittance of ₹150 a month from home, from which I paid the hostel fees of ₹90. I had no tuition fees as those were waived on 'merit cum means' grounds. The rest was pocket money. The ₹200, therefore, was enough for my needs. I was about six months short of twenty-one then, and I felt good that I could spare my family from having to send me money. However, my father insisted it was his duty to support me during my studies, no matter how much I earned. So after a lot of arguments, he decided to reduce the amount of my remittance to ₹100. But even then, with my earnings from my tuitions and my allowance from home, I became a pretty well-heeled student at the hostel.

My tuitions were in a part of town called Alipore. It was a rich neighbourhood, characterized by huge marble-clad bungalows set in large grounds surrounded by high boundary walls. Little did I know that many of these householders would be my customers some day and would treat me with huge respect – the amount of respect being inversely proportional to the state of their business. On winter evenings, by the time I finished the tuitions, the roads would already be empty, lit only by the street lights, with large cars gliding by and very few pedestrians around. I would often be the only one waiting for a bus at the Alipore Burdwan Road bus stand. The Alipore branch of the State Bank of India (SBI) was located bang opposite the bus stand. As I waited for my bus, I would often see groups of people leaving the branch, obviously employees of the bank going home after the day's work. As they came out, I would notice the camaraderie, the laughter, the way they called out 'goodnight' before separating. Some would cross the road to the bus stand. Others would zoom away on their motorcycles. Some would regularly visit a fruit stall at the corner. I had heard bank employees were well paid. As I stood at the bus stand, I would watch these guys longingly and imagine what it would be like to be part of that group, with a secure, well-paid job and a loving family to go back home to.

This was November 1976. That day I stood at the bus stand like every other day, waiting for the bus to take me back to the hostel. The bus was taking a long time to come. There were very few people on the road. It was cold and a little smoggy. The road past the bus stand led to one of the largest crematoriums of Kolkata, called Keoratola. Often, I would witness dead bodies being carried in a procession towards the crematorium, accompanied by chants of 'Bolo Hari, Hari Bol'. That day a similar procession was passing by, and just as they came abreast, the cloth used by one of the pall-bearers to cushion the bier on his shoulder fell off. The group came to a halt. The bier was lowered right in front of me as the pall-bearers fanned themselves and wiped their brows. The smell of the incense sticks burning at the feet of the body assailed my nostrils, and I closed my eyes and prayed for the peace of the departed soul. As the procession went on their way, my bus arrived and I boarded it.

The entrance exams for the banks' probationary officers was a few days away. In those days, there were no guide books or coaching classes for these exams. But there were some magazines for general knowledge called *Competition Master*, and my roommate Shubhra and I had decided to study late. After dinner, we sat down to study till we heard the shrill whistle of a train that passed by at 3 a.m. and was our signal for going to bed. We put aside our books, and Shubhra went off to use the toilet. I approached my bed to pull down the mosquito net when a strong smell assailed my nostrils. In a trice, the smell transported me back to that evening's encounter at the bus stop as the pall-bearers stopped in front of me. It was the same smell! I couldn't believe it. I shook awake Supty, my other roommate, who was fast asleep. 'Can you smell something?' I asked her. Groggily, she sniffed the air, declared that someone must be doing a puja somewhere, turned over and promptly fell asleep. As Shubhra returned to the room, I thought about mentioning this incident to her, but then decided against it. She was inordinately scared of ghosts and the smell seemed to be concentrated on my side of the room. Also, somehow, it made me feel at peace rather than scared. So I crept under the net and was soon asleep.

I mention this incident because after joining the bank at Staff College in Hyderabad, when our postings arrived I was amazed to find that I had been posted to that same Alipore branch in front of which I had stood many days, wishing to be part of the team. Maybe my wishes had fructified, or maybe a good soul had blessed me on its way to eternity. Of course, on the practical side, my tuitions did help me with the entrance exam. The girls I tutored were extraordinarily weak in maths. In desperation, I had started them on mental maths for half an hour each day. That exercise really paid off for me as well in cracking the paper on logic, as speed and clarity of thinking are required for this.

On the day of the written test, we went off to the venue, which happened to be the local head office of the bank. I was a little anxious and so hardly ate any breakfast. On arriving, I found my seat on the tenth floor. The exam hall was well organized. The chief invigilator was, Yasmin Das, who I gathered was an officer in the bank. I admired her assured style, and the fact that she seemed so much at ease in her surroundings. The tests were not as difficult as I had feared they would be. I finished in time, but by then I was ravenously hungry. I waited impatiently for the elevator, but all were too crowded for me to get into. I decided to take the stairs instead, and quickly discovered that climbing down ten flights was not easy. I was almost faint with hunger by the time I reached the hostel.

I rushed to the dining hall to find that the only items still available were rice and a chutney made of a fruit called 'chalta'. It was horribly sour, but even that tasted heavenly that day. I gorged on the rice and chutney, then went to my room and fell fast asleep. I woke an hour later to a sick feeling in my stomach. I rushed to the bathroom somehow and threw up. The retching wouldn't stop. Alarmed, my friends called the doctor. By the time he came, I was curled up into a tight ball and couldn't seem to lie straight for fear of setting off the retching again. Anyway, the doctor diagnosed severe acidity, gave me an injection, told me to be less stupid about what I ate on an empty stomach and left. I was fine the next morning, but felt that after having gone through so much trouble to take the entrance test, the least the bank could do was to shortlist me for an interview.

The bank obliged! The day of the interview dawned. I felt both excited and nervous. We were to reach the same building where we had written the test, except I was assigned to a room on the eleventh floor. On arrival, we were told that we should keep the noise down as it was here that the top guy – the chief general manager – had his office. There was a plush green carpet on the floor; the corridor walls were panelled in a rich walnut-coloured wood. The rooms were pristine with white walls and quality furniture. There were few people on the floor, and everyone seemed to be tiptoeing around. It was quite impressive and intimidating. However, we soon got into the swing of things. The first round was a group discussion, which I, with my background in debating, quite enjoyed. The second round was an interview. The only question I remember was the one someone asked about drawing a parallel between what I had learnt in my special paper, that is, Greek mythology and the fall of the government after Emergency. 'Hubris?' I replied a little tentatively, not quite sure whether political discourse could be carried out openly in such a forum. The answer, though, seemed to please the board and I left with a feeling that I had aced the interaction.

On coming out, however, I was quickly brought back to earth. I could hear raised voices coming through the door of the hallway. They seemed to be familiar, so I quickly made my way out. Sure enough, it was a group of my friends demanding that I be let out, as I had asked them to collect me on their way to a movie for which we had tickets and for which they were getting delayed. I apologized for the commotion, and herded my friends out as quickly as I could.

University didn't excite me on the academic front. But I had a busy time, what with classes and tuition. We had lots of good times as our circle of friends grew bigger. The intense discussions we had on the steps of the Arts building or sitting around in the hostel or in the AC (Amenities Centre) had all the fervour of youth and none of the practicality of real life. The 3 a.m. train was our signal to disperse. I also joined a drama club and the last play that I would act in was as a member of this group.

I had been scanning the newspapers for a few days, anticipating the declaration of the results. Newspapers were delivered in the common room and there would be one copy of each publication. But as boarders wandered in and out looking for the paper to read with their morning tea, it would soon get disaggregated and pages would frequently go missing. As a result, I had to get up early every day to get hold of the full newspaper. This proved a little difficult for I was going to bed at 3 a.m. And so, one morning, I was rudely shaken awake by a friend, telling me that the State Bank of India results had been published. I rushed down three flights of stairs, flipped through the pages and, lo and behold! There was my roll number in black and white.

# 4

# SBI: The Journey Begins

I was ordered to report to the SBI Staff College at Hyderabad on 5 September 1977. My MA classes ended on 31 August. I had to board the East Coast Express on 3 September as it would take thirty-six hours to reach Hyderabad. I had just two days to pack and sort out my affairs before I left for three weeks. I was terribly excited to be travelling in first class with my own money for the very first time in my life. My friends made my departure an unforgettable experience. It felt as though the daughter of the house was leaving for her in-laws' place. A huge group of my friends came to see me off, and I was delighted to receive such a grand send-off. My parents couldn't come to Kolkata, and so my brother was deputed to stand in for them. We arrived at the station in a fleet of taxis. Once we figured out which platform the train was on, and, of course, double-checked the reservation list stuck outside compartments for my name, we all piled in. I was in a two-seater ladies' coupe. There was no one else in the coupe, so my friends decided to serenade me with some of our favourite songs. I don't think the East Coast Express had ever heard such raucous renditions of 'Oh my darling Clementine', 'Summer wine', 'Congratulations and celebrations', and others of its ilk. We soon had a bunch of curious onlookers peeking in through the doors and windows, but nothing could deter my friends as they bounced around on the cushioned berths and interpreted the songs in ways I would have thought impossible. After trying helplessly to make them understand that they were seriously embarrassing me, I gave up, sat back and joined in. It really was the best send-off I have ever had.

My brother had been instructed by my father to keep an eye out for fellow travellers to the same destination – someone who could help me if required. So we all scanned the faces of everyone else in my compartment. There was a family standing a little to the side, surrounding a guy who looked like a typical 'good boy'. My brother felt that he seemed a likely candidate. He wandered over to talk to them, and in some time brought him over to introduce him to me and my large group of friends. One look at the group, however, and he scuttled back to his seat, promising to get better acquainted with me during the journey. Thus, I met my first batchmate, Atanu Sen, who still maintains that he seriously questioned whether he was entering the right job after taking a look at me and my boisterous friends. Regardless, we did become friends for life – the only difference is that he has lost a lot of his hair but has maintained his size, while I have lost a lot of my hair and trebled my size.

On arrival at Hyderabad, we took an auto together to Begumpet, where the Staff College was located in the midst of a verdant campus. We were quickly allotted rooms after completing the formalities. Two trainees were required to share a room, and my roommate was a girl called Baruni. She too was from Kolkata. We became good friends in the course of our stay. Soon after joining SBI, she took a transfer to the northeast and married one of our Assamese batchmates, one of the successful relationships that bloomed during the training period.

The best experience I had there was what woke us up the next morning. There was a tap on the door at exactly 6.30 a.m. We were greeted by a waiter, dressed in a white coat and gloves, bearing two small thermos flasks, cups and saucers, and a plate of biscuits. On being invited in, he politely enquired, 'Should I pour out the tea, madam, or would you prefer to do it later?' I was awestruck. I had arrived from a hostel where we had to rush down three flights of stairs clutching our mugs tightly, to pour our morning tea (thick from having been boiled too long) from a large, blackened kettle. This was a serious improvement from those days.

There were about fifty of us in the batch, mostly straight out of college and heady with the thought of having landed one of the best jobs (definitely then, and maybe even now) in the market. There were lots of lectures and gameplay and talks from seniors. Two incidents remain fresh in my memory. One, was an exercise when the class was divided into three groups. A volunteer from each group was asked to leave the class with an instructor. The rest of us were told to come up with three promotional strategies for a product in twenty minutes and then choose a spokesperson to present it. Three strategies in twenty minutes – it seemed impossible. We quickly sketched out three possible methods and then divided the team into three groups, so that we could all simultaneously work on all three ideas. Sometime during this period, the group member who had been sent out returned. He wanted to know what was going on. Nobody had the time to tell him as we were in the thick of it. We were frantically trying to create a storyline and the last thing we wanted was to waste time going over the matter with him. He checked with all of us, but we shooed him away. His suggestions fell on deaf ears as we raced the clock.

When the twenty minutes passed, the instructors called for order and then instead of calling us to present our work, they called on the three volunteers to narrate their experience and how they felt.

'I felt totally unwanted and unwelcome.'

'I felt like a pest that the team wanted to swat away.'

'I felt I was invisible to them.'

'I felt I was useless and irrelevant.'

And so it went on, till one of the instructors stopped them, turned to us and told us that is this is how we could expect to feel when we join the branches. 'You would be jumping in midstream, among a group of people engaged in doing a job. They will have no time for a rookie. So, now, we will teach you how to make your place in the team, and not only that, how to become a valued member of the team.'

It is a lesson that has stood me in good stead through my career.

The other matter that stands out in my memory is the inauguration speech given by our course coordinator, Balakrishna Iyer, a charismatic senior official. He told us about his journey in the bank, how he had followed the same path that we were starting on, and that every chairman in the bank had done the same. 'One of you could be chairman one day,' he told us. And so a seed was sown. It lay dormant for many, many years, forgotten in the hurly-burly of life's daily challenges. But it was there in all of us, and I wouldn't believe it if one of my batchmates told me that we were not all thinking the same thought: 'Maybe, just maybe, it could be me.'

The ten days of the induction course flew past, and the time had come for the group to split up and head for the training centres for our hands-on lessons. Luckily, most of us who had become good friends by then were allocated to the training centre at Banjara Hills, Hyderabad. The centre there was an old building that looked like a ship. And it was also rather ramshackle, especially compared to the swanky new college building. But it had an old-world charm. Besides, Banjara Hills in those days was beautiful. The most outrageously gorgeous rock shapes were all around, balanced impossibly on tiny bases. As one walked up the hill, the silence felt solid and I realized why literary pieces talked about silences so profound they could be 'cut with a knife'. The nature of the silence there was soothing yet mind-blowing. Not a blade of grass moved, nor a whisper of wind blew. Surrounded by huge boulders – some canting over at crazy angles, others majestically straight – it felt like I was at the beginning of time itself. I loved going for walks amongst the rocks, by myself or with a friend, content to just sit there and soak in the beauty. Words were unnecessary, and almost felt sacrilegious there. When I return to Banjara Hills these days, the beautiful bungalows I now see drive home a deep sense of loss – a loss of youth, beauty and innocence itself.

The bonding that occurred in those days has remained intact through the years. Every batch today has its own email group, and even those who left the bank after some time to pursue other careers remain part of it and are often the most prolific contributors. They remain our most balanced critics, but their critique is invariably constructive as they still feel for the institution. The training days had the right ingredients for cementing these ties. In fact, SBI's Probationary Officers' Training programme has often been hailed as the model that we got right.

Besides, Hyderabad was a great city for our training, as it provided ample entertainment over the weekends. We went through the Salar Jung Museum for a whole day. I am fascinated by antiques – and just one day at the museum felt insufficient. The next weekend, we explored Golconda Fort. Another weekend was spent at the Nagarjuna Sagar Dam. We came close to a tragedy on our visit to the Hussain Sagar, though. We had gone to the lake for a picnic, and it had been decided that the boys and the girls would separately prepare some items of food. Accordingly, we were hard at it. In the midst of this, Padmaja, Shashi and I wandered off to the edge of the lake. A lovely breeze was blowing, and all seemed peaceful and quite. Little waves lapped at the rocks on the edges. As we stood there, Padmaja put out a foot to dip it in the water. The next moment, she slid right in. One would have expected shallow water at the edge, but obviously that was not the case here as she went under fully before she came up puffing and splashing desperately. The next moment, Shashi too was in the water. I don't know how that happened. Maybe she leaned over to catch Padmaja, or she may have slipped herself. It happened within seconds and she too went under. I felt as though I was moving on autopilot. I lay down, splayed my arms and legs for better purchase and held out my hand. Padmaja caught on to it as Shashi clasped her shoulder. I tried pulling them out. But it was an unequal battle. I was all of 39 kgs and pulling out two girls made heavier by their soaking-wet clothes seemed a tall order. I could feel my feet slipping as my body inched forward, pulled by the weight of the two girls. And then suddenly somebody caught hold of both my legs. I could hardly turn around to see who had come to our rescue, but I saw someone dressed in a shirt and trousers. The man pulled on my legs, and slowly I could feel my body moving backwards as both girls slowly emerged from the water.

Padmaja had a huge leather tote bag on her shoulder. She came out with the bag swollen with water, looking like a *bhisti* (a person who uses large skin bags to supply water from wells to houses in rural areas). Closer to the shoreline, they caught on to the rocks and hauled themselves out. Padmaja opened her bag to pour out the water and inside, floating forlornly, was a packet of cigarettes and a box of matches that she had been hiding from prying eyes. By the time I got over the shock and then the relief of seeing that my friends were okay, I looked around to thank our saviour but he had disappeared. I was thoroughly puzzled. When we had walked up to the shore, no one was there. Where did the man come from and why did he leave in such a hurry? Where had he gone? There was no one in sight. None of our other batchmates had even realized we were missing or the near tragedy that had befallen us. There was no sign of our saviour. As I said before, I have kept my guardian angel pretty busy.

On the last day of the training programme, there was a suppressed sense of excitement all around – the excitement of going into battle at last. There was also a frisson of worry as our postings were to be soon revealed. And to my surprise, I got posted to the same branch in Alipore in front of which I had stood on many a long evening, waiting for the bus to take me back to my hostel, envying the people who came streaming out of the branch! The universe was indeed working to fulfil all my wishes.

My first day felt as though I had crashed into reality. The Alipore branch at that time was the largest treasury branch in the country, serving the largest district of undivided 24 Parganas (later on, it was divided into North and South 24 Parganas). The treasury branches were responsible for paying all government cheques and bills. I joined the branch on Panchami, a day before commencement of the Durga Puja holidays in Bengal. This is the largest festival in eastern India, and all employers try to pay their employees before the festivities begin. The government too tries to release all its dues, so that companies that have done work for the government or have supplied the government in some way are in a position to pay their workers. When I arrived at the branch, at half past nine in the morning, there was already a huge crowd gathered outside. There was a lot of jostling and shouting. I tried sneaking in through the side door but the guard wouldn't let me in. I kept displaying my appointment letter to the sceptical guard till other staff members came over to find out what the problem was. With their help, I was at last allowed to step inside.

Most people inside took one look at me and heaved a sigh of relief, as if to say, 'Oh good, here's another pair of hands to help.'

The branch manager took me to the government section, organized an empty table and chair, and presented me to the in-charge, as though he had personally arranged for my appearance to help out the section in what was going to be at best a difficult day, and at worst a nightmare.

I was given a two-headed ballpoint pen, blue at one end and red at the other, a pad of 'government scrolls' – consisting of blank pages with several rows and four columns – and a box of carbon paper. I was to write down details of twenty-five instruments in triplicate per page. This entailed numbering the page, writing a serial number, the number of the instrument and the amount. When the twenty-five instruments were written down, I was to add up the amounts and close each scroll, before moving on to the next one.

The first thing I realized was that one had to press down really hard to make the third copy legible ( I got a corn on my middle finger in the three weeks I was in this department). The second was that one had to be really fast. The paid government cheques were being carried from the cash department in baskets and poured on to my table at an unimaginable rate. I struggled to keep up with the pace, but the mountain of cheques kept growing. My anxiety increased to such an extent that adding up the twenty-five numbers became a major hurdle. The officer in-charge had luckily decided to check my initial work. After seeing the results of my effort at addition, he let out a long-suffering sigh and asked me to desist from adding, and to just write down the details correctly. On seeing my deeply concerned face, he assured me in a kindly manner that I could do the additions in the evening. I quickly lowered my head because I didn't want him to see the horror on my face at having to add the numbers in the evening.

But there was more to come. By 7 p.m. that day, I had finally finished adding up all the numbers, even though payments had stopped at 2 p.m. as per the banking hours in those days. The messenger brought me a long, slim book in which there was a thick bunch of vouchers and cheques. This was the dreaded 'day book'. I was required to sort out the instruments by account number, enter the details – taking care to put the debit amounts in the inner column and the credit in the outer ones. The struggle was on. After one and a half hours, the accountant came by to check on my progress. The poor man couldn't believe the mess staring at him. I had the vouchers in little piles all over my desk. In many of the entries that I had entered, the account numbers appeared in the column meant for the amount and vice versa. The debit amounts had crept into the credit columns and the credit amounts had strangely slipped into the debit columns. Being a practical man, wanting to close the branch at a reasonable time of, say, 10 p.m., he decided to dictate the details to me, rather than leaving me to my own devices, in which case I might have spent the entire night in the branch. I was deeply grateful and we did finish by about 9.30 p.m. As I left the branch, grimy and exhausted, hands blackened from handling carbon paper, neck aching from poring over numbers and papers for close on to twelve hours, I had to ask myself where on earth I had landed up.

During the day I had noticed that the staff had three toilets marked 'Gents', 'Ladies' and 'Officers'. Unsure of which one to use, I sidled up to one of the ladies and asked. She looked up from the pile of papers in front of her and informed me rather disdainfully that lady officers always used the toilet attached to the branch manager's (BM) room. This was rather embarrassing. I had to wait till the BM was free to request him to allow me the privilege. He was a kind man and obviously schooled in the ways of women probationary officers (PO). He informed me that henceforth I need not ask or wait for him to be free, and that I simply walk in and use the facilities. On hindsight, it was an eminently practical way to handle an otherwise delicate matter. Though I sometimes wondered what the customers sitting with the BM thought of a lady walking in without so much as a by your leave, disappearing behind a door, reappearing after a little while, only to leave the room without acknowledging anyone sitting there.

The other incident on my first day was equally strange. As I was struggling with my work, sometime during midday, somebody came up from behind, opened my table drawer without even asking, thrust something inside, banged the drawer shut and left. I was mystified. In our school days, this was how the really adventurous boys would pass on their love missives. I was quite offended too. After all, I had been sitting right there – how could someone open my drawer without asking? I opened the drawer to see what was inside. It was a packet made of an old newspaper, stuffed with puffed rice with a few roasted peanuts. I took out the packet, utterly baffled. Our section in-charge had seen the entire incident and he called out, 'Take good care of that packet. It's the only thing that will keep ulcer at bay. In these seats, you cannot leave for lunch at a fixed time. Whenever you feel hungry, just have a fistful of *muri* and peanuts. It will keep you going. Hari, the fellow who put the packet in your drawer, supplies us daily, and you can pay him at the end of the month. Today is your first day. Remember always that this is a very high-pressure job and it is difficult to make time for yourself. So you will have to multitask without ignoring your health. If something happens to you, the organization will manage. But what about your near and dear ones? So never neglect yourself. You can do both – look after the organization and yourself – if you do it intelligently.'

It was a great lesson to learn on my first day.

The probation period flew past. There was never a moment to relax. New challenges were thrown at me daily. I struggled and fought, but one way or the other, the job got done. I always remembered the exercise we had done at the Staff College about how we would be viewed as unwelcome intrusions. So when someone made the effort to handhold and guide me, I was truly grateful. Meanwhile, my post-graduation exams loomed ahead. I was still staying at Jadavpur hostel. My friends were extraordinarily helpful. I would leave for office by nine after a hurried breakfast. All the small chores, such as collecting the clothes put out to dry, keeping them folded and ready, ironing some of them, keeping my tea warm and collecting hot water for the nightly cup of Complan, were taken care of by them for days on end. Luckily, this hostel also had no curfew, and so I was able to manage even when I had to stay late at office, which was about every day.

My family, especially my aunt, were insistent that I had to appear for my final post-graduate exams. No matter how much I tried to convince them that my job didn't leave me any time to study, they would not listen. I had no time to read up reference books and make notes. One of my roommates at that point was Anju, who had also been with me in college. She had a hoard of reference books at home on account of having an uncle who had majored in English and was heading a major publishing house in those days. She also had little time to study because she had just gotten into a relationship with a really nice guy (whom she later married). So we made a deal. She would get the reference books and I would underline or highlight the major points, and then we would study directly from these books.

The plan worked well. I would return at 9 p.m., have dinner and fall asleep. One of the girls would wake me up at eleven, give me a steaming cup of Complan, and then Anju and I would sit down to study till the 3 a.m. train went chugging by. This was our signal to dive into bed, to catch another three to four hours of rest. I did manage to sit for all my papers, but on the day of the oral examination, I was running a fever. My friends had to arrange for a rickshaw to take me from the hostel to the department building. The viva board very kindly came downstairs to interview me as I was in no shape to climb up the one flight of stairs to the department. And thus ended my studies and my hostel sojourn. Looking back, I realize it was one of the best periods of my life. Even today when I meet those friends, we can behave as though we had met just yesterday. And my parents and aunt were right. Had I not completed the post-graduate course then, I doubt I would have been able to do it later.

The situations that I faced during the two years of probation turned me into a battle-hardened veteran. For instance, in my second branch, I was told to balance ledgers. Ledgers in those days were heavy loose-leaf binders weighing about 6 or 7 kgs each. The branch had 100-plus ledgers. Balancing them entailed taking down the balance of each account, and then tallying them with the summary of debits and credits made to that ledger during the month. It was sheer drudgery, and it was a job that all of us POs tried to avoid. We knew probationers were usually the fall guys who had to take on these jobs. So it was no surprise that I was asked to balance ledgers. What was disconcerting was that I was told to sit close to the counters, as these were live ledgers in which transactions were expected every day, but there was no table or chair that could be fitted into the narrow space behind the counters. Some out-of-the-box thinking was called for here. So I stacked five ledgers for me to sit on. In front, I stacked enough ledgers to create a 'table' and placed the ledger I was working on on those. It wasn't an ideal way of working – far from it. But we were expected to deliver, come what may, and we did.

Sometimes we did get stuck in really difficult situations. Once, while doing my rural training, I had gone to a village in the branch jeep. We were trying to convince farmers to repay loans so that the bank could help them with further loans and that they should not wait for elections when they may or may not get waivers. On the way back, the jeep got stuck in mud. The villagers had to use all their resources to push the vehicle out. By then, it was already seven in the evening. The driver drove as quickly as he could to Chinsurah station from where I used to take a local train to Kolkata.

As we approached the station, we could sense that something was wrong as huge crowds had gathered everywhere. On enquiring, we were told that the overhead wires had snapped and train services had been suspended for the past three hours. The driver reassured me that he would put me on a bus. However, as I rummaged through my bag, I realized that though I had the Indian Railways monthly pass, I seemed to have left my purse back at home. The driver didn't have much money on him as well. So I suggested going back to the branch and prayed that a few people were still around to lend me money. As we neared the branch, my heart sank – the shutters were down. We still went to the staff entrance in the hopes that somebody would be inside. Nobody was, but the night guard, hearing my predicament, told me that he had some cash to pay for his dinner and fare back home. He insisted that I take the money – he said he could buy dinner on credit as he was a regular customer and he could borrow the money to go home from the staff who came in the morning. Finding no other alternative, I accepted the money from him and we set off for the bus station again. It was way past ten by then. The buses were so crowded that I couldn't even get close to one, forget boarding it. It was after an hour's jostling and pushing and pleading that I managed to get on a bus. By the time I got back to my uncle's home where I was staying at the time, it was 2 a.m. My uncle was standing on the road in front of his house, wondering whether he should report me missing. Nowadays, with the advent of mobile phones, these worries rarely occur. In those days, it could be sheer agony if you were waiting for someone to come home and they didn't return at their usual time.

Not all experiences had happy endings. Three of us probationers were posted to a rural branch. Before leaving for our posting, we were told that the branch was being investigated for having given loans in an irregular manner. It appeared that the documentation of the loans was not done properly and we were specifically instructed to get these in order. On arrival, I was given the keys to the cupboard which contained the incomplete documents. When I opened the cupboard, an avalanche of papers greeted me. They were loan documents with thumb impressions all over and the land-record documents called *parcha* inside. It seemed no one had had the time to fill up the details, and that was what we needed to do now. But God forbid if the *parcha* got detached from a document. There was no way of knowing which *parcha* belonged to which document. On our trips to the villages, however, we found out that most of the locals revered the branch manager. It seemed he always helped farmers in distress, often with his own money. But despite his inherent goodness, nothing could save him.

A few days later, both he and the loan officer were suspended. It was a lesson for us, letting us know that we needed to follow laid-down procedures and processes. It also highlighted the fact that banks had not found a way of addressing lending in rural areas – moreover, regular loan programmes did not address those with little or no disposable income to see them through downturns or personal crisis. The issue has still not been addressed. We also became aware of the pressure on banks to deliver volumes of work that was almost impossible to do manually; back then, computerization was still some way off. The personal risk that bankers ran was painfully brought home to us.

A year had passed by and my batch of trainees was due for our intermediate PO programme to learn about the intricacies of credit or of giving loans. I was asked to report to the Vadodara training centre. It was July 1978 and many parts of the country were devastated by floods. Despite my best efforts, I could not get a train ticket. When I called the head office to share my woes, the personnel department promptly advised me to fly to Vadodara. In those days, only senior management was allowed flight expenses. I was elated and, at the same time, a little anxious. It was the first time I would be in an aircraft. I soon learnt that three men from my batch were also going to Vadodara for the course and they too had been instructed to fly. In an instant, all my worries disappeared as we planned to embark on this journey. Though since then I have flown hundreds of times, that flight remains special in my memory. It was a typical Indian Airlines plane, but for us it was a great experience. Starting from putting on our seat belts to choosing a meal, everything felt new. I am a person who hates turbulent flights (as I am sure most do – though some show it and some don't), but that first flight gave us no cause for complaint. However, we had to go via Ahmedabad as there was no direct flight to our destination back then. Upon reaching Ahmedabad, we had another challenge facing us – that of getting to Vadodara. We managed to secure tickets on a train that arrived at Vadodara at three in the morning. The training centre told us to stay put at the station till dawn.

On arrival, we requested the stationmaster to arrange for a place to stay. He offered us the retiring rooms. But there were separate rooms for men and women. The men came along as I was shown to a cavernous room, which had a few old-style cane recliners with heavy frames. The room smelt of mice. There was not a soul about. The stationmaster told me to get in and latch the huge doors from inside. My friends promised me that they would come and call me as soon as first light broke. I spent the next few hours curled up in one of the recliners, imagining all kinds of horrors that could befall me. I don't know when I fell asleep, but I was awakened by a loud banging on the doors. It was morning and my friends swore that they had been banging on the door for the last fifteen minutes, and were on the verge of breaking it down.

I remember little of the training course, except that we had a great time. On Friday evenings, we would take an overnight train to Ahmedabad and take an overnight train back on Sunday, so as to get back in time for classes. It was on one of those trips that I visited the swaying minarets of Sidi Bashir Mosque. These were originally four minarets made of stone, of which two were reportedly dismantled and taken away by the British. But the amazing thing about the minarets is that even though made of solid stone, with a circular staircase within that took one to the balcony about two or three storeys high, the minaret swayed when pushed from within. Not only that, the other minaret would sway in resonance, even though it had not been pushed. I have seen and experienced this, and was totally amazed at the technology that must have gone into its building.

Soon enough, we finished our course and it was time to return to Kolkata. I booked my tickets with the three friends who had accompanied me. Our return journey was on the Ahmedabad–Howrah Express. A forty-hour journey, it was amongst the longest in India. We shared a coupe and the journey, though slow, was enjoyable. There was no puri–aloo sabji at any of the stations en route that we didn't taste. We partook of everything we could get our hands on – be it the bananas of Bhusawal or the *batata* (potato) fritters – we experienced the sheer variety of food one can find in India. The only problem was the washrooms, but one of my friends was nice enough to clean it thoroughly every morning - the only thing we needed to do was contribute our bottles of shampoo, which was the closest thing to a cleaning agent we had. The four of us remain fast friends, and the journey remains one of the best train rides that I have ever undertaken.

Our probation days ended soon and the time had come for our first permanent posting. Each one of us wanted to get into the credit wing. It was considered the most glamorous department and also a sure-fire way to kick-start a great career. But to my disappointment, I got appointed to the foreign exchange department, which was the second choice for everyone. Looking back, I think two things militated against my choice in the credit wing – my background in English literature and the fact that I was a woman. At the time, I blamed the latter reason, as I felt that my performance had been quite superior. Now that I have more of a macro view, I think being a girl had less of a part to play than my qualifications – though I can't say for sure it had no role at all.

Anyway, I was posted to the forex division of the main SBI branch at Kolkata, the largest hub of such activity in eastern India then. To say I learnt a lot from this posting would be minimizing its contribution to what I am today. For instance, I learnt how good some of the clerical staff were. I had a head clerk whose English was so perfect that I couldn't find a single mistake in his work. However, there was a promotee officer (an officer promoted from the clerical cadre) under me, who felt that he had to justify his existence by making corrections to the drafting done by our head clerk. My job was to undo his corrections. This made the department quite dysfunctional till I decided to confront the issue. I waited till six that evening when the clerical staff left for the day, before calling in the junior officer and reading him the riot act.

Then we had another clerk who wanted to interview the staff to see who would work in his place when he went on leave. I was quite peeved at such a peculiar request till he took me to his seat and showed me the ledger and his calligraphy therein. Indeed, it was perfection. 'I can't allow anyone with bad handwriting to write in this ledger, ma'am. Please understand,' he pleaded. I almost had to feed him the concept of detachment as written in our scriptures to get him to proceed on his leave.

And then we had a head messenger who came by one day and complimented me on the fact that I wouldn't drink water brought to me by the water boy. The fact was that in the morning and afternoon, the water boy, whose sole job was to give us water, would come around with large aluminium glasses of water. These glasses looked most unappetizing, and drinking all that water would inevitably lead to frequent visits to the ladies' room which was right across the banking hall. With time I got over the embarrassment, but back then I was still quite sensitive. As a result, I refused the water. However, our head messenger, a Brahmin from central India, had concluded that I wasn't accepting it because I wasn't sure of the caste of the water boy. I was horrified at his interpretation and thereafter made it a point to accept the water whenever it was brought around.

The branch in those days was a very large one, with around 3,500 employees. The clerical staff were split into two unions, the incumbent ones symbolized by a conch and the newbies who had adopted the hand as their symbol. Officers often got caught in midst of their skirmishes, and it took all of one's wits to ensure that one played a balanced role. In those days, very often, overtime payment would be given for getting a job done rather than for actually working overtime. On one such instance, it appeared I had employed staff mostly pertaining to one faction. The leaders of the other side came calling soon enough for what they termed a 'display of partiality'. I was taken aback as the matter pertained to one particular section in the bank, in which it so happened that the staff belonged to one faction. But this explanation didn't satisfy the leaders. They wanted me to find some other work for which overtime could be given to *their* loyalists. I was fed up with these unreasonable demands and told them that I would never again give anyone overtime. If a job needed doing, they would jolly well do it or else I would issue a memo seeking an explanation as to why it was not done yet, because they also knew that most jobs could be completed within the allotted time if undertaken seriously. I also predicted that such abuse of a facility could not last. As it happened, within a couple of months an embargo was enforced by the bank on overtime. Though I had nothing to do with the new rule, when I heard gossip about how I had predicted it and so must somehow have been involved in the decision making, I looked the other way – neither denying nor confirming it.

During this period, I also learnt how to manage over-enthusiastic male colleagues. I found talking about family dampened their friendliness quickly. I would talk glowingly about my father and brother (I find talking about your husband and children even more effective – but at that juncture, I had neither). Suffice it to say, I never got into a situation from which I could not extricate myself gracefully. But I also must mention that such people were few in number. Most male colleagues were helpful and cooperative. Many a time, they would delay their own departure in order to see me home safely. Many of them spent extra hours going over the nuances of difficult credit applications and gave me the benefit of their hard-earned experiences.

The officers' lunch room in the main branch was something of an institution. It still had cooks and khansamas who looked ancient but, as per the records, were still far from retirement age. They could cook fairly delicious Continental meals. It used to be a sit-down lunch of three courses – soup, a main course of fish, poultry or mutton, and a dessert (I liked their desserts the best – soufflés and puddings and creme brûlées or biscuit and fruit custards). The one major contribution of this lunch room was to get us to pass our Certified Associates of Indian Institute of Bankers (CAIIB) exams. Most of us came from diverse disciplines. Therefore, it was mandatory for us to take the CAIIB exams to become eligible for the next promotion. The exams consisted of two parts of eleven papers, spanning various areas pertinent to banking such as contract law, Companies Act,

Negotiable Instruments Act, accountancy, management and even one on English. The CAIIB was notorious for failing people, and the lunch room conversation centred on who passed and who failed whenever the results were published. The most failures were in English! In fact, we had a senior official who had done a master's degree in English (not me!) but failed to clear that paper eleven times and then gave up. This custom of divulging our results had the salutary effect of making us study, so that most of us passed these papers within the first two years, thus smoothening our journey in the bank. Many bright officers lost years of promotions as they lacked the peer pressure to pass these exams.

The other lessons I learnt in that branch came from its heads. There were two of them – one who looked after the credit and forex divisions, the other after the rest. Their treatment of senior officers was much more demanding. However, with us juniors, they were quite indulgent. The seniors dared not enter their rooms without full preparation. We, on the other hand, were allowed to not know certain things and, in most such cases, were guided about what we needed to do. One of them went on to become the chairman, and his management skills were on display from his days in Kolkata. When he got transferred to the local head office (LHO), he also asked for my services to be transferred to one of his departments. And so I got a stint at the LHO.

Over there, however, I had a different kind of experience. My immediate superior insisted on changing almost every second word of any letter or note that I drafted. In six months, my confidence was shattered, and life was becoming more and more miserable. Out of sheer desperation, I decided to seek a transfer. However, as luck would have it, the very same day when I decided to approach the human resources department, my boss got transferred. I thanked my lucky stars that I had managed to hold off for long enough for the problem to get resolved by itself. Seeking a transfer on the grounds of inability to get on with one's boss would definitely be viewed with some degree of suspicion. One of my seniors put it rather well – he said one can't choose one's parents or bosses. The only redeeming feature was that bosses changed often.

The one reason for which I enjoyed this stint was the number of women probationary officers at this establishment. We were a large group of around seven or eight women, which was by far more than most other offices. The relationships we formed here have stayed with us through our careers. We would all lunch together, made especially memorable by a woman named Yasmin Engineer, who had a cook and khansamas at home, whose lunch would arrive in an enormous five-tiered tiffin box that she generously shared with all of us. We often went for movies and other after-work shows together. When we couldn't make time to see Richard Attenborough's *Gandhi*, we all decided to bunk office one afternoon and watch it. The plan was executed to perfection – some of us had to visit a doctor, while some of us got a toothache or a tummy ache. The result was that we all watched the matinee show together. Though, before the hall darkened, we kept looking around surreptitiously – lest we spot someone we knew. We comforted ourselves by reasoning that if our colleagues spotted us there, then they too would have been playing hooky, would be equally embarrassed at having got caught and, therefore, unlikely to acknowledge our presence.

By this time, I was around twenty-seven years old. All my male friends were already married. My parents would bring up the topic of my marriage whenever I went home. Since they themselves and my siblings had chosen their own partners, they hoped I would do the same. But somehow, I couldn't quite make up my mind on the matter. Out of desperation, they had advertised my eligibility in the papers. In response, we got some good, some bad and some outright strange responses. Luckily, in Bengal, the dowry system is not strong. The maximum demand, at least in our community, was restricted to household furniture and fixtures, and at most a few saris to give to elderly relatives. But there was someone who wanted to marry me so that he could get a loan to buy a flat. Or there was another who liked everything about me except my job. There was another family that objected to the fact that my parents had an inter-caste marriage. And so it went on till we chanced upon Pritimoy.

He was teaching in the newly opened Department of Computer Science and Engineering at Indian Institute of Technology, Kharagpur. He had just recently attended a younger cousin's wedding where his uncle had suggested that he should look for an alliance with one of the many girls that had not been found suitable for his own son. This riled Pritimoy to no end. So, the next Sunday, he sat down with his morning coffee and a newspaper to look for a bride. There were two advertisements that he marked. One was mine and the other was also a bank employee. I asked him later about his preference for bank employees. 'I always thought that the ladies who work in the bank must be getting home early because the bank entertains customers only till 2 p.m. And also, it is common knowledge that bank employees are well paid. I thought that bank employees, especially women, never get transferred as I have been seeing the same ladies in my local branch from the time I was a student. It seemed to tick all the boxes for me,' he told me. He was very clear about one thing – he was sure he wanted a career woman as his wife. He felt that the demands made by spouses who didn't work were too high and he felt that he needed his space. Hence, the search for a partner with a regular employment. But here his research fell awfully short of reality. The going home early part and the lack of transfers pertained to our clerical staff. But by the time he realized his error, it was too late. We had decided to marry.

Both our fathers were retired. So we refused any financial help from them to defray marriage expenses. We realized this only after the wedding as each looked to the other to fund the honeymoon trip, only to realize that our financial positions were identical. Later, when we got to know each other better, we often regretted not talking about marriage expenses earlier. Had we known each was spending their hard-earned savings, we could have had a simple ceremony and gone for a trip ourselves, instead of feeding all and sundry. But the deed was done. So our honeymoon was in the third-floor apartment that my husband stayed in, in the IIT Kharagpur campus. A good start to a partnership that would need many such adjustments and compromises.

# 5

# Kharagpur: Of Friendships and Finding a Partner

My next challenge was to find a way to get transferred to the Kharagpur branch of our bank, which was conveniently located within the IIT campus. Normally, branch postings are done by the regional office to which the branch reports. When I checked with that office, they told me that with my seniority I would need to be posted as the accountant, and that was not acceptable to them as it was a very difficult branch. I went to the general manager in charge of human resources with my plea. He understood my predicament, but told me that the branch was a very disturbed one. 'Did you know, the last branch manager was lifted from his chair by his collar? It's no wonder they don't want to post you there as the accountant.' But I was desperate for the posting. So I retorted, 'Well, I don't have a collar, so they won't be able to do that with me.'

The long and short of it was that under 'spouse grounds' the LHO posted me directly to the branch. The grapevine started buzzing at this development, and I was told that the branch manager had taken his grouse to the regional manager and had received permission to not allow me to join when I reported to the branch (though he later told me that this was not true). For me, this was a real challenge and I was wondering how to overcome it when I received a phone call from the branch manager. He was polite, and asked me to join at the earliest. I was taken aback at this sudden change in his stance, but decided to not look a gift horse in the mouth. I later found out that the accountant was in such a situation that the union had demanded he be removed in a week, or they would begin an agitation against him. My release from LHO was slated for that week anyway, and so I reported for duty immediately.

My welcome at the branch seemed normal enough. The BM, however, had one stipulation – that I relieve the outgoing accountant within a week. The accountant had to take charge of many things – not least of which was the cash in the currency chest. The Kharagpur branch was a feeder for many branches and so had a huge chest, the size of a small Mumbai apartment. It was lined with cupboards containing cash, blank security forms (such as drafts and cheque leaves) and items such as gold against which loans had been given.

Stories about cash and cash handling in the bank are countless. First of all, I don't know how many people have stood in front of rows of cupboards with cash stashed neatly in tightly bound packets and bundles from bottom to top. The sight can be quite intimidating, especially when you realize that you are required to count it all as a part of the 'taking-over' ritual! There were no cash-counting machines in those days. As chairman, I did, however, inaugurate our first completely mechanized cash-counting centre, where one put in cash at one end and the machine would sort it by denomination into ATM-fit, issuable, non-issuable and of doubtful quality. It would then package them and spew them out in bundles of ten packets –

a dream that I dreamt in the cash vault that day. But to return to my struggles in the stuffy cash vault of Kharagpur, no matter how hard I tried when I counted the notes in each packet, I would always end up with either 99 or 101 notes! The chief cashier, who had to be present during the exercise, tried hard to hold back his laughter but then just gave up. After having a good laugh at my ham-handed efforts, he told me to clip a few of the notes in each packet. Then he called in a cashier and told him to count the unclipped notes and write down that number before passing it to me. I was then required to only count the clipped notes and check whether it came to 100. This was definitely a more workable solution. By the time the cashier had counted ninety or ninety-one or eighty-nine, or whatever be the amount in the unclipped portion, I managed to count my share of nine, ten or eleven. And so we got through the cash.

The remittances for the chest would come from various places – and sometimes from the Reserve Bank of India (RBI) branch at Kolkata. On one such occasion, we were expecting a large consignment. It was to be sent by train. A special goods wagon was to be attached to the Howrah–Puri Express that arrived at Kharagpur at four in the morning. I had requisitioned a bus and a large police contingent to convey the consignment from the station to the branch. Every such consignment sent from the RBI would be accompanied by one of our cashiers, who would witness the preparation of the consignment. An RBI cashier would witness the receipt of the consignment and our counting. So, that day I was on the platform with the police force at the appointed time. The train arrived. But there was no special wagon attached. Panic surged through me. I ran to the station master, but he had no information either.

In those days of no mobiles, there was no way of contacting the RBI personnel. With trepidation I rang up the GM in charge of our region, and he promised to send someone to the RBI as soon as it opened to enquire. I returned to the stationmaster, who too was trying all means to locate the missing wagon. After calling each station in between Howrah and Kharagpur, he got some information: one wagon of the Howrah–Puri Express had been detached at Santragachi as its springs had given way. Nobody knew the importance of that wagon, and so it was dragged to a siding to await instructions from the dispatcher, which of course couldn't be received till offices opened. After being told the nature of the problem, the officials at the station acted immediately. A local police force was deployed while a new wagon was arranged. We later found out that the huge number of coins that were being remitted – which weighed tons – may have led to the breakage of the springs. But the few hours that I had spent trying to locate the lost 'treasure' aged me at least by five years.

We had, under Kharagpur branch, fourteen 'single-man' branches. These were branches with only one officer and a small cash balance. Normally, cash was required to be in 'joint' custody – meaning, it was kept in a safe with two sets of keys and had to be accessed by both custodians operating the keys at the same time. However, in single-man branches, cash was held by one person only. Accordingly, I was required to visit the branch at irregular intervals to check the cash. My first such visit was to a branch called Rohini. Its building was the only pukka structure in the whole village. As I entered the branch, I found one fellow sitting on the floor in the corridor. He seemed to be pulling on a rope that went through the top of the wall of the room in which the branch was located. But I was totally unprepared for what I found inside. It was a punkah – a sheet of woven bamboo, with a red frilly border, suspended from the ceiling. A rope was attached to it, and the person outside was pulling on it, causing the punkah to move back and forth, thereby providing a faint breeze to relieve the heat inside.

I had read about punkah-pullers who worked in the offices and residences of the sahibs of the British Raj. But it was astounding to find one in the premises of a modern bank. The branch manager confirmed that there was no electricity in the village and he lived on the floor above the branch. At sunset, he would light a lantern and retire with his dinner to his bed, which had the protection of a mosquito net. Or else, he rued, he would be afflicted with malaria in no time. I got the branch manager to apply for a generator for both the branch and his residence, which I approved there and then. The punkah-puller was delighted at his elevation to generator-operator as were the two other staff members who stayed with the BM. Only the BM appeared worried – his next problem was carting the diesel for the generator to the branch and then improving the bank's business to be able to pay for the added expense.

Life as a BM is always interesting, if nothing else. I remember another visit to Banspahari – another of the single-man branches. This one was located amongst the sal forests of Jhargram. On arriving, I found the collapsible gate of the branch locked. The BM and staff sat just inside the gate carrying on the transactions through the gate. On enquiring about this very unwelcoming way of conducting business, the BM informed me that they were helpless. 'We have more bears here than human beings, and if you leave the door open, they wander in!' he exclaimed. It was an explanation to which I had no counter.

Once, an official came to Kharagpur to inspect a branch called Ramgarh, similarly situated deep inside a forest. I arranged for a jeep to take him there. Three hours later, he returned looking as though he had been hit by a hurricane. He was in no condition to speak. So while my staff sat him down and brought him water to drink, I called the driver of the jeep to find out what happened. It seemed that midway to the branch, they had been confronted by a huge crowd of villagers carrying spears and scythes. On seeing the vehicle, they had rushed towards them. The road at that point was so narrow that there was no place to turn. So he had driven the jeep in reverse for about a kilometre and a half before he could turn the vehicle around and flee. Later, enquiries revealed that an old lady had been hit by a jeep at that spot earlier in the day. Hence, the gathering of agitated villagers, who were out to avenge the wronged. Two days later, we arranged for a police escort to get the inspecting official to the branch.

Being in the inspection department was no picnic. As per the rules of the bank, an inspector could not inspect branches in the circle (roughly equivalent to a state) they belonged to. As a result, they would rarely get the food of their choice, and so the default diet of inspectors was curd rice. Surviving on curd rice for a period of three years required enormous discipline. But the fear of failing health kept our inspectors in line. Branch managers of most small branches like Ramgarh and Banspahari either gave up their beds to the inspector or desks were pulled together to create a bed of sorts. All in all, their life was hardly a bed of roses.

I was to have two stints at this branch in Kharagpur, one as an accountant and then again as the branch manager. The branch soon became my best teacher, especially in the art of management. There were about ninety people at the branch, of which eleven were officers and sixteen were messengers. The rest were clerical employees. The union was extremely powerful and would often decide on what would be done or not done by the staff. Staying ahead of them was a constant battle.

A tedious job every month was the posting of salaries into the accounts of IIT employees or pensions in the accounts of railways' pensioners – and we had many of them. The staff often tried all kinds of delaying tactics so that they could leave the job half-done, which would then have to be completed by the officers, as overtime was strictly controlled and none could be given for regular work. The moment the lists arrived, one had to monitor the work constantly to ensure that the task got completed.

On one such occasion, I found one of the leaders standing at the counters where the ledger-keepers were working and intoning 'stop writing, stop writing' the moment the clock struck five. I was thoroughly peeved, but I knew that it was being done deliberately to rile me. So after the staff left, I asked the leader to come to my room. I then complimented him on his conscientious stand. Could he do the same every day? He was a little nonplussed by this request. I elucidated further, 'I also want you to stand at the same place at ten in the morning, and announce "start writing, start writing" in the same manner. We could extend the announcements for lunch time as well. However, you have to agree to doing it all or else …' That did the trick. I had no more hassles with that gentleman going forward.

On another occasion, there was a big commotion early in the morning just as the branch opened. I was about to go out and check when a delegation from the union arrived.

'We can't work today,' they announced.

'But why?' I asked in all innocence.

It appeared that the windows of the branch had not been opened and 'people were suffocating'.

'Why were the windows not opened?' I asked.

'It was the cleaner's job and he is absent.'

'Okay, then who closes the windows?'

They told me it was the guards' job.

'Let's ask the guards then …'

'Oh no! You can't do that. The guards are only required to look after security. Closing the windows is important to secure the branch, but opening them is not part of branch security. So you can't ask them to perform a job that has not been allocated to them.'

Then another voice chimed in. 'Ma'am, can we refer to the Corporate Centre for directions as to who opens the branch windows? It is not mentioned in our book of instructions.'

I looked at the crowd in front of me, stood up and marched determinedly towards the tall windows. 'The book of instructions says that all jobs not allocated can be done by the branch manager. So if you guys don't think this is something you can do, I will open the windows myself.' As I proceeded to do that, several other employees who had been watching the entire drama unfold from a safe distance came forward to help me. All the windows got opened in the next few minutes and peace was restored. Work commenced soon after.

The constant friction with the union members was taken as par for the course. My husband used to pick me up from work every evening on his way back home from the college. My room was next to the rear entrance of the branch. He would normally park under the window of my room and toot the horn of his scooter. I would wave to him from the window, wind up quickly and step out. This was in the early days of our marriage. One evening, I waited at the usual time for him to come, and I was beginning to wonder why he didn't turn up. I received a call from him on the internal IIT phone. 'Shall I call the police?' he asked in a hushed voice.

'Whatever for?' I was totally puzzled.

'I heard a huge *hungama* in your room. People were shouting so much that you didn't even hear the sound of my horn. What do you mean "for what"?'

I burst out laughing. 'That kind of stuff happens every day. Now please come back and take me home.'

Then there was the time the bank decided to start the computerization exercise. It was supposed to be only back-office computerization on a stand-alone system. (This does sound like the Stone Age, doesn't it?) We were asked to keep our books balanced and ready for the migration. This was easier said than done. Most branches were struggling with balancing arrears and so a decision was taken to outsource the activity. 'Outsourcing' was a no-no word in those days. The moment the union got wind of it, they declared that they would lie down on the path leading out of the branch. We would need to carry the large trunks in which the vouchers had been packed by walking over them if we wanted to take them to the agency we had employed to do the job. After about an hour's heated argument that were inconclusive, I gave in. We all went home. However, a few days later, the vouchers, this time packed unobtrusively in small cardboard boxes, were despatched safely after office hours to the agency and the first step towards computerization got underway.

Industrial relations not was only the preserve of unions; any local political party could also hold the bank hostage once in a while. One of those days, when I was the branch manager, I arrived at my usual time of 9.30 a.m. to find the gate closed and a large crowd sitting outside. I was surprised as none of our employees were visible till I spotted the canteen workers, who were part-time employees of the contractors running the canteen, in the crowd. The crowd was led by netas and their demand was for full employment of these workers in the bank immediately.

I tried pointing out that this was a pan-India issue and that a wildcat strike was neither warranted nor legal in the existing situation. The tenor of communication from the other side was a revelation to me. I had never even heard such words in the past and I didn't even know the meaning of a few. I offered to hold discussions and explained that closing the branch provided no relief to anyone. But they would have none of it. Meanwhile, other employees and officers had arrived. So had the cashiers from IIT Kharagpur, for the cash that they took for their daily expenses. They all stood at a safe distance watching the fun. I tried calling my controlling office, which was in Burdwan at that time. There were no mobile phones; hence, I needed to go into the IIT offices to make the calls. The connection was feeble, and it took a lot of screaming and shouting before I could convey my situation to my boss. His instructions were clear. The controlling office was too far away to help. I was the person on the ground and so I should take whatever action I deemed fit to 'protect the bank's interest'.

Thus empowered, I called on the local police outpost next. Their first query was what colour was the flags the protestors were carrying. 'What colour do you think it is?' I asked in response.

'If it is what we believe is most likely, then we are sorry we can do nothing,' came the response.

'What about the inconvenience to IIT? Are you not here to protect their interest?' I didn't mention what was worrying me the most. Our vaults contained the question papers of the Higher Secondary Examinations of the Kendriya Vidyalaya Sangathan, the organization that headed the network of schools managed by the central government. The question papers had been sent to us for safekeeping. My inability to produce those if the bandh continued would have caused a national-level crisis.

But my pleas for help fell on deaf ears. Fortuitously, I remembered that one of the senior police officials at the district level had been a probationary officer of SBI. He had joined the bank a year after me, and had left after a year to join the Indian Police Service. I called him up directly and requested his help – if nothing, for the sake of his erstwhile employer. He was most helpful and half an hour later, I was in a police car heading towards the branch. After due warning to the protestors, the way was cleared for us and the gates were opened. By this time, it was already 3.30 p.m. I quickly opened the vaults and had the question papers safely transported to a smaller branch nearby. Thereafter, we did a few transactions ourselves to record that the branch had functioned that day. It's the last time I was in the middle of a lathi charge; I must add, I don't want a repeat of the experience.

But were the union activities always negative in my experience? Not at all. When I took over the branch, the incumbent group at the state level also headed the branch unit. But there was a young claimant to the throne back then. This person went around methodically deploying his team to work with the employees to make their lives easier. He had one guy who was an expert at helping you make out your regular allowances bills. Another specialized in leave fare concession matters. There was a man who knew everything that was to be known about medical bills. And yet another who guided the employees in their efforts to secure a home loan. With such scrutiny and oversight, every single bill or loan application was received in apple-pie order with all required documents in place. This made it simple for the applications to be processed quickly, and when the next election came around, this young group won hands down. It was a lesson in strategizing and perfect execution.

Not only in such matters, but in other areas too the union played a role. Our branch maintained a list of willing blood donors with the dates of the last donation made by them. Many students from IIT volunteered to be on this list. In fact, people drew so frequently from this list that when the wife of the chief medical officer of the railway hospital was undergoing an operation, they approached us for help as she had a rare blood group. This, despite the fact that the railways had a huge operation in Kharagpur.

During one of my father's visits to Kharagpur, he fell grievously ill. IIT had a rudimentary hospital and so he was moved to the intensive care unit (ICU) of the railway hospital, where he stayed for twenty-two days. Back then, a family member needed to stay with the patient in the ICU. I stayed the first night, but thereafter, for the next twenty-one days, the union guys organized employees who took turns staying in the hospital with my father. Their logic was clear: 'You need to run the branch, madam, and how will you do that if you can't sleep?' Time and again, and especially during a crisis, I have found that SBI employees seamlessly closed ranks in order to help out the afflicted person and their family. It is a trait that one only realizes when one is in trouble, but it is something I greatly value in this organization and which I think not many other organizations possess.

The workload, however, was terrible. During my entire tenure at Kharagpur, I never got home before 8.30 p.m., even though my travel time was barely five minutes. Once, when the branch needed to be closed in the early afternoon on account of the riots that took place in the wake of the assassination of Prime Minister Indira Gandhi, my staff joked that I should not step out in the daylight as the crows would peck out my eyes. I didn't quite get the joke till I realized that they were comparing me to an owl that never came out in the day.

On most Saturdays too, I wouldn't get to leave until very late in the evening.

At times, I had to resort to black humour to get me through the huge workload. I am a short person. And as the work piled up on my desk – as it tended to do, with amazing speed at that – I would often be hidden behind the fat ledgers and registers plonked down on the table by the messengers. As I finished working with each ledger or register, I would yell for the messenger to return it from wherever he had brought it, but he would never be available at exactly that moment and I would end up heaving the heavy registers and place them on the floor next to me. I often worked standing up, because managing these heavy books while sitting down was just not possible. Plus, I could hardly talk to my customers from behind the mountain of books stacked in front of me.

When the time came for job rotation, which happened every six months, the then branch manager asked me which messenger I wanted to be attached to my seat. Of the sixteen messengers in the branch, ten were named after deities – Shankar, Madhav, Hare Krishna, Narayan, etc. I told the BM that I would manage with any as long as they had the name of some deity. He was puzzled and asked me to explain my strange request.

'Well, my workload leaves me no time to even take the lord's name and my mother had always told me to multitask. I, in any case, have to yell for these messengers throughout the day,' I explained. 'So I thought this would be one way to do both. However, I think the lord is more likely to respond before them.'

When I took over as branch manager, my office was towards one side of the building. The side or rear entrance used by employees after customer hours was next to my room. A room opposite mine was used by the guards to change into their uniforms and store the guns they carried. One afternoon, as I sat down for my lunch around 2.30 p.m. I heard a gunshot fired. I jumped out of my skin fearing the worst – that miscreants must have entered the premises through the side door. As I shot out of my room, I noticed a wisp of smoke emanating from the guards' room. I looked inside to see one of our guards with a bemused look on his face, his rifle pointing at the ceiling. There was a hole in the ceiling where the concrete had chipped off.

I was flooded with relief upon realizing that the guard had misfired the gun. That relief, however, was short-lived when I found out the amount of paperwork required to be done in the wake of such an incident. I had to file a first information report (FIR) with the police, report the matter to my controllers and our security department, arrange for retraining of the guard, as well as give explanations regarding any delays observed in the training of all the guards in the establishment. I even preserved the spent casing of the bullet for inspection by the next inspector (it was not specified in the rule book, but I was taking no chances).

The union, sensing an opportunity to add to my woes, came calling with the demand that this guard not be allowed on duty during working hours. 'What if he shoots the gun again?' they asked. 'This time, we were lucky that he shot at the ceiling. Can you guarantee he won't fire his gun again and this time hit someone?' Of course, I couldn't make any such guarantees, though knowing the guard I thought it highly unlikely (he couldn't hit a truck 10 metres away was my personal assessment of his capabilities). And yet, I had no way of letting him off duty as I didn't have the luxury of extra guards to take on his shift. Some adroit manoeuvring, sending off the guard for training the next day, and the union's short span of attention (as they concentrated on finding their next cause) helped me get past this particular problem.

Then there was the day as I struggled to complete my response to a pending audit report, a staff member came running into my room yelling, 'Snake, snake!'

I looked up with alacrity. Kharagpur was once a sal forest, and there was not a room in our house where I had not encountered a snake. I had even found a Russell's viper in my bedroom curtain.

Luckily, these snakes are slow, but their bite can be deadly. I had also seen a magnificent king cobra once in my backyard. It was very early in the morning and my husband, who was an early riser, had just made his cup of black coffee when he caught sight of the snake just below the kitchen window, burrowing into a hole obviously looking for a mouse or frog. He shook me awake to see the sight. By the time I got up and rushed to the window, the snake was gliding away. Perhaps something alerted it. Maybe our voices, or the sound of the window being opened. It reared up an impressive three-and-a-half feet above the ground. Its banded body glistened in the morning light as it turned its head towards the sound. It held a splayed frog in its mouth. I couldn't help but let out a yelp of surprise. In a trice, it let go of the frog, there was a whoosh of air and it disappeared into the tall grass covering our backyard that I had been exhorting our gardener to cut for the last ten days. Only the swaying of the grass attested to its majestic presence. Surprisingly, the frog hopped away!

So, hearing that there was a snake on the office premises didn't surprise me at all.

'Where?' I asked.

'In the record room.'

Abandoning the inspection report, I got up to take a look. There was a small crowd of people outside the record room. This was a longish room with racks on both sides on which were neatly tied packages containing each day's vouchers. Registers and ledgers were stacked at the far side of the room. There was enough space for two people to walk abreast between the racks. The room had a window and a door at the far side – the window was generally kept open, but the door was kept locked. The snake must have been about four feet long. It was of a muddy-brown colour on top and had a pale belly. The size and thickness made me believe that it was a rat snake. Rat snakes are generally harmless, but there wasn't a braveheart there who would want to take a chance in that confined space. We decided to lock the door through which we entered, and then bang on it so that the snake would leave by the same way it had entered, which was probably the window at the back. But I had not accounted for what happened next.

Once the door was locked, nobody was willing to open it. I allowed the matter to drift for two–three days. The room remained unopened. In those days, for cancelling drafts, one needed to take out the original draft application voucher, tally the signature and then cancel the draft. This was to ensure that if someone got hold of a draft that had not been bought by them, they wouldn't be able to encash it. With the record room closed, no draft could be cancelled. How many times could one send back a customer with the excuse that there was a snake in the record room? So on the fourth day, I decided that action needed to be taken. I called the guard on duty (incidentally, it was the same one who had misfired his rifle) and asked him to bring a bottle containing carbolic acid. I told him to liberally douse the entry to the record room. Thereafter, I opened the door just a crack and then slowly opened it wider. No snake was visible. I asked the guard to liberally spray the acid on the floor. However, as he did it, I noticed the smell was different. 'Stop! Are you sure that's carbolic acid?' I asked.

'Yes, madam. See here; it says so on the label.'

I called another member of staff to the room, took the bottle and asked him to smell it. 'What is it?' I asked. He hesitantly replied, 'Smells like kerosene, madam.'

Just as I thought. Imagine spraying a record room with kerosene! Our guard might as well have brought along a lighted match. I couldn't control my laughter. The ridiculousness of the situation was just too much. But I thought that the union in this case had a point. This guard was a walking disaster.

Then there was the day a customer entered my chamber with a sorrowful face. I asked him the reason for his distress. 'How would you feel if you were suddenly transformed from a Bengali to a Tamilian?' he asked. I was confused, but nonetheless, I tried to put on my most helpful face and asked him to repeat himself.

'My name is Jay Gopal Mukherjee,' he said. 'That was how it was appearing in my account and in my passbook. Then, when a new page in the ledger had to be opened after the earlier one got exhausted, my name was carried forward as Mukherjee, Jay Gopal. Even at that time I had objected, but was told by the ledger-keeper that this was the new norm adopted by the bank. My surname or family name would appear first, followed by my first name. I accepted the bank's logic. When the next page was added, my name was further shortened to Mukherjee, J. Gopal. When I queried about it, your ledger-keeper said that he was highly overworked and didn't have time to write out the full name on every page. I accepted even that. But today, when I asked for a new passbook, my name had been shortened to M.J. Gopal. Now, tell me, have you ever heard of a Bengali with such a name?'

Another time, while I was still the accountant at the branch, I was asked to hold dual charge as the BM was on leave. He was a nice man, but quite unwell and needed to go on leave often. In those days, urgent communications were still sent by telegram. At the peak hour, when I was battling the work and the crowds and the staff issues, I received a telegram stating: 'PLEASE RELIEVE SMT. A. BHATTACHARYA ON ... TO ENABLE HER TO ATTEND THE INTERVIEW FOR PROMOTION TO SCALE III. YOU WILL BE HELD PERSONALLY ACCOUNTABLE FOR FAILURE TO CARRY OUT THESE INSTRUCTIONS.'

Imagine the situation – I was supposed to relieve myself of a dual charge, and if I did not do so, I would be held accountable! And this, when Head Office knew quite well that I was holding charge as both the BM and the accountant. It was by looking at the lighter side of such situations that we managed to bear the load of our daily work routines.

My husband taught me a valuable lesson in those days. As an accountant, I used to carry seven bunches of keys. One for the main vault, one for the lockers, one for the cash cupboards, one for security form cupboards, one for the cupboards containing pledged gold, etc. At the end of the day, I would ensure that each of these was locked, then put the seven bunches in the right-hand drawer of the hand safe (which was about my height), close and lock that door and carry only the key to the hand safe door home. The ritual had become such a routine that once in a while when I tried to recall on returning home whether I had followed all the steps or not, I would be unable to do so. One such day, I became convinced that I had left the hand safe unlocked – meaning that anybody could access the keys. My anxiety mounted as the night wore on and I couldn't sleep. At around 2 a.m., I shook Pritimoy awake, narrated my fears and asked him to take me to the branch to check. 'Absolutely not!' he exclaimed. 'But why ever not?' I wailed.

I thought he was being mean. 'Consider this. If there is a mishap on account of a mistake committed by you, by going now, you will not be able to rectify it. In fact, it will draw suspicion, and if they find both of us there, you know where we will end up. If you stay at home and something does go wrong, only you will be under suspicion. But at least you will have me on the outside to bail you out.' With that bit of practical wisdom, he turned over and was soon fast asleep. I watched the darkness of the night fade, the stars disappear and dawn spread across the skies. I went to the branch at my regular time to find everything peaceful and every cupboard, safe and vault properly locked.

That evening, at dinner, Pritimoy asked me what was it that actually preyed on my mind, and made me so worried and fearful in such situations. Was it loss of power, prestige, reputation, daily comforts or something else? 'Well, it was a little of all that I suppose,' I replied.

'Imagine you lose all of that. What is the worst that could happen? Nobody can take away your education and ability. At the most, you may have to live in a slum. Imagine one room with a wooden bed, covered with a blue-checked bedcover (these were the most common and cheap handloom bed spreads available across India back then). Maybe to earn money you can start tutoring again. Imagine such a life. Do you think you would never enjoy yourself? Never have a good day? Do you think people living in slums don't enjoy themselves? They don't laugh or smile? Ask our maid and she will tell you that they too are subject to the same emotions as ourselves, they have good days and bad days.

'They have days of sadness and days of happiness, and many are content with what they have. They too dream of their children's success; they too do charity, maybe not with money but by giving time, which is much more valuable. So stop flaying yourself with these worries. Imagine how truly bad it can get and then accept it. Once you have done that, the worries will cease.'

I kept this piece of wisdom close to my heart and have come back to it many a time over the years. Imagining a doomsday scenario and then accepting it did help me cope. I called it Pritimoy's 'blue-checked bedcover theory', and it became a refuge for me when I felt that there was mighty little I could do to control events.

My stint as accountant also taught me self-reliance. There was the time when the wiring just outside the cash department caught fire. Luckily, it was at floor level. I shouted to the guard to run and turn the main power switch off. At the same time, I ran for the extinguisher. By that time, people were screaming and shouting all around, and there was a stampede for the door. I wrestled with the heavy canister to get it out of its wall holder, but it was way too heavy for me. Luckily, amongst the staff, there was an ex-serviceman. He rushed to help me and together we hauled the canister to the fire, which was still not very large. I think I didn't even have the required strength to hit the plunger hard enough. So Gokul Pal, the officer who had helped me, asked me to hold the hose steady as he hit the plunger. There was a whoosh of white powder and, by the time I opened my eyes, the fire was out. But every single thing in the vicinity was coated with a fine layer of white powder. I think I must have waved the hose around a little – or maybe a lot – but it gave me immense satisfaction to direct the clean-up operations from my chair, which, given the bravery displayed by the others, they carried out sheepishly.

Another time, a part of the branch was plunged into darkness late in the evening. A call to the electrician, who handled small jobs for us, proved futile as he was not in town. People were getting restive and packing their bags to call it a day. But it was month-end and a lot of work still needed to be finished. I was an electrical engineer's daughter after all. So I took a large torch from the guard and started checking the fuses in the junction box. Lo and behold, there was the offending fuse. The next step was to find a fuse wire and a set of screwdrivers. The guards showed me where the electrician kept his kit and, in ten minutes, the lights came back on. I had a set of disappointed staff, who had been looking forward to an early night, and I almost licked my chops at having got the better of them.

Lessons in self-reliance happened not only at the workplace level but also at home. Till the time I had got married, my forays into the kitchen were rare. Except for the one stint of a few days when I was in class six, I had never cooked except under the supervision of either my mother, aunt or sister. At the time of my marriage, I was more interested in getting my mother to pen down the recipes of everyday meals than in finding out what jewellery, if any, she would give me. She did oblige, starting from how to make out whether the rice was cooked or not, to the various kinds of dal preparations, the *chorchoris* (vegetable dishes) and the standard *macher jhol* and *jhaal* (fish curries of Bengal). She also wrote out the recipes of a few more exotic dishes, such as devilled chops, braised cutlets, meatballs, vindaloo and mango ice cream. The diary was a lifesaver. I still have it with me, and have added to it over time. Maybe one day I could share that as well with the many youngsters who are setting out on their individual journeys. I learnt to cook well thanks to it, though, at the end of the day, I sometimes felt I was in a labour camp of some sort. I would wake up at 4.30 a.m. in order to get my cooking done in time for office. But by the time I cleaned up after dinner, it would be past midnight.

I also learnt the trick of doing some dish out of the ordinary when we entertained. I got the maximum likes for my mayonnaise salads. I had learnt to make mayonnaise at home from a book I had picked up at a second-hand book shop in College Street. In those days, people who had not gone abroad had never tasted mayo, much less had any idea as to how to make it – though the IIT campus had probably more people who had been abroad than many other places. But even these foreign-returned friends had never tasted mayo in India. And yet, it was one of the easiest things to make. Pritimoy rather enjoyed these small tricks I employed to earn quick plaudits, but I am not sure as to whether the womenfolk among our friends held quite the same opinion.

Our first Durga Puja after marriage was looming when my husband came home with a slight fever. When it refused to go away in a few days, he saw a doctor who prescribed him typhoid drugs and asked him to get the Widal test – a blood test to detect typhoid – done. The test was negative, much to my relief. But the fever would not abate. By then, the puja holidays had started. The campus emptied rapidly, as both students and teachers left either to join their families or to take a break from the familiar surroundings. With my husband unwell, we were in a quandary. Luckily, my husband's older sister and her spouse, who was employed with the railways and also resident at Kharagpur at the time, invited us to spend the holidays with them. I accepted with alacrity as the last thing I wanted was to be on my own in a deserted campus. On the first day of the puja, my sister-in-law insisted that I go out with them to do what was called 'pandal hopping' – travel from pandal to pandal to see the different likenesses of Goddess Durga and her family. This was a standard practice for most families during these few days as the puja committees left no stone unturned to make their pandal the most beautiful. I was loath to leave Pritimoy at home, but gave in when she insisted.

On returning that night, I found Pritimoy fast asleep. So I too got inside the mosquito net. I felt I should check his temperature before turning in for the night, and so I touched his forehead. I nearly jumped up as it seemed hot enough to burn my hand. I quickly fetched a thermometer and regardless of whether I woke him up or not, I pushed it under his arm. When I took it out and tried to read it, the mercury line seemed to inch further and further. It finally stopped at 106° F. For a moment I felt paralysed. But the next moment, I rushed to my sister-in-law's room and banged on their door. My brother-in-law immediately understood the situation. He asked me to get a towel and put it under his head. 'Get a bucket of water and a mug, and keep pouring it on his head. I will try to find a doctor,' he told me. 'I know the best doctor is out of town for the holidays. But I will phone another doctor friend and ask what is to be done.'

I went back to our room and pulled Pritimoy to the edge of the bed, till the top of his head was just clear of the bed. Then I started pouring water over his head. My brother-in-law came in to inform me that his doctor friend was on his way and would arrive shortly. My sister-in-law meanwhile kept insisting that we call an ambulance and transfer him to the hospital. But my brother-in-law was totally against the idea as he felt that during the festivities the hospital would be running with a skeleton staff as most would be on holiday. There would be hardly anyone to take proper care of an emergency patient. He began pouring water on Pritimoy's head, and asked me to check his feet. They were ice cold, indicating that the fever was still rising. I found a pair of socks and put them on his feet, and using a hot bag tried desperately to warm his limbs.

By this time, the doctor arrived. He quickly administered two injections and told us to keep bathing his head with cold water. The next fifteen minutes were difficult as I ran around rubbing his hands and feet, and replacing the water we were pouring over his head. Slowly, the temperature of his palms and feet rose. After another half hour, the doctor instructed us to stop bathing his head and start using a wet compress instead. After another fifteen minutes, I found that he had started sweating. The fever had broken and soon beads of sweat as large as peas rolled off his face and body. My brother-in-law and the doctor gave him a thorough wipe down and then lifted him on to another bed. Soon after, the doctor left, promising to return in the morning. For me, however, there was no rest. Every half hour, I would check his temperature.

About two hours later, I found that the temperature was sliding below normal. I didn't want to again awaken my in-laws. So I went to the kitchen and made a cup of strong black coffee. Then I pushed teaspoons of the same through his lips. It seemed to have the desired effect, and the downward slide was arrested. I have spent some difficult nights in my life. This goes way up in that list. The next two days I spent in sheer terror of the temperature shooting up again as there was still no diagnosis. His fever would abate with the paracetamol, only to rise once the effects of the medicine wore off. On the third day, Dr Ghosh, the doctor my in-laws relied upon, returned from his leave. A few minutes of checking later, he declared it was typhoid. I told him that the test had been negative and that he had been given typhoid medicine right at the beginning to no effect. 'The Widal test often gives a wrong result if done early during the onset of the disease. So repeat it again, and we shall see. As for the medicine, he was given too small a dose for his bodyweight. Please give the medicine at the dosage I prescribed and he will be afebrile in two and a half days,' he said.

Pritimoy's fever did abate after exactly two and a half days and a full twenty-three days after it started. The test also turned in a positive result. On the doctor's next visit, when I asked him how he did it, he said, 'I started my career in villages where we didn't have the luxury of tests. Plus, I am a paediatrician. Most of my patients can't really tell me what's wrong with them. Therefore, I have learnt to rely on symptoms. Do you know that even the nature of children's wailing can tell me what's wrong with them. In medical school, we learnt to diagnose by looking for symptoms and recognizing them correctly. Tests are meant to confirm one's diagnoses and not for making them.' Since then, I have often played this game of trying to understand the future course of events from tiny symptoms that may otherwise have been overlooked. Initially, I would frequently jump to wrong conclusions, but over time I unconsciously began to get things right. It has become one of my strengths.

But this ability to look further than one's nose had not yet developed fully when I was heading the branch at Kharagpur, and led to one incident that has left me with a deep sense of regret. Much of my branch banking I had learnt from a senior clerk called Manoj. Not only did Manoj understand the accounting entries perfectly but he also wrote in a neat, legible script and was one of our most sincere workers. About a year after I took over as accountant, I was sitting late one night, tallying the books with Manoj. I could feel that he was very disturbed as his usual attention to detail seemed lacking. After he had made the fourth small mistake that night, I turned to him and asked him what the matter was. It seemed that he hailed from a village, and was the first person in his family to do well in academics and land a job with an organization such as ours. Early on in his life, he had married a girl from his village. She had not studied much, and he had been attracted by her vivacity and her ready laughter. He was himself a serious person and an introvert, and initially he had loved her easy manner of making friends.

They had two young sons, but his wife's inability to get down to the grind of life bothered him. She hated supervising their sons in their studies as she had little interest. She would often forget to buy essentials and would remember about it only when she started cooking. Thereafter, she would rush off to a neighbour's house to borrow whatever she needed, but once there, would get so engrossed in chatting that by the time she returned home, whatever she was cooking would have burnt to a crisp. Once he began speaking, Manoj seemed unable to stop. I could sense his frustration as well as his helplessness in tackling the situation. I counselled him as best as I could, reminding him that it was this very same vivaciousness that he had loved most initially. I also asked him to relax, that probably he was seeking a level of perfection in her that was unrealistic. He didn't seem quite convinced, but did agree to be less critical and more accommodating.

A few days later, just before noon, a few of our clerks came over to my desk. Shock was writ large on their faces. Manoj's wife, it seemed, had died by suicide. It appeared that before leaving for office that day, he had had a terrific row with her and had flung his breakfast to the floor before storming out. It seemed that his wife had drained the petrol from a moped that he had left at home, doused herself with it and immolated herself.

It was a huge shock to our branch community, which was very close-knit. Nobody had any inkling that matters had come to such a pass. A few days later, when Manoj joined work once again, he appeared even more morose and withdrawn. I found a few minutes to talk to him, and he roundly blamed himself. 'I was the better-educated one. It was my duty to have moulded her. Instead, I drove her to her death. I must be punished. But everyone only commiserated with me. They don't realize what I have done,' he said. I tried hard to convince him that everyone who is born also dies as per their destiny. There was no reason to think that he was powerful enough to have changed the course of her life, but he would have none of it. I felt truly concerned at his state of mind, and called some of the union leaders to my desk to discuss the matter. They confirmed that they too were worried for him. It seemed that his younger brother and his wife had come to stay with them as someone needed to take care of the two little boys at home. They were also planning to force him to see a psychiatrist to help him cope with his loss.

The psychiatrist prescribed some medications which made Manoj sleepy and lethargic. He began to gain weight and the quality of his work suffered. We tried to give him a light desk, but that would hurt his ego as he was used to handling the toughest and heaviest assignments. And yet, he was in no shape to handle a large workload.

One day, he just decided to give up the medications. 'I can't bear to be so drowsy through the day. I feel like a zombie, like I am sleepwalking through the day,' he said. But as soon as the medication was stopped, his obsessive thoughts returned.

A few days later, there was a commotion at the branch. It appeared that Manoj had tried to leap off the roof of our two-storeyed building. We had a canteen on the terrace, which people visited during lunch hour. It appeared that he had gone up early and was climbing the parapet in order to jump when a messenger who had wanted an early lunch spotted him and held him back. The matter was brought to me with the recommendation that I send him home as no one had time to watch over him in order to ensure he didn't harm himself. Given our workload, I thought that was the best course of action. I asked one of the messengers to escort him home and he left without a word. A few hours later, we received news that he had hanged himself at home. How did this happen? His sister-in-law and his brother were staying with him. It transpired that they had stepped out as they didn't know he was coming home early that day. The messenger who had accompanied him had not enquired whether anyone was at home, nor had we asked him to do so. We all just took it for granted that he would be safe at home without taking the steps necessary to ensure his safety. I will never ever be able to get past the regret of not having thought through that situation.

A bank job, though stable, had its downsides as well. During my first stint as an accountant, this was brought home with considerable force as we fell victim to a fraud. It was an ordinary day like many others. My desk was piled high with ledgers and registers. There was a large number of cheques and withdrawal slips that had been referred to me for various reasons. One of them was a withdrawal of ₹20,000 that had been referred to me because the account holder was taking out large amounts within a short period. He had already withdrawn a similar amount earlier that week. The account appeared to be for pension and superannuation benefit purpose, and had been opened recently. The first credit was from a large cheque representing provident fund proceeds.

The counter clerk had sent it to me because as per the standard operating procedure we needed to counsel such a person and persuade him to save/invest for the future. However, when I called his name, there was a flurry at the counter as some person pushed through the crowd and ran off. The guard too had taken note of a fellow rushing out. The matter needed investigation. We scrutinized that account. Nothing seemed amiss, though no phone number was provided (in those days, this was not mandatory). I had the cheque which funded the account retrieved. It appeared genuine. I then looked for the person who had introduced the account, and called him at the address and phone number provided. However, the person who answered the phone stated that a person of that name had indeed resided there for a little while but he had passed away about a year ago. A further scrutiny of the introducer's account revealed that it too was opened within the year and had been funded by a cheque of ₹15,000 that had also been issued by the same department at IIT that handled the terminal benefits. This money too had been withdrawn, leaving behind a small balance. But the introduction to the account we were investigating had been given recently, so obviously someone was misusing the identity of the dead man.

We next looked at the introducer of the dead person's account. It was an officer from the air force base at Salua. When contacted, at first he couldn't recall any such incident. But after we jogged his memory and gave the details that showed that the account was opened on the same day when he appeared to have visited the branch, as evidenced by transactions in his own account, he recalled the incident. It was a typical confidence scam, when a fellow had approached him saying that he needed to open a bank account to encash the proceeds from the sale of his land, how the hard-hearted, callous bank employees were not helping him open an account in the absence of an introduction, and could he please oblige as he did not know any other account holder of the bank. The officer felt he was doing a good deed by helping someone in need, and so the modus operandi was established.

Of course an FIR was lodged, and both the local police and the Enforcement Directorate (ED) investigated the affair. While the local police were sympathetic to our plight, the ED appeared much more sceptical about our narration of events. They appeared to approach the matter with a view that there had to be internal collaboration and would not accept this was not so. On the day they arrived, my BM was unwell. He was running a fever and I had no option other than to tell him to go home. So I met the officials of ED and, in spite of the open distrust, narrated the entire chain of events again.

After handing over the matter to the police and referring it to the fraud investigation cell within the organization, our role in the incident ceased. However, the worry about the resultant action continued to gnaw at my mind because this was my first-ever encounter with the law, and the ED's suspicions were unsettling.

About six months later, I was again holding joint charge of BM and accountant. It was a particularly heavy day as the branch had reopened after three days of closure. There were piles of cheques that had come in for clearing (that is, those drawn on our bank but received by other banks for credit of their customer's accounts). There were sheafs of cheques issued by IIT. One such cheque of a pretty large amount caught my attention as the deputy director (DD) who normally signed these cheques had used his short signature again. He had been doing so frequently and I had often warned him that I would stop paying cheques issued by IIT if he did not use the signature on our records, which was his full signature.

He complained that it took him too long, but I refused to accept that plea. Either he needed to change the signature recorded with us or else he had to sign in full. I gave him my example. I had a pretty long signature. What with IIT students purchasing drafts by the dozen to apply abroad, there were days when I had to sign over 500 drafts. He asked me curiously why I merely wrote my name for a signature, and did not have something shorter and more stylized. I told him that God had not conveyed to me what my surname would be after marriage to enable me to develop a better signature (one of the travails of being a woman in those days).

Besides, within a month of my marriage, I was to move to Kharagpur. My signature needed to be circulated if I was to be an accountant or BM. As per the bank's rules, the signature had to be legible yet uniform, and so after trying a few times, I gave up and opted to just write my name in my regular handwriting. Again, I doubt whether men have ever faced such an issue, but for women, it was one of the passages to adulthood – we would suddenly have a different surname and would have to change our signatures to adapt to this change. Another lack I have always felt as a woman is the lack of pockets in our attire. Even in Western wear, women's slacks often have no pockets. Jackets may have the pocket flap, but again those are usually for show. I realize that vanity is probably to blame for this. Our shapeliness can get distorted by bulky items stuffed into pockets, and so it was decided not to have pockets at all. As a result, we are doomed to purses and handbags that seem to have magnetic properties for attracting odds and ends. Ultimately, they grow so heavy that a tryst with spondylosis is almost assured.

But enough of the digression. I contacted the DD, who heard my tirade patiently and then told me that post our last interaction, he had not issued any cheque under his short signature. But I was holding one in my hand! The cheque appeared to have been issued just a few days ago. But as I stared at the cheque, I felt that there was something amiss. The handwriting, though apparently the same, appeared laboured, as though someone had written it very slowly. The DD took down the cheque number and promised to revert with more information. He called back within the next ten minutes to tell me that the said cheque leaf seemed to have been torn out of the cheque book and IIT had not issued the same. The college and the bank swung into action. We contacted the police and the collecting bank, and then a trap was laid to catch the person who would come to withdraw money from that account. Sure enough, on the second day, a person turned up and was promptly nabbed. He led us to the leader of his group, a young on-probation clerk at IIT.

A search of his place revealed reams of sheets on which he had practised the handwriting on the cheques and the DD's signature. Luckily, the DD used his short signature for all circulars and the long signature only for financial instruments. So the fellow had only been able to obtain specimens of the short signature, but not the longer one. When interrogated, he also owned up to an earlier fraud he had committed by opening fictitious accounts in the names of payees of cheques whose terminal benefits remained unclaimed for a long time. Thus, the earlier incident too was closed. I thanked God again and again that something had triggered my suspicion and stayed my hand from passing that cheque. I could easily have passed the cheque, given the history and the fact that I was sorely overworked and running against time. I recognized that as always my guardian angel had their work cut out to keep me safe.

Over this entire period, the bank remained cognizant of my need to stay in and around Kharagpur, and over a nine-year period, I did three stints there: first, as an accountant at our Kharagpur branch, then as a branch manager of another small semi-urban branch called Nimpura and then again as the branch manager of the Kharagpur branch.

Nimpura was a small semi-urban branch, with two officers and five staff members. It was a different kind of experience, leading a small group of people – but totally enjoyable. The staff had each other's backs. And unlike the common perception about public sector organizations, there was no slacking off at all. During my stint at the branch, we had witnessed one of the worst storms in my life. It was the tail end of a massive cyclone that made landfall further to the south of India. By the morning after the storm, there was no power and water. Most roads were blocked by uprooted trees. I had to get to work though. I managed to cajole my husband to give me a lift on his scooter. Soon, we found out for ourselves how dangerous it could be. There were live power lines hanging across the road. One had fallen at the side and was showering sparks. There were trees and branches on the roads that were still slick with rain. We proceeded at snail's pace, so that we wouldn't be beheaded or electrocuted by the dangling wires. Pritimoy questioned my wisdom at having ventured out while I narrated stories of how some of our guys had crossed a river in spate in an iron cauldron to open a branch, or cadged a ride on an elephant when the roads got washed away. But a state banker never – and absolutely never – left a branch closed unless it was a scheduled holiday. Not only me, but all of my staff including the guard and messenger arrived in due time, and the branch did open, though the customers didn't put in an appearance that day.

As BM of Nimpura, I had to often stay late in order to complete work before leaving. I never had to request any of my staff to stay. They took turns if required, but never once brought up the matter of overtime. It was as though they had decided that given the remote location of the branch, my well-being was their responsibility and I never had to remind them of my seniority to make them do what needed to be done. Though, strictly speaking, they could have refused to cooperate.

Recovery of loans was a problem even in those days. We had to go out and follow-up some borrowers on a regular basis. I remember my interactions with one such person. He was a man of considerable influence, and my staff were very averse to my interacting with him. But I was young and felt that such caution was of little use if it did not get the job done. I did meet the person and our interaction was anything but pleasant. Veiled threats were delivered from both sides. Shortly after, I was travelling to the branch in a cycle rickshaw – a mode of transport I often used as other modes of public transport were unreliable or unavailable, and because I don't drive (I still don't, to my deep regret).

As my rickshaw approached an empty stretch of land between the last outpost of the town and the branch, I saw a procession of people who appeared to be rehearsing for some upcoming festivities. They had open swords in their hands, which they swung about with ferocious abandon. As my rickshaw approached, most of them courteously stepped aside, but not our recalcitrant borrower. He was, in fact, leading the group and he continued with a display of his swordsmanship right in front of my rickshaw. I can't say that I didn't feel intimidated, but I also felt that showing fear was the last thing I should do. I asked the rickshaw to pedal slowly, so as to allow people to move out of the way. I smiled and acknowledged a few others whom I knew in the crowd as well as our borrower. When the procession moved on, I finally breathed a sigh of relief.

My staff, on hearing of the incident, felt that I had not acted with due caution while following up with this borrower, but I could think of no other course of action. A few days later, I came across him again on the way to the branch. This time, I stopped the rickshaw, got off and complimented him on his leadership abilities. I asked him to consider how that status would be sullied if we took action against him as a defaulter, as his followers would surely know that he had not paid despite having adequate ability to do so. I appealed again to his good sense, and asked him to set an example. Ultimately, we did recover the loan without any further incidents.

Since Pritimoy didn't work on the weekends, he would drop me off to work on Saturdays. One such Saturday, I had been dropped off and had just opened the cash safe with my cash officer when a fellow came rushing to tell me that Pritimoy had met with a bad accident and that the locals had taken him to a nearby medical store where a doctor was normally available. I forgot the fact that the cash safe was open. I asked one of the staff to take me to the spot on his scooter, and we rushed off. I found my husband – his face bathed in blood – sitting in the shop, while a fellow was trying to staunch the flow. The local guys had managed to get a hold of a vehicle, but were awaiting my arrival. We quickly took him to the nearest nursing home.

Only after the doctor had put in a dozen stitches, given him an anti-tetanus shot, cleaned him up and declared that he was in no danger did I remember the branch and the fact that I had left the safe open with the keys still hanging on the door. I used the nursing home phone to call up the branch. My staff assured me that matters were under control. A nearby branch had been requested to send a replacement for me. The replacement was on his way to take charge, and I should just concentrate on getting my husband the best care without worrying about the branch. I felt deeply grateful to my team for stepping up so seamlessly to the challenge.

This happened again when I was hit by a bug that caused high fever and stomach cramps. As I lay on my table in my room, which I rarely used, preferring to sit in the banking hall instead, my team efficiently organized my replacement, a doctor to come and see me immediately and a vehicle to take me home.

The way each member of my team backed up one another was exemplary, and memories from my time there are some of my best. Youngsters often ask me how I managed to stay in one organization for so long. I stayed because I felt challenged and alive every day. There was so much to learn and so much to do. It was a never-ending struggle, but a rewarding one.

I had by then spent nine years in and around Kharagpur. I had arrived as a Scale II officer, in March 1984, had been promoted twice and in April 1993 had just become a Scale V officer – at which level there were no more positions in Kharagpur. In between, there was an occasion when I had been asked to be ready for a transfer. Pritimoy proactively had secured a deputation to the Indian Institute of Management (IIM) Calcutta. But after he joined there, my transfer didn't come through. So I stayed put in Kharagpur, while he spent nine months in Kolkata before he could arrange to end the deputation and return.

He had tried teaching at IIM but as computer science and engineering were not in the mainstream curriculum of that institute, he had not enjoyed teaching there. So this time around, we decided that he would continue in Kharagpur while I went to Kolkata. The matter of leaving my job and staying on in Kharagpur did come up in discussions. I even went to see the then director of IIT, who was otherwise well disposed towards me. Earlier, on hearing of my ambition to do a PhD, he had offered to help me do it from that IIT itself. Towards that end, I had chosen a guide and even visited National Institute of Bank Management at Pune to determine a suitable topic. However, the IIT senate – a body that determined the policies and strategies of the institute, both academic and non-academic – refused to allow me to do the PhD unless I spent six months full-time on campus attending various courses. I offered to sit for the exams and acquire necessary credits, without attending the classes, by studying on my own time. But the offer cut no ice, and I was refused permission. When I went to see the director, he was quite apologetic. However, he had no position to offer me except that of an assistant registrar, which I politely refused. As not working was not an option, I prepared to leave Kharagpur for Kolkata.

# 6

# When Challenges Lead to Opportunities

In April 1993, I left Kharagpur for Kolkata. I had been posted to the commercial branch which had its office on Park Street. I was allocated a ground floor flat in Golf Green, and I set up house for the fourth time (I had done so thrice in Kharagpur as Pritimoy got promoted and we moved to bigger houses) since my marriage. I would do so many more times in the coming years. The houses in Kharagpur had been unsatisfactory. Each house had its own distinctive design. I often wondered whether they were parcelled out to the students studying architecture to test their ideas on. Of course, today those old bungalows have given way to modern multi-storeyed apartment buildings. But in those days, such apartment buildings were few and far between. In one of our houses, one could see the stars as one lay in bed as the walls near the ceiling had developed large cracks. In another, the kitchen was as large as a basketball court. But the bathroom was so small that one had to go on one's toes like a ballerina in order to get in and close the doors. But all said and done, the bungalows in Kharagpur were large. The water tank behind our house was the size of a small paddle pool. Compared to that, the rooms in the Golf Green apartment appeared to be handkerchief-sized. This was another problem I would face again and again in the coming years. The size of our dwelling space expanded or contracted with every transfer, depending on my rank and the city that I was in, causing me much aggravation as I had to constantly give away various items of furniture and buy new ones. In this Golf Green apartment the bigger problem, however, was its location on the ground floor. Not only was it a little damp but security too seemed to be an issue.

One night, as I sat down to eat, I found someone staring at me through the dining room grille. As I called out to ask what he wanted, he flashed me. I yelled in fright, and then quickly dialled my neighbour, who lived in the adjoining apartment. He immediately came out and banged on my door, but when I tried to open it for him it wouldn't budge. We discovered that the miscreant had latched the door from the outside. The next morning, I engaged a carpenter to come and put another hook on the door, so I could latch it even if it was open. I applied again to be shifted to a higher floor, but to no avail. Instead, I employed an old lady as a full-time caretaker so that I didn't have to be alone in that flat.

It was during this time that one morning as I entered office, I found a person from the Steel Authority of India Limited (SAIL) office waiting for me with an urgent message. It appeared that my father had passed away the night before.

How does one respond to such news? All the insecurities of childhood emerge in a rush. I remembered that as a child I would hate going to the movies unless my parents were with me. Even then, I used to fear the disconnect I felt without them, and the question as to what would happen if something befell them and I could not be contacted as I was locked away in a dark cinema theatre used to plague me. It took me a number of years to outgrow these fears. But now, my very worst fears had been realized. My father was no more and for twelve long hours I had no inkling of this tragedy. It was like someone had bludgeoned me. My knees seemed to give away and I couldn't respond. I was informed that he was watching his usual 9 p.m. TV serial – *Neem ka Ped* – when he passed away. My family had been trying to get in touch with me, but somehow the phone calls didn't go through – there was some fault in the system, which, in those days, was not uncommon. Hence, they had sent a message to the SAIL office on their private network.

I left for Bokaro immediately. The train journey and then the bus ride seemed interminable. It was early May and blisteringly hot. My father had just celebrated his eightieth birthday in April. He had always been convinced that he would die before he retired (like his own father and grandfather had). As a result, he had not built a house nor made adequate retirement plans, even though he had no pension. It was lucky then that both my mother (from her homeopathy practice) and my aunt (from a school she had set up) continued to earn an income, or else it would have been a difficult phase for them.

By the time I arrived, the last rites had been completed. I was overwhelmed by the guilt. The last time I had seen him was in March, and I had noticed some changes in him then, which probably should have warned me of the things to come. Normally, my visits home were the high point of his days. But the last time, he had seemed less aware of my visit. He had given me attention for about fifteen minutes before forgetting my presence and becoming immersed in his own daily routine. In fact, it was because of this that I had not called him up to share with him the news of my elevation to assistant general manager (AGM). I thought he may register it better if I told him face to face. But was it only because of that reason that I had kept the news from him, or was it because I wanted to see the delight on his face, his eyes light up and his face glow with pride at my achievements? But now he would never know.

Once we finished handling all the formalities of my father's passing, I returned to Kolkata and immersed myself in work. The Commercial branch handled large corporate credit, and the person I was taking over from handled one of the largest portfolios in the branch. He was also the undoubted favourite of the head of the branch. This was with good reason. I have myself rarely seen a more competent and well-meaning officer. I was to handle large credit for the first time and I was quite apprehensive. But Arijit Sanyal, my predecessor, took me through every step patiently, instructing me on the finer nuances of credit appraisal as we went through the files of each account. In all my years of a dozen or more assignments, nobody has done a more thorough job of handing over charge.

In time, I took over completely. The head of the branch, however, had still not warmed up to me. He could barely handle the loss of his favourite officer, and then to find out that a woman was replacing the man he valued so much was the unkindest cut of all. Whenever I went to his room, I was never invited to sit down. I was told that he allowed only the people he approved of to sit in his presence.

Shortly after I joined this branch, the bank launched its maiden Global Depository Receipt (GDR) issue. Our branch was given a target for the amount of investments we needed to garner. One of my accounts was that of the largest miner in India. While their corporate headquarters was in Kolkata, their Provident Fund Trust, which was a large investor, had its office in the neighbouring state. I took the help of my relationship with the corporate to visit their PF office and seek their investment in our issue. After three days of hard work, I managed to convince their investment committee and returned to my branch with a cheque that was big enough to cover not only the branch's target but also that of the circle. However, at this point, our neighbouring circle woke up and complained to our chief general manager (CGM) that the Bengal circle had taken what was rightfully theirs. The CGM, who knew me well from my Kharagpur days (as local board meetings of the circle were sometimes held at the IIT there), told the head of my branch to resolve the issue. My boss called me to his room and, for the first time ever, asked me to take a seat. Thereafter, I never faced any issue with him and he was most supportive of all my initiatives. On the GDR issue, I refused to back off. Ultimately, my bosses decided to share the amount 50:50 between the circles, but I had proved my abilities and my reputation as someone who could be relied on to deliver got a great boost.

My interactions with the large corporate customers showed me a world of finance very different from the one I had handled till then. Decisions needed to be taken for exposures in crores of rupees and the amount of diligence required was commensurately large. A good practice I saw at that branch was it had a dedicated team for inspection and another for documentation. It helped in creating expertise in areas which were otherwise not well understood, but which had a great bearing on the health of the account and protection of lenders. I also met some great leaders who went on to head large companies, and the business practices of a calibrated approach to risk that I saw them follow provided great learning opportunities for me.

The challenge of balancing work and home had become greater by now. I would catch the Coromandel Express on Saturday evenings to go to Kharagpur. It would take about three hours if there were no disruptions, which, unfortunately, happened frequently. Once when the overhead wires snapped, I got to Kharagpur at 2.30 a.m. Pritimoy invariably picked me up from the station. That day, he was not on the platform. On exiting the station, I saw our car parked at the very end and discovered my husband fast asleep at the wheel. He had been mistaken for a taxi driver for half the night, and, as each train came in, he had his work cut out refusing passengers wanting to hire the vehicle. He was unable to see what I found so funny in the situation.

Every Monday morning, I would take the 5 a.m. Sri Jagannath Express. The train would often run late, though it still meant that both Pritimoy and I would need to get up at 4 a.m. I would bathe and dress in Kharagpur, so I could go straight to work on Mondays. The life of a daily passenger, though tortuous on account of the challenges of train delays, still had its high points. There was a lot of camaraderie amongst the regulars on these journeys. The younger amongst the lot would clamber on before the train came to a stop. The idea was to capture empty berths so we could catch a bit of shut-eye on the journey. Once when we get stalled in the middle of nowhere, the group rounded up some locals, got them to pluck the small cucumbers from the fields and sell them to us to slake both our thirst and hunger. We often shared our successes and troubles with each other. It often reminded me that people's needs were really not all that huge, and sometimes being part of a group that seemed to gel well was enough to reduce our angst at the daily grind.

I had hoped to have a child earlier in the marriage. It would have been ideal to have had one at Kharagpur, where support would have been easier to arrange. But as someone rightly said, 'If you want to make God laugh, just tell him your plans.' We had consulted doctors, done the regular rounds of clinics and been through umpteen tests. Most of these were in the 'irritating' category, but a few were downright painful. Getting posted to Kolkata enabled better follow-up at least. My father's demise seemed to sharpen my sense of mortality and the feeling that time was running out. Around a year after my father's demise, I conceived. My husband opined that my father's soul had opted to be born to me, for no other soul would want to be born to us – we had such little time on our hands. Jokes apart, this increased the challenge of keeping the family together. I found it difficult to travel, and so Pritimoy started coming to Kolkata over the weekends. For him, it was slightly easier as he had two-day weekends. He would come on Friday night, help me with the shopping and other household chores over the weekend and return on Monday morning.

After a while, my mother came and stayed with me, as managing on my own became increasingly difficult. I had to temporarily hand over charge and take a break. I had a difficult time, complicated by the fact that I was well past my best child-bearing years. Given the fact that the risks were higher, I asked for an amniocentesis to be done. But the doctors thought that the risk of miscarriage would be greater and so refused to do so. Till date I do not know whether that was a wise decision, or whether I should have insisted and got my way. Anyway, the only person who can raise my blood pressure was born soon – my daughter Sukrita.

Returning to work after the maternity break proved difficult. My mother and aunt took turns to be with me and supervise the household. I had a separate nurse from 8 a.m. to 8 p.m. for Sukrita. At night, however, she was in my charge alone. I slept little for the first eleven months. When I think back, I don't know how I managed it. But I did manage, and I think women get endowed with superpowers when they hold a baby in their arms. Many times I would sing to keep myself from falling asleep. Sukrita has an excellent sense of tune, and I often think that my singing was what gave her this gift. However, she is at pains to inform me that I can't hold a tune to save my life.

The lives of young mothers today have improved with the advent of diapers and other baby aides. In those days we did have diapers, but not only were they costly, they were available only in one size. The ones I could procure almost covered Sukrita's entire body. There was one night, for instance, when I changed her seventeen times! But the next morning, I was at work on time. During this period when I sat with Sukrita in my arms, trying to lull her back to sleep, a white owl would frequently come and perch on the bedroom window. It would drift down, quiet as a snowflake, peer inside and then would be gone again, as silently as it had arrived. It used to make me think of the many wonders of the night I never knew of.

The other challenge was to get a proper posting on resuming duty. The first suggestion that came up was from Central Accounts Office that looked after balance sheet preparations for the entire bank. I soon learnt, however, that the proposal had met with mixed response for people in this department often needed to work through the night. Posting a woman was therefore considered inappropriate. I thought of objecting to this, saying that this could not be considered a major factor in my posting. On second thoughts, however, I realized that a customer-facing position would do more for my career than a back-office operation, and so I maintained my silence. Subsequently, I was posted to the overseas branch to look after private-sector clients. This too involved large corporate credit, but clients here had large export or import requirements typically. So, along with credit, knowledge of forex was also required. I had enough background of working in both credit and forex, and so I was quite happy with the posting.

What I had not bargained for was the person heading the branch. This was his first posting at a credit-oriented branch. Normally, under such situations, people simply got down to the job and learnt what to do. Not so for this gentleman. He took to underlining every sentence in the notes and comments we put up, initialled and returned them, without any value addition. 'Can anyone looking at the note ever allege that I was not completely diligent?' he asked while holding up a page where every line was underlined in red.

He was prone to a lot of grandstanding as well. He sent a note to his manager one day saying that as he appeared incapable of contributing to my or my department's work, he should be transferred. His boss must have been flabbergasted to receive this message. Another time, I found all four of my credit analysts missing. I was told that they were in my boss's room. Two hours later, they were still not back at their desk. I went to see what was keeping them. As I knocked and entered, I found all four of them sitting upright on the sofa. The head of the branch was disposing files at his desk. I looked at them and asked them why they were wasting time.

'They have come because I asked them to. Do you have a problem?' my boss asked.

'No, not really a problem, but they have work to do ...'

'Whose work should have precedence, yours or mine?'

'Yours, of course, but ...'

'No buts. Can't you see they are busy?'

'They don't look very busy. They are having tea and biscuits.'

'Well, I am about to give them some important work. So please excuse us. You will need to manage on your own.'

When the guys got released at six in the evening, they came up to me apologetically. We had a good laugh at the stratagem employed to make my life difficult. My team assured me that the day's work would get done by the morrow. Knowing that I couldn't rely on my manager, who could suddenly take my team away for the day, I learnt to handle a computer, and learnt both Word and PowerPoint for myself. I had no teachers, but found that none were required. I remain a two-finger typist though and continue to envy those who type fluidly using all their fingers. But as far as two-fingered typists go, I am pretty good. This independence from the tyranny of typists made me feel empowered. It also enabled me to take home more work, so that I could leave by 7.30 p.m. and get back home at a tolerably decent time.

The redeeming feature about my boss was that he was a dog lover. He had a pet dachshund, who would often come to the office to pick him up at day's end. She sported a bindi and was very friendly. I was of the opinion that a dog lover is bound to be a caring person. But as far as we at the branch were concerned, his caring side was not evident. It so happened that both of us got called for interviews for foreign postings by the bank. Both of us got selected, but all hell broke loose when the postings finally came. I had been posted to New

York, whereas he had been posted to a location where we had very small operations. This magnified the issues he had with me.

During this time, I was fighting multiple battles. The first was regarding Sukrita. She had been born six weeks premature as my blood pressure had suddenly risen. While most premature babies gain weight rapidly, this was not happening in her case. Her milestones were delayed. With further investigations, doctors diagnosed multiple other problems, such as stenosis of a valve in the heart, weakness of abdominal muscles causing umbilical hernia and strabismus (squint eye, again caused by weakness of the eye muscles). Added to this was her slow growth, which doctors felt could lead to learning issues. When all this was told to me, I turned numb for a little while. Words were being spoken, but I couldn't comprehend their import. All that kept echoing in my mind was the doctor's opening sentence. 'You have a long battle ahead of you. But where there is life, there is hope. Never forget that and never give up.'

The other stress point was of course my job and, to compound it all, I fell ill. The problem was diagnosed as surgical jaundice caused by a blocking of the bile duct by stones from the gall bladder. Pritimoy was at Kharagpur then. So a neighbour and colleague took me to the hospital and admitted me. The doctors wanted to operate on me without delay. I sought twelve hours from them so that at least Pritimoy could get there. My biggest worry was Sukrita. What if something were to happen to me? Who would look after her? However, at the end of the next few hours, the sheer pain made me want to die. I realized then that at the end it is all about the self. No matter how involved one is doing various things, one comes alone and departs alone, and sometimes a release from life can be considered a blessing. But the moment the pain receded, my worries for my little one loomed large again. As soon as Pritimoy arrived, I was taken to the operation theatre.

By God's grace, the operation went well and I returned home in due time. I was to leave for the USA in three months. There were many preparations to make and things to put in order before we left. I had a classical open-abdomen operation as there had been some other complications. Doctors forbade me to strain myself for at least six weeks. But I just didn't have the time to take it easy. We had to get our passports readied and then our visas. Tax and security clearances had to be obtained. I had to wind up my Kolkata residence. I turned to my family to help me with Sukrita while I sorted out my affairs. Moreover, I needed someone to look after her while I was at work. Luckily, my aunt had just retired from her job. She offered to accompany me to New York for six months, during which time we hoped some permanent arrangement could be made.

Pritimoy was just about to be promoted to a professor and we didn't think it right for him to accompany us immediately. This meant that I would be shifting to a foreign country with a one-year-old baby and a senior citizen. Through all this, my boss was thoroughly uncooperative. He refused me all leave, and would not even allow me to attend the training one underwent before departure. We were entitled to a leave fare/home travel allowance before going abroad. People used it to wind up their establishments and transport what needed to be stored to their hometowns. In my case, though, this too was denied. My last working day at the overseas branch ended with a consortium meeting I chaired at 4.30 p.m. My flight was at eleven that very night.

It was a mad scramble. My mother and aunt came over to help pack up my Kolkata residence. Through all this, challenges continued to mount. We had a really nasty experience at the passport office. Never having travelled abroad, none of us had passports. Getting one in those days was not easy, and often the officers handling the matter would behave as though they were doing citizens an enormous favour. After going through the grind, including providing the fingerprints of my very young daughter, my husband, daughter and I received our passports without any hitches. But my aunt's passport seemed to have run afoul in the system. When it didn't arrive after several days, we used the bank's contacts to find out what happened. Ultimately, I secured an appointment with the passport officer and went to see him along with my aunt. He saw us after making us wait for half an hour, and then started grilling us as to why my aunt needed a passport at her age. When I explained my situation, he smirked and remarked that he knew what we were up to. I was quite foxed and asked him what he meant.

At this, he felt I was questioning his intelligence and he snapped at us, saying that he had seen many instances where maids were passed off as aunts, and he felt that this was a similar case. I lost my cool. I sprang up from my chair ready for a screaming match when I felt my aunt's restraining hand on my arm. In a cool and calm manner, she took out her academic degrees and passed them over. 'I have no problem being called a maid, but where do you think I got all these degrees from? Besides, is there a law in India that says maids cannot be issued passports? If so, if you can quote me the rule and section number we will stop bothering you.' The passport officer by this time, after checking the academic certificates, appeared to feel that he had overplayed his hand. So to get rid of us he quickly rang for his assistant and asked him to sort out the issue. As there was nothing to be sorted out except his own personal prejudice, we were allowed to leave and the passport was received the next week.

The next big hurdle were the health checks. While for the three adults things went smoothly, that was not the case for my little one. She had to go through numerous cardiac tests but, to our delight, it appeared that the valve stenosis was resolving itself. So also with the strengthening of her muscles, the umbilical hernia had gotten resolved. However, strengthening of her eye muscles would still need to be taken care of, as well as her developmental problems, but that wouldn't keep me from being part of the new adventure that beckoned.

So, with a lot of hope and not a few apprehensions, we set off. Quite a few of my colleagues, including my team members, had come to see us off. But this one was a far more muted send-off than the one given by my college mates.

As I trundled up the steps of the Air India flight with my handbag and my baby's bag, I looked back one last time at the life of certainty I was leaving behind. But the next moment I was breathless with anticipation, and as the flight took off, I sat back with the little one in my arms, a prayer on my lips and trepidation in my heart.

# 7

# New York: Discovering a New World

The flight seemed endless. We had departed Kolkata and deplaned at Delhi, and now we had embarked again on the flight to New York. Travelling with a small child, especially one with several health issues, is not a picnic. When its travel into the unknown – as mine was – it is even more daunting.

I was going off to New York to take up a four-year assignment, accompanied by my very young daughter and my aunt who had just retired. I tried not to conjure up images of the challenges I would face once I got there. Instead, I concentrated on the many stories of New York I had heard and read – its famed museums, Central Park, Broadway, Greenwich Village, the city's cosmopolitan outlook and its vibrant financial markets.

I felt sick – was it excitement or anxiety? I couldn't tell. I only knew that I had rolled with the punches and a new world awaited me.

Of course, one reassuring feature was the security net of the bank. I knew someone would receive me at the airport and I wasn't too worried on that front. In those days, US immigration authorities were far more hospitable and there were hardly any instances of unwelcome incidents on arrival. In line with my expectations, we breezed through immigration, collected our many pieces of baggage and made our way out. One of the senior functionaries of the branch, Indrajit Gupta, and his wife, were waiting for us. He was a batchmate of my regional manager A. K. Das, when I was at Kharagpur, and had been especially requested to look out for me as I was arriving with a baby and an elderly aunt. He was there with his wife and a large SUV to accommodate us, baggage and all. As we moved out of the airport, I marvelled that my first international flight was at last over.

My first view of New York enchanted me. The cool air accentuated by golden sunlight, the green, neatly trimmed lawns, the red-brick row houses with sloping roofs … I absorbed it all with a newcomer's eyes. The neatly trimmed trees, the bright bursts of colours from flowers along the road, the fat chipmunks that scurried on the green grass – it all appeared to be just as I had imagined it, and better! Reality would dawn only later, especially when I saw my temporary lodgings.

The bank's transit allowance was insufficient for us to rent a service apartment. Accordingly, interim arrangements had been made for us to put up with an Indian family that had settled down in the US. Their apartment in Queens had a large living-cum-dining room, two bedrooms, one common bath and an attached half-bath. This was the Khanna family – which included the parents, their son, daughter-in-law and two grandkids. They allotted one bedroom (luckily the one with the attached half-bath) to us. The other bedroom was occupied by two junior India-based officials, who had landed just a few days before me.

The Khannas, all six of them, used the living room as their bedroom. With eleven people in a two-bedroom apartment, it was a bit of a crush to say the least. One needed to wake up precisely at a particular time in order to be able to use the toilet and take a bath.

As many as eight people needed to leave for school or office in the morning. There was no privacy to speak of; every once in a while, somebody would knock hurriedly and barge in without waiting for an answer as they needed to use the restroom. But Mrs Khanna soothed over many of these irritations with her smiling hospitality. She would be the first to wake up at 4 a.m. She would cook a hearty Punjabi breakfast and pack eight tiffin boxes. We had free access to the kitchen, and she kept the fridge well-stocked with fruits, milk and ice cream, which she would urge us to consume whenever she could. We didn't have such large buckets of ice cream back home, and the variety of flavours available were enough to blow our mind. Those were the days before India saw the advent of large malls and supermarkets. Things are very different now – at least, I can say that the US may have lots of ice-cream flavours, but the ones available in India, including the one with green chilli, are surely not available there. I once gave Pritimoy a spoonful of the green chilli ice cream, and he demanded to know if I was poisoning him!

Mrs Khanna showed my aunt the ropes of shopping at supermarkets and looking out for deals for various produce by clipping the coupons that cluttered the mailbox regularly. In fact, I think the US postal system was only used by shopping establishments to send out catalogues and coupons that allowed one to have a glimpse of the shopping paradise that America was. Sukrita at that time was still not strong enough to sit up, though she would roll from one end of the room to the other. So whenever my aunt went for her bath, Mrs Khanna would look after Sukrita, and would often volunteer to look after her during the day as well so my aunt could catch a little shut-eye in the afternoon. However, having to live in such cramped conditions needed patience of a kind I have not been asked to display anywhere else in my life.

Mr Khanna had a penchant for flea markets. It was an activity that he introduced me to, and he soon discovered that I had a good eye for quality curio pieces, which on account of neglect or the sheer dust covering them, on first glance, looked like junk. Through my four years in New York, I would often foray out to these markets on Saturday afternoons, after my family retired for a post-lunch nap following a hearty home-cooked meal. Most of the good flea markets could be found in downtown Manhattan. I would take the 7 train to Queensboro Plaza and then change to the N train before getting off at 28th Street. I especially loved those days when the sun shone brightly and a cool wind whistled down between the skyscrapers of Manhattan. I imagined the streets, on both sides of which loomed enormous glass and steel structures, as canyons, and the skyscrapers as the craggy mountains of the Wild West. Generally, on such afternoons, there would only be a few people around – so it was easier to imagine I was out in the wild. The wind would whip past me, making me draw my trench coat around me tightly. The flea markets would be held in vacant parking lots (the last time I was in New York, I found that most parking lots had disappeared and more skyscrapers had come up in their place).

Rummaging through tables loaded with knick-knacks was a great stress buster. I didn't discover good pieces every day. But when I did, it made my day. Once, I found a small piece of shining magnetite with a beautifully executed pewter horse perched on top. It was a three-by-two-inch piece, and its exquisite craftsmanship captivated me. Another time I paid 25 cents for a Kabuki scene made up of tiny plastic dolls stuck inside a shell-like structure. Then there was a lovely Chinese carving I discovered. The curvature of the piece made me suspect that it could be bone or ivory. But it was black with grime, its intricate carving caked in dirt. The young man selling the piece had no idea what it was. We started the bargaining from $30. I finally walked away with it after paying $19. I was really excited with my find, though my family took one look at the blackened piece and wondered why I had wasted my time and money on it. However, the challenge was to clean the piece – and I didn't want to clean it any which way and then damage it, especially if it was ivory. As always, when stuck, call a girlfriend. Manjira, who was also posted to New York a year after me, had a practical suggestion. 'Use your daughter's toothpaste and toothbrush,' she suggested. 'Ivory is tooth after all, and the soft and fine brush will ensure that the dirt gets dislodged.' I took her advice and soon had a beautiful carving of a Chinese village scene. I don't know whether it is bone or ivory or something else entirely, only that for $19 I got hours of pleasure admiring it.

The scene at the office, however, was a little dull. I was to take over the function of branch coordination and would report directly to the head of US operations. Our US operations in those days comprised five branches, an agency at Los Angeles and a small subsidiary in California. One of my main jobs was to look after the performance management of the entire US operations. I was a little surprised though that the gentleman from whom I was taking over seemed to only work for about half an hour per day, photocopying instructions and passing them on to various departments. For the rest of the day, he would sit at his desk with his eyes closed, thinking of the next poem he could write. Having just arrived from an assignment where I was working fourteen hours a day, this seemed like a travesty. I was often reminded of my previous posting. I finally went to my boss, Mr Govindan, the head of US operations, to tell him that I was finding the lack of work very frustrating.

I still remember what he told me: 'Arundhati, there is a time for everything. In most assignments in the bank, you will be working for more than twelve hours a day. But there will be a few assignments in which you will have the luxury of time. Make full use of it. Read the papers, find some courses that can help you improve your skills and knowledge, and don't complain. You should feel privileged that you have been sent for an assignment that exposes you to such a vibrant financial market. Make friends, meet people and understand the markets. There is so much to learn, and now you have the time to do it. How can you complain? Look around and broaden your understanding – it will stand you in very good stead going forward.'

Indeed, I deserved this rebuke. Here I was in the most vibrant financial market of the world, complaining that I didn't have enough files to push! As rightly pointed out by him, such opportunities were rare and I needed to make use of my time here fully. I changed my outlook and started scanning courses that I could quickly complete to understand the US financial and banking regulations, I made friends with various bankers in other banks and learnt the ropes of regulation and compliance. After work, I would visit the library, the museums, Central Park and, of course, the famed shops of New York. Each of these fascinated me, and indeed are some of the best in the entire world. New York's libraries, for instance, were a reader's dream. One could theoretically borrow up to ninety-nine books or CDs for three weeks at a time, and these could be renewed for a further three weeks simply through the phone (I normally borrowed six). Any book that you wanted but was not available could be requisitioned, and once the library received the book or bought it, you were advised by post. From my childhood, libraries have fascinated me. Some of my fondest memories of school were to do with browsing in the library. The New York libraries always reminded me of Ali Baba and his cave of untold treasures. My posting proved to be the 'open sesame' to unearth these riches.

As for museums, one could visit them umpteen number of times and still find new things to see. The Natural History Museum was a favourite. They recreated various natural and man-made structures that were simply wonderful. I remember they once recreated an entire underground coal mine. I cherish my memories of afternoons spent at the museum. Of course, the Metropolitan Museum of Art with its massive collection was always awesome, but I also loved the galleries like the Frick, which had a collection that was small enough to cover without feeling completely drained out. It also had a mix of beautiful paintings and sculptures, and unique pieces of furniture with pre-recorded audio commentaries that enabled one to understand the intricacies of the pieces on show.

One other place attracted me greatly. It was the showroom at Christie's, the auction house, which at that point was just a block away from the SBI office. Three days before an auction, the collections would be put out for preview. Anyone could visit and, best of all, there were no entry charges. I visited it during lunch hour the very first week of my arrival. I found that they had on display eighteen paintings by Pablo Picasso, which was from a couple's collection. They had passed away, and had left the paintings to charity with the proviso that they be auctioned and the proceeds used to serve good causes. Having come from a place where Picasso is highly revered, but where we had never seen any originals by the master, seeing eighteen of them in one place was mind-blowing.

Besides, this was not a viewing from a distance as one normally encounters in a museum setting. Here, one could actually get close to the painting and study it minutely. Not only that, there was also a small pencil sketch by Picasso which had a reserve price of $2,600. As I looked at it, I thought to myself, 'Oh boy! A few of us could get together and actually bid for a Picasso!' The thought was so thrilling and so outlandish that I burst out laughing, much to the astonishment of the viewers standing close by. Thanks to these auction previews, I saw several other things that filled me with awe, like a full Lalique crystal dining table and chair set, various rare paintings, and diamonds the size of pigeon eggs during the 'fabulous jewels' auctions held twice a year. Interestingly, the only people checking out these jewels (which all had tags that discreetly said 'price on demand'), with a loupe tucked into their eyes, were Jews or our very own brothers from Gujarat. I think I was one of those who really felt sorry when the auction house moved to Rockefeller Centre, putting an end to my lunch-time recreation.

The medical system in the USA was another matter altogether. You were assigned a doctor close to your home who accepted your insurance. In case of any urgent need, one had to go and see the doctor – no question of a home visit at all. If you fell ill outside office hours or on weekends, the only place to visit was a casualty department in a hospital. If tests were ordered, the results went directly to your doctor. If he called directly, one could be sure it would be to give bad news. If results were normal, the doctor's office would call. One could sometimes wait for weeks to get a test done if it was not considered an emergency. However, in an emergency, things could move superfast.

Also, I learnt to my chagrin that if you had an accident, you should just stay put and help would be forthcoming shortly. As soon as a 911 call is made, either a police car, an ambulance or a fire truck are dispatched as per the nature of the emergency, and they reach the spot in three minutes or less. Further, the ambulance chasers – that's what the attorneys who file compensation cases are called – would be with you in a trice. If negligence can be proved, then the amount of compensation can be quite handsome. In my last year of stay, I slipped on black ice on the side of the road and fractured my arm. The incident happened quite close to my residence and my only thought was to somehow get home. I did manage to stagger back. Pritimoy called 911 and the ambulance was with us shortly. The first question that the paramedic asked me was whether the fracture was a result of domestic abuse.

One should have seen Pritimoy's face when he realized what was being alleged. But I also made a similar face when the attorney told me that by leaving the accident site I had considerably reduced my chance of any compensation, which could have been as much as $10,000. They were right. I never did get any compensation. In any case, I left the country shortly afterwards, and it would have been foolish to go back and fight a case where I had little chance of winning.

But coming back to my initial days in the country, settling down and setting up home in the US was hard work. When the person whom I was replacing vacated his residence, fifty-four days had already passed since our arrival. I was so eager to get away from the Khanna residence with its one proper bathroom and half-bath that I moved in the very next day. But that meant that while the walls were getting painted, and the carpets and furniture replaced or cleaned, we were already inhabiting the place. And there were surprises galore. The kitchen was overrun with small cockroaches. I had naively believed that cockroaches inhabited only developing countries. When we lifted an old sofa, we discovered the desiccated carcass of a mouse.

But the guys doing the cleaning and painting did a professional job, and the apartment looked spic and span within three days. There was very little to remind us of the tough beginnings, other than the lingering smell of fresh paint. The next step was purchasing the items required for running a household. One had to buy mattresses and pillows, bed sheets and towels, as well as pots and pans for the kitchen. One also needed to buy various appliances such as coffee makers, microwave ovens, toasters and such others. Normally, I enjoyed shopping – though, it could be a very tiring activity. Hauling all the stuff back home was no easy job either.

Often on my way home, loaded down like a pack mule, I would feel a wave of homesickness wash over me. On one such occasion, I had just visited a sale at Macy's and was standing at a crossing, with bags of all sizes heaped around me and feeling very sorry for myself. Just then a plane flew overhead, and I imagined a ladder coming down and me clambering into the plane to be whisked back to India. I felt tired beyond belief. I squeezed my eyes shut tightly to stop the tears. And just then, I heard a babble in Bengali right behind me. I turned around, completely shocked, to see a largish group of Bangladeshis behind me. They spoke their own variety of Bengali, for sure, but it was the same language – my language. In a split second, my homesickness waned as I realized that I was not that far from home after all.

When I got transferred to the USA, my colleagues often told me I should be thankful that I was going to an English-speaking country. No doubt. But when you actually converse with an American, you realize that the Queen's English and American English are miles apart. For instance, I visited several shops looking to buy a perambulator for Sukrita. Wherever I asked, they looked at me blankly and shook their heads to indicate it wasn't available. At the last shop I tried, the saleslady cocked her head to one side and asked, 'What's that, dearie?' 'You know, a push cart that you put a baby in when you go out for a walk,' I explained. 'Oh!' she exclaimed. 'You mean a stroller. In the basement, dearie.' And there you have it. In the USA, a 'flat' means a 'flat tire', not an 'apartment'. A footpath is probably understood as a walking track in a forest and not what they call a 'sidewalk'. There are various other differences. Medicine bottles for instance come with unusually precise instructions. All oral pills come with the instruction 'Take by mouth'. I didn't realize oral medication could be taken in any other way! Besides, switches have to be flipped up to turn on the lights and down to turn them off. Hot water taps are on the right side. Locks open when you turn the keys clockwise and, of course, they drive on the right-hand side of the road. All these differences can drive one mad.

The local norms of behaviour and sensitivities are also vastly different. For instance, on a complaint of sexual harassment received by us, a local agency was hired to investigate it. They concluded that the male worker (an Indian expat) was not at fault when he asked the lady co-worker (a US citizen of Indian origin) to accompany him to a ball game, as this is accepted behaviour in the American workplace. But he had also approached her with a proposal for the marriage of his son with her daughter, and this fell under the definition of sexual harassment. In India, probably an invitation to go watch a game would have been treated as an unwelcome advance, whereas a proposal for a child's marriage may actually have been treated as normal behaviour. I learnt some valuable lessons regarding the need to be sensitive to language and customs, and these are as relevant to the different parts of our own country as they are internationally.

It took about thirty days of hard work to complete setting up the house. The difference between India and the US is that in India you have manpower, but no gadgets and other required materials. In the US, on the other hand, one has no manpower but all the gadgets, appliances and materials one may conceivably need. Everything was self-help, and to us, unused as we were to taking up the role of a carpenter, plumber or electrician, it was highly challenging. Help was available, but quite expensive, and so one learnt to call them in only where true expertise was required.

Pritimoy came over for a month's vacation once we had settled in. I was hopeful that now that we were in a country where smoking was prohibited in most places, he would give up this habit. A few days down the line, I realized that was not to be. In the smoking areas outside office buildings, one mostly found women puffing away. Quite frequently, Pritimoy was the sole man there and he quite liked the friendly attention he received. He made some friends and would often narrate the interesting parts of their conversations, and I soon realized the futility of my hopes.

In the initial days, Pritimoy would take Sukrita to the park in front of our house in the morning after I had left for work. Most children at the park would be accompanied by their mothers. Pritimoy elicited a lot of interest as he was asked at various times whether he was a widower or whether his wife was sick, or had deserted him and the child. Most of them became a tad less sympathetic on hearing that the mother was at work. Then the queries would turn to what he did. Pritimoy quite enjoyed describing himself as a homemaker, whereupon he was often given loads of tips on how to manage a household. He did say that he was tempted to experiment by narrating a sob story of his wife having run away, but that entailed remembering all the stuff he would have to make up – so better sense prevailed.

If there is one experience that is quite unique in the US, it is that of shopping. One could find all sizes and shapes and things to fit each budget. The best was the liberal 'exchange and return' policy. This encouraged one to take home stuff you were not fully sure about, content in the belief that the item could be returned. Most of the times, though, it didn't get returned, as one felt too lazy to go through the hassle of queuing up to return an item or two. But if one compared shopping to the Indian experience – at least where clothes were concerned – it fell short by far. In India, should you feel depressed, you only need to step into a sari shop. The shelves spilling over with magnificent colours of all hues, the textures of the silks and crepes and the finest cottons all work together to lift your mood instantly.

In the US, the colours of women's dresses left much to be desired. I had heard that black was considered eternally fashionable. While that proved to be true, much of the other hues bordered on black, such as grey or charcoal or ebony and the like. Browns and navy blues were also up there, as was white, cream, ecru and ivory. Once in a while, one came across a dress or coat in fire-engine red. But such instances were few and far between. The only thing that came close to the colour palettes seen in a sari shop were the cosmetic counters with their myriad-hued lipsticks. No wonder it's said that when women in New York feel depressed, they buy a lipstick.

There was another thing that made me feel a little sad. Whenever we went to shop for Indian food stuff at the Asian shops, we got produce which was far superior to the stuff we got at home. So be it Basmati rice or pulses or spices, the quality seen on the shelves of the shops in Queens was by far better than what we were used to in India. I felt quite bad for our countrymen, who laboured to produce such beautiful stuff, but couldn't afford to consume it.

Shopping for food was an experience in its own way. Most of the fruits and vegetables were beautifully arrayed, and a sight to behold. The red of the Red Delicious apples, the light green of the Granny

Smith apples to the bright orange of nectarines and the yellow–green of the pomelos – the colours and the sizes of the fruits were simply breathtaking. But where taste and smell was concerned, I felt our local produce back home was far superior. I would remember my childhood days, when Ma simply stepped out to our vegetable garden and picked a few cucumbers, tomatoes, a bunch of coriander and a small lemon to make a salad. As she chopped up the items, the smell of cucumber and coriander would permeate through the house signalling that mealtime was close by. The produce that we got from the supermarket shelves of Queens looked great, but lacked aroma and, to our jaded tongues, seemed to fall short on taste as well.

We were used to freshwater fish, and there was no lack of fresh fish in the shops of Queens. Most of the sea food would be neatly presented in rows on large beds of ice, with just the head and a small part of the body showing above the ice shavings that covered them. Behind these racks were large water tanks containing live freshwater fish, as well as lobsters and crabs. While the latter were trussed up and sold live, the fish would be brought out with a small net, stunned with one swift blow to the head and then cleaned, gutted, sliced and delivered in a trice. The men wore heavy rubber galoshes (gumboots in India), gloves and overalls. While these were far cleaner places to visit as compared to the fish markets in India, somewhere I missed the women dressed in gaily coloured saris, with their produce laid out in cane baskets and pieces of burlap, as the sun beat down fiercely on them. However, there is no doubt that because the hugely off-putting smell and the cacophony of bartering of Indian fish markets were absent, I preferred the Western experience.

Soon after his arrival, Pritimoy was offered a good job. He sought a sabbatical from IIT, for which he was eligible, but the college insisted he return and then make an application for it. A little hurt by the fact that IIT had in the past entertained many such proposals, and also given the fact that my career would not allow me to return to Kharagpur, he decided to resign. It was a huge decision and would prove a very big help to my being able to stay on in the bank. For him, it could not have been easy. He had been in IIT Kharagpur for five years as a student and then another nineteen years as a faculty member. He had been one of the founder members of the Department of Computer Science and Engineering. He had been made a full professor just four months before he joined us in New York. He had not even fully savoured the perks of being a professor at IIT yet, one of the most prestigious educational institutions in India.

The professors participated in the IIT Senate. His not having participated in even one of those meetings, I think, remained for him a matter of regret. But he always insisted that it was not a sacrifice, as many of his friends liked to characterize it. I am glad he felt it was a decision taken by him after due deliberation, as the term 'sacrifice' carries with it a little seed of discontent and bitterness that can drive a fatal wedge in relationships over time.

It's not as though the decision was made in a hurry either. In any case, his paperwork for the necessary work visa had to be submitted and the process for receiving the approvals took time. During this period, for days on end, he would hang out in the balcony, smoking one cigarette after another, trying to decide what to do. He later told me that after considerable thought he realized a few things: he knew Sukrita would need a kind of support not available in Kharagpur, and he also understood that his compensation would be much more if he stayed on in the US, which could mean much more financial stability for the family going forward. As I was in a steady job already, he felt it was up to him to take a risk and venture out. Being professionally qualified in a field that was highly sought after in the US, he felt it would be foolish to let the opportunity pass. And of course, he wanted the family to be together as long as we could possibly be, though he did realize that at times we would need to stay apart.

On the other hand, resigning meant giving up a lifestyle he had got used to for the past twenty-five years. It meant giving up friends and the dhabas – haunts where they would meet at least once a day to talk about work, politics and sports. Some of these places were open round the clock, and their limited menu of omelette and toast or French toast or local bread with *ghugni* (the Bengali variety of chana) followed by steaming tea served in little earthenware pots was in great demand.

Nowadays most of the dhabas have morphed into serving instant soups and noodles, but back then the menu was strictly local. These places would always be filled with students and teachers, and were the most visited spots on campus. The lure and magic of these dhabas are difficult to deny. Beyond that, there was also the consideration of stepping out into the unknown. He had completed nineteen years of service and just one more year there would make him eligible for partial pension. The amount may not have been anything substantial, but still it would be some support for when one grew older. As against that, he needed to balance a few year's earnings in the US and also the fact that the opportunity he had now may or may not be available at a later date.

Ultimately, staying on won and our life as a kind of semi-immigrant family commenced. It was a hard life. Pritimoy had to commute to New Jersey, and as office started at 8 a.m., he would leave home at 5.30 a.m. to get to work on time. This meant waking up at 4 a.m., By the time he went to bed, it would be past 11 p.m. But the trains functioned like clockwork and I could predict his time of return every day. Therefore, any change of routine could lead to huge worries. One such day, when he had not returned an hour after his regular time, I grew frantic. Calls to two of his colleagues whose phone numbers I had gave no comfort. He had left office on time. They suggested I call up the train helplines to find out whether there were any delays. I didn't have the number of the train he travelled on, but the helpline told me that there were no weather events and no generalized delays.

As I was wondering whether to call the police or not, the phone rang. It was Pritimoy telling me that there had been a suicide on the tracks involving the train he was on and till all police formalities were completed, the train was not allowed to move. He had hoped that the matter would be cleared up quickly, but as it appeared to be taking time, he had borrowed a co-passenger's mobile phone to call and reassure me. That same weekend we went shopping for a mobile phone, though they were very expensive in those days. But I did not consider them too costly if it spared me a few hours of worry in this alien land.

The timings eased a little after he got his own car, but the commute was still a long one and I would be on tenterhooks till he got home. On top of that, both Pritimoy and I were bad at directions. When going out with friends, we almost always missed the right exit and had to travel a few extra miles to return to the correct one. Once we missed the exit – our blame game would start and then we would end up having a full-blown fight. We never did ultimately decide who was supposed to keep track of the right exits – the person driving or the person sitting beside him (sometimes with a map opened on one's lap). It sometimes could get quite bad, like the time we kept driving round and round Williamsburg Bridge – we could see it, first to the left then to the right and then even above us at one point, but we simply couldn't get on to it. Our friends would refuse to ride with us, knowing our routine. I often feel that the creator of Google Maps must have been inspired by a couple like us.

As we settled down into our jobs, the next worry was Sukrita. We found an excellent Indian paediatrician close to our house and we needed him frequently for her various health issues. She was underweight and prone to bouts of cold and cough, leading to breathing distress. Her food intake was very low. Most of her milestones were delayed. Though she started sitting up soon after we moved into our place, she was yet to walk or talk. The doctor's jabs, however, she did remember very clearly. Our car turning into the alley leading to the doctor's chamber would immediately trigger an ear-splitting bout of bawling. Not that the doctor was not gentle and caring. However, on her very first visit, he had to give her a number of shots as per her immunization programme. She never forgave him for it. On looking back, I do feel that more could have been done for her with early intervention methods. The doctor alluded to them vaguely, but it was our fault that we did not pursue them with more vigour. I think both Pritimoy and I were in denial, and were yet to fully accept and internalize the problems that our child faced. We were still naively confidant that this was a phase and she would overcome it. From the doctor's side, I think he would have also pushed harder had we been US residents. Knowing that we were there for just a few years probably made him less eager to spend state resources. The problem though was much more on our side than his.

Sukrita was admitted to a playschool close to our home, and my aunt would drop her off and pick her up. She was happy there, but her progress was slow. She picked up the language, despite the fact that she spoke very little. The doctor kept insisting that we leave her in a standard environment as long as possible, as she needed to be challenged in order to improve. But my biggest issue with regard to her was just around the corner and came from a totally unexpected quarter. My aunt's visa was that of a visitor's and was valid for six months. On expiry, we requested for an extension and it was granted twice, each time for a further period of six months. When we routinely applied a third time, the immigration attorney called us to say that he felt that we should not reapply as the authorities were unlikely to grant a third extension.

He also felt that should her application be rejected once, it would be difficult for her to enter America ever again. Knowing my circumstances and how much I needed her for Sukrita's sake, he suggested that she return to India for a year and then come back again for my remaining term of one-and-a-half years.

For me, this was like a bolt from the blue. Sukrita was still not strong enough to be put into day-long child care – at least not the kind locally available. I could go for high-end child care services, but those were beyond our means. Both Pritimoy and I spent about twelve hours or more outside the home – we were either at work or commuting. How then would we look after the child if there was no one at home?

My aunt's solution was to take Sukrita back with her for a year. My mother and sister promised to pitch in and urged me to consider this option. My mother also told me to sit down and think through our options. The first was for all of us to return to India. While that would mean we would stay together, it would do nothing for my career and Pritimoy had just given up his job in India. We would not achieve our goal of financial stability, and all the trouble taken to move to the US would be for nought. The next option was to stay on in the USA and only my aunt would return. This entailed arranging child care. Sukrita had got used to my aunt as her caregiver. In fact, her first spoken word was what she called my aunt – not 'Ma' – because she spent the maximum amount of time with her. To deprive her of my aunt's company and then put her with someone who may not be as sensitive to her needs was a call I needed to take. The last choice was to let her go to India for a year. I tried very hard to determine whether the objection to this was to do with her well-being or mine. Was I resisting this because I would miss her terribly or I would feel guilty, or was it because I felt that it was important for her well-being? I discussed my arguments for and against this with Pritimoy while he played the devil's advocate. But in the end, I knew the decision would have to be mine. I also knew that whichever way I decided, I would never know whether I made the correct decision.

After a few days of agonizing over this problem, I decided at last to send her back with my aunt for a year. It was heartbreaking to pack her things as she looked on innocently. Which of her clothes should I send? What about her toys? Which were her favourites? I must remember to pack her medicines. She wasn't eating well and the doctors had asked us to give her Pediasure, which was not available in India then. So how many tins should I pack to last a year? I didn't know how I would cope. I would sit down and take a deep breath, and remember to take it a day at a time. Before her flight to India, I held her whenever I could – I couldn't quite imagine what the house would be like without her. I would be out of the house most of the time, right? So why was I making such a big thing out of it? In any case, even when I returned from work, how much time did I spend with her exclusively? But a thought at the back of my head kept gnawing at me. Was I doing the right thing? Right by her, not me. My rational mind would say yes, but I still couldn't feel good about it.

I had decided to go to India and drop them back as I couldn't imagine them undertaking the flight on their own. Sukrita was quite pleased as for her it was a great outing. Realizing that her father wasn't accompanying us upset her a little, though I knew that Pritimoy was feeling far more upset. But I kept a stiff upper lip as we stepped on to the flight.

This time she insisted on walking around the moment the seat belt signs got turned off. I trailed behind her to ensure that she didn't disturb any other passenger. There were a few youngsters chatting and smoking at the rear of the plane and one of them asked me with mock politeness whether we intended to walk all the way to India.

Returning home is always such a pleasure but the impending separation sat like a heavy weight on my heart preventing me from enjoying that experience.

The day when I was to leave for the journey back arrived soon enough. As I got into the taxi, everyone crowded round to say their goodbyes. Sukrita was in my aunt's arms. As I opened the door of the cab and got in, she leaned forward and stretched out her arms. I looked away – was it so that I wouldn't see her face crumple or was it to hide my own eyes that were threatening to overflow? I can't tell any more.

The next 365 days were spent in agony. In those days of no mobiles or FaceTime or Skype, the landline was the only mode of communication. And it was highly undependable, as the slightest rain would disable the line for days. Then there was something called a 'false ring', where when I called I would hear the phone ringing on their side, but they would hear nothing. When that happened, I would imagine the most horrendous scenarios – that Sukrita had had an accident and the whole family had rushed off to the hospital leaving no one to attend the phone, or that she was so unwell that my family was not taking the call for fear of having to tell me. I took to calling up the neighbours in such cases. Realizing that this could be a regular occurrence, they kept track of Sukrita's status and would reassure me. By and by, the whole neighbourhood seemed to participate in her upbringing and care.

As soon as the year passed, I reapplied for my aunt's visa. I was on edge until it came through. As soon as it did, I was on the first flight I could find to India to pick them up. As I made my way to Bokaro by road from Kolkata, another fear reared its head. 'What if Sukrita had forgotten me?' As the taxi chugged to a stop outside the house, my sense of dread deepened. I paused to take a deep breath and then unlatched the gate, and walked up the path through the small garden to the veranda. There she was, sitting on the floor, intent on a few toys strewn around. As I opened the grille door, she looked up. For a moment all was still and then, with a tentative smile, she lifted up her arms just as she had the day I had left.

I gained a lot of insights into the way of doing business in the US. For one, I learnt the importance of planning and documentation. In India, in the mid-1990s, we were often given the deadline for a project first. The details were fleshed out after that, and the policies and processes came last. Not so in the US. Every single product was thought through in full detail, studied to ensure risks and mitigants were properly identified, policies written and approved, standard operating processes created and staff trained, systems checked to ensure correct outcomes and then the launch date was the last to be discussed.

The use of legal help over there was quite a revelation as well. Even if a short sentence was to be put in the public domain, it had to be vetted and cleared by legal. But, and most tellingly, the compliance team had the final word. If they objected to something, even the CEO would give way. Subsequently, I am told that risk had taken over that mantle – but that was after the Lehman crisis. On the other hand, while the practices I learnt there were valuable, I felt that too many people were ticking boxes and not applying their minds. Because all matters were done so systematically, people probably didn't feel the need to think much. Otherwise, it is very difficult to understand how the risks leading up to the 2008 global financial crisis got built up in the system.

Some of our experiences really brought home the emphasis on process and documentation, and some of those experiences taught us valuable lessons. The Government of India had decided to launch a deposit instrument called Resurgent India Bonds (RIB) to garner forex deposits from the non-resident Indian population. It was very much on the lines of the India Development Bonds that had been launched a few years previously, which NRIs had lapped up eagerly for it paid an attractive rate of interest. Both Citibank and our New York branch were the nodal offices for the launch of the deposit programme and collections. In the US, one had to clearly distinguish between deposits and securities. While deposits were regulated by the banking regulator, to launch securities, we needed the Securities and Exchange Commission (SEC) to provide approval. These were deposits, but even then as a measure of abundant precaution, we decided to visit the SEC at Washington, D.C. and advise them of the matter. Accordingly, we wrote to them, providing details of the deposit programme and sought a meeting to which they acceded.

I happened to be part of the delegation that was present at the meeting. After hearing us out, they advised that while they could give us no written approval, they were okay with us going ahead. The precise words, if memory serves me right, were: 'Well, you may proceed. We don't think we will jump up and sue you should you do so.' Armed with that assurance, and after complying with all regulations pertaining to deposits, we went ahead, and the collections proved that the programme was a resounding success.

The day the programme ended, the *New York Times* covered it on the front page, more so as India had just conducted the Pokhran test and the US had clamped down on the country. Credit lines to all Indian banks, including ours, had been cancelled and Chase – our clearing banker – had told us unequivocally that they would not allow us even inter-day overdrafts, so we would need to ensure that that there was sufficient balance in our account with them at all times to clear cheques. In the midst of this, India raising such substantial dollar deposits was indeed a matter of both pride and importance.

The consequence though was that at 10 a.m. sharp we received a call from the New York SEC saying that they were launching an investigation into how we did this programme.

In the US, these are matters of grave concern. The last thing one wants is to fall foul of regulators, as it carries grave implications, not to mention the large penalty they could slap on us.

We wrote in detail to the SEC in New York and quoted our conversations with SEC Washington, specifically stating that this was a deposit programme and therefore not covered under securities regulations. But they would have none of it. Reams of information were requested and delivered, and then they sought depositions from the people handling the programme.

As I had been part of the delegation to Washington, I got a notice. A deposition is an experience that is one of a kind. Arduous, sustained grilling may describe it best. But before that, there was the preparation for it. The law firm handling the case asked us to come in for a briefing. I still remember the day. It had been snowing. A few days ago, I had sustained a bad fall down a flight of stairs and had torn a number of ligaments in my leg, requiring it to be put into a cast. Lots of people asked how I had slipped, and I was too embarrassed to tell them that I had put on a pair of Pritimoy's trousers by mistake (they were the same colour, so it was an honest mistake!). He is not much taller than me, so I didn't notice till I stepped out and the legs of the trousers hampered my movement and I took a tumble. So there I was, slipping and sliding through the large open foyer, with a cast on my leg, leaning against Manjira (who I am sure must have been praying that she didn't end up with a cast as well), but the preparation was all important and I had to attend it no matter what.

The lessons I learnt that day still remain with me:

i. Never ever say something of which one has no personal knowledge. I think that Indians have a tendency to answer based on second-hand knowledge – something said by a friend or colleague, something overheard – because we just don't want to appear ignorant. This is dangerous and to be avoided at all costs.
ii. Write down accurately all that you know about the event in as much detail as you can remember. This is important because we have selective memory and we forget, whereas one needs to answer as accurately as possible.
iii. If the questioning becomes relentless, take a break. One can ask for a drink of water or to visit the restroom or simply stretch one's legs. But it is good to be able to take questions and give answers after due thought and deliberation.
iv. Stick to the truth and stick to what you personally know. Answer the question as precisely as you can – long-winded explanations are not required.

The deposition was a difficult experience. It went on for what seemed like hours, but actually lasted about half a day. I was lucky – Manjira, who handled the NRI division, went through it for an entire day. The same questions were asked in various ways, sometimes nicely but mostly not. I understood the meaning of the phrase 'in your face' at that deposition because that is how it was at times, with the questioner leaning across the table and literally shouting into my face. I think the gentleman must have thought that I had an active bladder syndrome as I called for so many restroom breaks, but our lawyers assured me that no one would mind as this was standard procedure. The learnings from that experience underlined the need for documentation and for following due process.

It also created understanding about the sensitivity to language and the meanings different words have in different countries. For example, in India, the RIB would have been called a 'deposit scheme'. In the US, the word 'scheme' is linked to 'scheming', and has a bad connotation. So one uses words like 'deposit programme' instead. I remember one of the questions that the interlocutor asked: 'Your Resurgent India Bond looks like a security, smells like a security and even sounds like one (because we called it a 'bond'). How then can you say it is a deposit?' Sensitivity to language therefore became second nature to us and saved us in many difficult situations. The New York branch was fined at a later time (not because of the RIB) because the regulators felt that the fact that we had no violations was 'an outcome of luck rather than design'. We learnt to proactively follow and adapt to evolving regulations the hard way.

Competition amongst the banks was fierce. Even internally, bankers used to confide that they feared taking their mandatory leave as another colleague may offer to do their job at half the cost and they would return to find a pink slip awaiting them. This was considered fair game, as they themselves would do the same given the opportunity. I used to find this intriguing, as I couldn't imagine backstabbing a person I sat next to the moment he turned his back. Such thoughts in the American situation would probably be considered unprofessional, though I do think that grace and empathy are required in a workplace and I am sure they are equally valued at US workplaces. I do not know how far this was true, but competition was probably one of the many reasons, along with large incentives, that goaded people to push ahead for short-term gains, sometimes to the detriment of long-term business goals.

Time passed quickly. While the work load for me had gone up substantially – I had followed my American counterparts and merged the role of one other officer looking after correspondent relations into mine (not by eliminating the role but because the officer got co-opted to run a branch whose manager needed to be repatriated) – I still felt I had the bandwidth to do more. I was now overseeing planning and performance of US operations, overseeing internal audit scope and coordinating external audit, looking after training requirements, handling correspondent relations, and helping out the chief of US operations in his activities. But I still felt underutilized. I soon realized that it was more because I enjoyed roles in operations rather than in planning or platform functions. As assistant to the chief of US operations, I would be part of most meetings which were normally held in our boardroom. Mentally, I called it the 'bored room'. Taking down minutes was the most tedious job I ever did. I tried to make this interesting by recording the minutes in as flowery a language as possible, only to be told that I was not doing an assignment in creative writing. I was to record bald facts baldly and in full detail (including the yawns and the sneezes? I never got an answer to that).

As the four years came to a close, I got ready to leave. I did not want to overstay even for a day for fear of my aunt's visa issues and so, as the end of the fourth year approached, I was all set to return. We were worried that finding the right school for Sukrita back in India could be a challenge. Her doctor had urged us to look for an integrated school because he felt she needed to be challenged constantly to improve. A special school, on the other hand, was unlikely to challenge her the same way. I was not too sure about finding the right kind of school back home and so we decided that Pritimoy would stay back in the US for the time being, and Sukrita would return with me. Should I find the school we needed, he would rejoin us. If not, we would give some serious thought to returning to the US.

Closing up the household is always a difficult job at the best of times. But segregating all our possessions into four lots – the first lot comprising things that Pritimoy would need to stay on; the second lot comprising the stuff I would need immediately on return; the third would be the main portion of baggage that would be shipped back; and lastly, the stuff we would have to throw away – was indeed a challenge. But it all got done, and as I waved the US goodbye, another chapter of my life and career closed.

# 8

# Walking the Tightrope: Achieving Work–Life Balance

I was still an assistant general manager (AGM) when I returned from New York. I was posted to Kolkata again, at the bank's Foreign Department, which handled the treasury operations. It was a horrific experience to have to set up house all over again and all by myself. When my goods arrived from New York, the clearing agent told me bluntly that while he would provide me a receipt for the charges, he would not be able to do so for ₹5,000. When I asked why, he gave a vague answer. I was not so foolish that I didn't understand what he was saying, but there seemed no way out. I was alone with a small child, and there was no one else to help, and so after struggling with my conscience for a while, I gave in to his demands – the one and only time in my life that I have ever done so.

When my belongings arrived in the middle of the night at my quarters in Alipore, I was all alone. I needed someone to supervise the unloading of the packages while I monitored them as they were placed inside the apartment. Indrajit Gupta, who had helped me on my arrival in New York, stepped in again. He had returned a year earlier, and was heading the Foreign Department (FD) where I had joined. Till 1.30 a.m. he kept vigil, standing by the truck until the unloading was finally done. No one had expected it to go on for so long, so there were no arrangements for my dinner. Here, his wife Nupur Gupta, or Nupur Boudi as I called her, stepped in. An excellent cook, she whipped up a piping hot meal of rice, dal and egg curry. By the time we got done and I went to bed in their guest room, it was past 2.30 a.m. But all my stuff was home and I could begin setting up my new house in earnest.

At work, I had the task of implementing a software platform that would reconcile the entries in our various accounts maintained in the various currencies in which we dealt. At that point, the task was being done manually by what we called the 'Tik 20' brigade (Tik 20 was the name of an insecticide in those days). This huge group of people would sit with a pack of coloured markers and match entries by ticking them off manually in the statements of our accounts (called mirror accounts) and that of the foreign banks (called nostro accounts). Given the fact that we had hundreds of such accounts and millions of entries per day, the backlog was enormous. The threat of having to make provisions for all unreconciled entries was hanging over us and an IT solution was the need of the hour. FD was considered a hotbed of union activities and no one was sure how the staff would react to the computerization initiative. We started by installing thirteen personal computers (PCs). Soon, some complaints started trickling in that people were playing games on the machines.

Considering the fact that most people were still handling a mouse as they would a carom striker, I was happy at this development for it meant they were not averse to using the desktops and were becoming adept at handling them. I also noticed that people started coming in a little earlier, so that they could capture one of the PCs for their use.

Before long, it became a game of musical chairs because the moment someone left their seat, someone else would quickly occupy it.

The long-awaited delegation of senior staff arrived soon after – the ones whom I knew would object to computerization. I was expecting the usual fiery speeches about how we were destroying opportunities for labour. Instead, to my astonishment, the delegation had come to request that for the senior staff some training sessions be initiated, and that they be conducted early in the morning, before the arrival of the other employees for they did not want to display their ignorance in front of the younger staff members. To them, it appeared as though the next generation had been born with these skills. I was delighted and agreed to their request readily. I knew at once that we were entering a new era from which there would be no turning back.

Negotiation for purchase of the reconciliation application was already at an advanced stage by the time I joined. There was one matter that impressed me immensely during this time. It was the seriousness with which the vendor fought to reduce on-site staff support. The vendor was amenable to most of our conditions, including giving us a suitable discount. What he wouldn't agree to, however, was to position people for on-site support for more than seven days. When I asked him why, he clarified that human resources were his most prized asset and he was not about to squander that away without a fight. It made me look at our human resources with new eyes. We had never looked at them as the ones who really mattered in the running and success of the business. And I had to learn this lesson from a software vendor, who was arguing over every additional hour of staff support that I was demanding. It is a lesson I never forgot.

I also made another discovery about our own people. Whenever we came up with a snag in the implementation process, the bank's employees came up with the solutions before the vendors did. That drove home how little I understood or appreciated what my own people were capable of. The other discovery I made – and this has been validated many times in the years since – was that for any IT implementation, one needed to budget for three times the hardware recommended for it to work well. Somehow vendors always underestimated the sheer volume of our transactions and the speed of throughput required. These lessons were learnt well, and stood me in good stead later.

At this time, my promotion to deputy general manager (DGM), the first rung of senior management, came about. The position of the head of forex treasury was vacant, but there was some hesitation about posting me there as I had never been in treasury. I asked for a three-month probation period, and I assured my bosses that if they found any deficiency in performance, they could transfer me at the end of those three months.

It was a posting that I really enjoyed. The work was very different and entailed a lot of learning. But unlike credit, in treasury one could see the gains or losses of one's actions almost immediately. The people working there were also some of the sharpest that I have come across. The challenge was to learn as much as possible, and as quickly as possible – for you couldn't possibly lead a team without knowing the work being done by the department. So I spent all my efforts in the first few months to quickly internalize the nuances of the work at hand.

A few weeks after I took charge, a number of our dealers trooped into my room with a piece of paper which they placed in front of me. The letter was a request to allow all the dealers to fly to Mumbai the next day as there was a call for a bandh the day after and they would go to Mumbai to carry on their activities from the dealing room there. I was surprised that this was considered the most efficient way to deal with the bandh threat. I told myself that this would be the last time this course of action was adopted.

We had an advantage in the fact that we didn't deal directly with customers. So we decided that the next time a bandh was called, everyone would come to office before 6 a.m. We would pull down the shutters and work through the day. By eight in the evening, when conditions normalized, we would all return home. We talked to our internal union and association people. When I conveyed to them the vital role our department played in the bank's operations, they too understood the importance of not closing down a unit that was required to support all-India operations on account of local issues. During the next four years, we never again had a closure on account of any local bandhs.

There was also a feeling prevalent at many of our offices, especially in the Corporate Centre at Mumbai, that the staff at Kolkata would stop working at the flimsiest of reasons. I understood the difference between reality and perceptions when the lift men, who were part of the building maintenance contractor's staff, suddenly went on strike. Our offices in the building were from the tenth to the nineteenth floors. The general manager (GM) in charge at the time was suffering from a slipped disc. Therefore, he chose to sit in an SBI office on the first floor of an adjacent building.My office was on the fifteenth floor. I made my way up slowly, along with a few others. By 10.30 a.m. most people were in their place and working. At around 12.30 p.m., the GM called me with a request to take stock of how many people had come to work that day. On taking a roll call, I was surprised that attendance was better than on normal days, regardless of whether it was the tenth or nineteenth floor. It was also apparent that it was not only officers who had climbed the stairs to report for duty but our clerical staff and messengers as well.

Similarly, even among the lift attendants who were on strike (they were about to lose their jobs because the contractor who employed them had lost his bid), we had some excellent workers. There was one attendant who was always at his post on time. He had a winning smile and greeted everyone politely. On a few occasions, I noticed that though I was alone in the lift, he pressed the buttons for both the fifteenth and sixteenth floors. Curious, I asked him why he was doing that. 'Didi, you need to get off on the fifteenth floor. But this lift sometimes skips that floor. The maintenance staff have not been able to put this right. So I press the sixteenth floor button, so that even if the fifteenth floor is skipped, you can get off on the sixteenth floor and walk one floor down. I know how busy you are and I don't want to waste your time.' How thoughtful. I appreciated his ability to take pre-emptive action for something that was a probability. This was true risk management – no less important than any other risk management practice.

Our entire treasury operations were migrating from manual to electronic mode. Half of the dealing room – the piece dealing with all rupee operations – was already working out of Mumbai. Any computerization initiative would have to involve them, especially as the rupee treasury was far bigger than the forex unit. Moreover, migration to a totally computerized scenario was far more difficult than what had appeared at first sight. Many of the operations were done in a manner that was different from what we did manually, and one needed a thorough understanding of both the manual system as well as the new computerized process to ensure that entries were made in the right manner. We had almost weekly conferences at Mumbai, which I was required to attend. Not wanting to be away overnight because of Sukrita, I would take the first flight out – meaning that I left home at 4 a.m., returning by the last flight, which got me home at 1 a.m. That was the beginning of the twenty-one-hour workday, which I would need to keep doing ever so often from then on.

I had come to the logical conclusion that the treasury operations couldn't be carried out in two different centres for very long, and that the operations out of Kolkata would necessarily have to migrate to Mumbai. My regret stemmed from the fact that the efficiency of our Kolkata operations was really high and I felt it would be a pity to close the unit down. So I suggested that a number of new things be introduced in Kolkata and the dealing room operations alone could be spun off to Mumbai. But convincing the bosses was not easy, because FD still reported to the international banking group which dealt in forex, though their activities were that of treasury operations. It was difficult to see how the matter could be resolved unless the reporting lines were changed. But it was a fraught situation and created a rather stressful workplace. The suggestions I made took many more years to be actualized, and the last of them – moving our foreign branch's back offices to FD – could only be actualized after I became chairman. The fact that all my suggestions were implemented showed that they were useful ideas, but in the absence of a suitable environment for collaboration, the matter dragged on for years. Within the bank, people defended their territories with as much ferocity as one would expect from the big jungle cats. Later, I would sometimes say that one of the advantages of having female leaders was their ability to be much less territorial and far more collaborative. I don't claim it to be a virtue restricted to the female sex, but certainly the territorial streak is less pronounced amongst women.

While my work in FD brought a lot of satisfaction to me, the challenges on the home front were mounting. I had returned from New York with Sukrita and my aunt. The move was difficult and setting up the house again equally challenging. But the most important matter was finding a suitable school for Sukrita. She had learning disabilities and fine motor movement problems. She was very gentle by nature and a warm, loving person. She needed an environment that would nurture her, but challenge her as well. Her doctor had repeatedly told me to keep her in a regular school, but one also needed to ensure that the challenges she faced were not to a degree that they became counterproductive.

When I left the US, it was because we felt she would do better in India, where we had a better support system. But we would need a good school too – else the move would have been for nought. Finding a school suitable for her had become of paramount importance.

I don't remember who told me about Akshar. It was a school close to our place in Alipore, and followed the 'integrated method' of schooling. This meant that each class of thirty students had up to six kids with mild to moderate challenges. A second teacher sat in every class with this small group and helped them keep up with their peers. All activities were done together and all children in the class were taught to help each other. The first time I went to visit the principal, Mrs Noni Khullar, I was amazed to see a child helping another patiently up the stairs. Normally, school corridors had children racing and jostling each other. As I climbed the stairs behind the two, they respectfully stood aside to allow me to pass, did a polite namaste and then continued to climb.

I knew instinctively that I had found the school for Sukrita. Their sports days were equally amazing. Till class five, all races were held in a group. Each one would be run between the four houses that formed the four groups. For example, in one race an able child would push another in his wheelchair for, say, 25 metres. On reaching the line, the child in the wheelchair would have to string a bead quickly and then would be pushed back again, after which the next pair would repeat the activity. The group that finished first was the winner. The beauty was that every single child participated and each knew that it was a collaborative effort that made them winners.

As Sukrita settled down, other problems began cropping up. My mother was keeping indifferent health and my brother-in-law had met with a serious accident and was in hospital. My aunt felt that she was needed in Bokaro and I couldn't but agree. I had managed to hire a young twenty-year-old girl, Gudiya, to look after Sukrita, and my aunt trained her well. Pritimoy too decided to come back as not only was Sukrita missing him sorely but he too was facing health issues in the US. He always had a weak knee, but because of the cold weather his knee would suddenly lock, making him incapable of folding his leg. The biggest problem of course was driving. His office at the time was on Wall Street so it did not require much driving. But now he couldn't go out on weekends or holidays. America is not a place for non-drivers, and yet he couldn't quite take the risk of driving. He also realized that he was required back home. My mother-in-law was keen to come stay with us, as she had been living with her elder son for some time and wanted a change. So Pritimoy decided to return, my mother-in-law came to stay with us and my aunt went back to Bokaro. All of this meant massive changes. My mother-in-law needed a twenty-four-hour help as she was almost bedridden. Sukrita struggled to cope with the absence of my aunt and in her new school. Pritimoy struggled to determine whether he should return to IIT or do something on his own – and if so, what? – while I struggled to ensure that the family ran smoothly as I learnt the ropes of a new job and settled back into a six-day week. The US spoilt us not only with better compensation but also a five-day week. It enabled working women to devote a day to cleaning, shopping and other myriad household jobs for a day, and then rest the other day.

In India, I always went back to work on Mondays more exhausted than when I started the week. It was an experience that made me determined to work towards a five-day week if the opportunity ever presented itself. It did, during my chairman tenure, but ultimately we could only get two Saturdays off in a month. An improvement, nonetheless. I continue to espouse a five-day week as it makes a huge difference to family life. One feels recharged and ready to go after a day of rest, which for women is impossible if they only have a day off to look after the demands of the family. As chairman, I also used to discourage calling people during weekend for work. At times, it is inevitable, but making it a practice is detrimental to productivity as people are unable to recharge and resentment builds, causing friction both at work and home.

Matters had settled into a rhythm when another problem presented itself. One fine morning, Gudiya's mother walked in and announced that she had arranged her daughter's marriage as she was already twenty-two and waiting further was not possible. In the meantime, I had sponsored Gudiya for a beautician's course. Though she knew rudimentary English, I had helped her create the notes detailing the various processes. She was so proud the day she completed the course. I had also spoken to a beauty salon that I went to, asking them to take her on for three hours a day to enable her to gain practical experience. She had a natural flair for make-up and fashion, and often when we went out, she was far better dressed than me. Naturally, she was shocked at her mother's proposal and there ensued a real battle of wills in our house. But her mother would have none of it. Her daughter had told her she would never marry a village boy. So, in keeping with her wish, she had found her a match in Kolkata. The boy was respectable and worked as a sound mixer in the troupe of a middle-tier singer, and she simply would not take a 'no' for an answer. In the end, I could only console Gudiya that at least she had learnt a craft and, if the opportunity presented itself, she could fall back on it and earn her own money.

Once Gudiya left, the problem of who would look after Sukrita reasserted itself. My mother-in-law had a helper, but her duties were quite specific to her charge. I had never imagined the level of difficulty I would experience in getting someone reliable. The first person provided by a centre that helped find support staff turned out to have been a helper at construction sites. She put the biscuits in the fridge, and the butter and other perishables outside. In the heat of May, I came back to find the butter oozing on the shelf and the cooked items emanating a putrid smell, as she took a nap with the AC on in full blast. She was succeeded by another who mistook the 7UP in the fridge for water, and made Pritimoy his black coffee with it. The next was even better. She had long, luxuriant hair, and her custom was to get up at six in the morning and spend the next hour and a half at her morning ablutions. Then she would sit in the sun for another hour, with her hair spread over her back, drying it, while the tape recorder played bhajans. She would be only ready for work by 9 a.m., by which time all the morning jobs were completed.

I was almost at my wits' end about how to manage the situation and the possibility of leaving my job loomed large. And then, my prayers were suddenly answered.

I was narrating my sorry state of affairs to a friend on the phone during my lunch break with a desperate request for help, when a junior colleague knocked on my door. I waved him in and gestured for him to take a seat while I finished my conversation. When I got off the phone, Mr De, my colleague, hesitantly said, 'Madam, I just heard your conversation. I have a lady who has been with me for twenty-two years. She helped us raise our son and daughter as my wife works in another bank. But both my children are in medical school now. On account of the education loans and other liabilities, I cannot pay her as much as she deserves. Also, I no longer need the level of support she is capable of providing as my children are no longer at home. I still regularly visit my village and can get someone else from there to help me at home. If you wish, I can talk to her to take up a job with you.'

And that is how Sulekha came into our lives. An excellent cook, a person of high integrity and indefatigable energy with the ability to work unbelievably hard, she has been a real boon in our lives. Her only drawbacks are her strong likes and dislikes, and her controlling nature. I often joke with her that she must have been my mother-in-law in some prior birth. If she gives you lunch and you eat it all, the next day the quantity of food will increase – as she feels that you may have not had enough. On the other hand, should you leave a little bit of it uneaten, she will grumble at the waste of good food. I am yet to find the golden mean in this respect.

But no matter how much I complain about her overbearing manner, there is no doubt that without her steady presence at home, I would never have been able to continue to give so much time to my career. Even though she is unlettered, her sharp common sense often prevents my making social blunders. Many a time, I would have landed up at a social function without a gift had it not been for her timely reminders. She does the shopping, sets the menu, cleans and cooks, and keeps a wary eye on Sukrita's well-being. Once told at what intervals medicines are to be given, she follows it like clockwork, reminds when fresh supplies are needed and when the doctor is to be consulted again. The kitchen is her domain and none dare trespass. In her opinion, no other household help can clean as well as she can – and in most cases she is right – but it makes keeping other help difficult. When they leave in a huff, she picks up the slack with much grumbling till we're able to find someone else. For a while, she tries to win over their loyalty by overfeeding them, until she realizes that food is not incentive enough, and then the cycle repeats itself.

As equilibrium was again slowly achieved at home, a new challenge rose on the horizon. By then, I was due for my next promotion to GM. I was a little ambivalent – on the one hand, the careerist in me pushed me to do my best; on the other hand, the fear of a transfer on promotion loomed large. How on earth would I manage relocating the family again with a bedridden mother-in-law and a child who needed a special environment for her schooling? Pritimoy too was reluctant to uproot himself again. The challenges seemed too difficult and too many. But from somewhere, I found the strength to barrel on. My mother, aunt and sister were my unqualified cheerleaders, as were Pritimoy and Sukrita. They were proud of my achievements and never once, by word or deed, asked me to hold back.

My promotion to GM came in August 2005, accompanied with instructions to report to Lucknow as GM of eastern UP. It was, at that time, one of the largest networks with the maximum number of regions. There were no flights from place to place, and the only means of transport was cars or a few pest-ridden trains. I remember once stepping into a first-class coupe on a train to Gorakhpur. The passenger in the seat opposite mine was fast asleep under a blanket that covered him from head to toe while a mouse ran merrily up and down the blanket, getting its daily exercise. I spent the night in the corridor – I could handle cockroaches but I drew a line at mice, no matter how friendly Disney thought they were.

My biggest worry still was school for Sukrita. She had settled in well and was in class three. Would I be able to find something similar in Lucknow? I called the Corporate Centre and the chief development officer (CDO) – the head of human resources in the bank. I sought their understanding and requested I be posted to a metro centre where I stood a better chance of locating a similar school. A few tension-filled days followed. I could almost imagine the conversations they were having: 'These women! Why do they opt for promotion? They want their cake and to eat it too. When will they realize that we are in a serious business?' A few days later, the CDO called to say that my request had been discussed with the chairman and denied. Management felt (and quite correctly at that) that I had never served at a primarily rural centre and needed to do so. With no options open, I again started seriously considering leaving the bank. My mind was in turmoil; I didn't know what the best step under the current circumstances would be. My family members refused to take a call on my behalf. They stood by to support me in whatever decision I took. It was at this time that I rang up one of my earliest mentors, M.S. Verma. Mr Verma had been the CGM of Bengal circle and I had known him well. He had risen to chairmanship and had retired only a few years ago. When I posed my dilemma to him, he had only one suggestion: 'Giving up takes a few seconds. It's a matter of typing three lines and pressing send. But what is the hurry? You have always worked very hard, and you are at the threshold of the most interesting phase of you career. Why should you give up now without even trying once? Go to Lucknow, see if you can find a school for your daughter and then decide. You may surprise yourself.'

His words were indeed prophetic. I did find a similar school in Lucknow called Study Hall, headed by an exceptional educationist, Urvashi Sahni. Pritimoy decided to stay on in Kolkata, but as I would be moving away it was decided my mother-in-law would go back to live with his brother. She passed away there a few years later. Of all my decisions, this is one that I regret even today. She was happy in our house perhaps because she was inordinately proud of my achievments and also a little because of a mostly absent daughter-in-law, which enabled her to play the main role at home. She would have undoubtedly enjoyed staying on with us. She had also loved travelling, and when she was in better health, she would often go on group tours with her neighbours as her husband never obliged. She loved to see the freedom I enjoyed, and lived vicariously through my successes and failures – exulting in the former and consoling me in the latter. But with no direct flight to Lucknow (one had to go via Delhi back then) and in her state of health, I didn't quite dare to take her to a new place.

I now believe things would have worked out had I taken her along, but such afterthoughts are of little use now. Another deterrent to taking her along was also the fact that Pritimoy had decided to stay on in Kolkata. He had just joined an education group as a consultant, and they had offered that he could travel as required and were also willing to take care of his stay in Kolkata. The arrangement was loose enough for him to come and visit us more frequently. He decided therefore to not pull up roots again. This meant that while I was travelling, Sulekha would look after not only Sukrita but also my mother-in-law, should she come with us to Lucknow. In view of her advanced age and uncertain health, we thought the risks were too many. So reluctantly, she returned to her elder son's care.

Lucknow was a different ball game altogether. After a long while, I was back in a predominantly rural community. I was in charge of a vast tract of land, stretching from the badlands of Chambal to the sparsely inhabited foothills of the mighty Himalayas bordering Nepal. The area was notorious for smuggling and other anti-social activities. The strange thing was that the Gorakhpur module, which included the area bordering Nepal, was the best-performing module. Yet, I had the most difficult time posting people there on account of the poor living conditions. We had a large residential complex at Gorakhpur where most families stayed, while the officers would be away at the remote branches. Families quickly adjusted to the community life, but getting them to go from one of the better centres, such as Lucknow or Varanasi, to Gorakhpur was the real hurdle.

The Lucknow posting taught me a number of things. One was to handle the unpleasant stuff at the earliest, instead of pushing it to the bottom of the pile. The circle had recently experienced a major housing loan fraud. In those days when records were not digitized, registering mortgages was not centralized and reported to a single agency such as the Central Registry of Securitisation Asset Reconstruction and Security Interest (CERSAI), diligence depended on a lot of disaggregated manual processes. So avoiding such frauds was difficult. As a result, my table always had a few vigilance files. Taking a decision as the disciplinary authority or an appellate authority was a taxing job.

One needed to read the case thoroughly to ensure that justice was done to the best of our abilities. A miscarriage of justice or one wrong decision might mean ruining someone's career and the subsequent devastation of a family. On the other hand, the system suffered if the guilty went unpunished. Accordingly, these files had to be handled with due care. Imposing punishments that could range from a warning to dismissal from service was not a job that enthused one, and I would often try to put off the job. But there soon came a day when there was nothing other than vigilance files on my table. And then I had a visit from the wife of one of our 'charged officers', as the people undergoing disciplinary action were called. I was reluctant to meet her – imagining her pleas and tears. Instead, I was surprised when the lady said only one thing: 'Please complete the process quickly. Not knowing the outcome is killing us.' I realized how nightmarish the delays could be. I vowed to take up these files first thing in the morning when the mind is fresh, instead of getting to them later in the night when it's easier to convince myself to let it slide for another day. Thus, it slowly became a matter of habit for me to handle the most difficult piece of business as soon as it came up.

Another major lesson I learnt was to remain accessible. I would not have been able to foil another large car loan fraud had I not been accessible for people to walk in and give me vital hints that enabled timely action.

I travelled extensively by car during this period. I did take an officer along on these journeys. But no matter what is said of law and order in the state, I never encountered any problem, despite the fact I was on the road sometimes as early as four in the morning or as late as two in the night. I did receive a few threats – one on a postcard which had a badly drawn skull and cross bones on it (the guy must have read a few pirate stories) – but luckily for me, these remained just threats.

The assignment was as different from my earlier ones as one could wish it to be. Coming from the rarefied confines of air-conditioned dealing rooms with scores of blinking electronic screens, I was suddenly in the midst of tall fields of waving sugarcane, planted so close together that venturing in between the rows seemed quite dangerous. I could hardly make out the thought processes of these farmers, who sometimes torched the standing cane in the fields for lack of buyers and yet planted cane once again the next season. They knew only how to grow cane. Cane was the Goddess Lakshmi that gave them wealth, ran their households, enabled their children's education and marriages, and they were not open to hearing anyone who asked them to grow something else. One cynical employee told me, 'Ma'am, look at it from their point of view. This is the famed Indo-Gangetic belt. The land here is so fertile that you just have to sow the seeds for crops to grow. The water table is barely 20 meters below the ground and most of these people don't pay for power. They switch on the pumps in the cane fields before going to bed at night and switch it off when they wake up. It's that easy. Why should they give it up?'

I asked, 'But doesn't such flood-irrigation tactics wash away the top soil into nearby water bodies, silting them up? It erodes fertility. And with water bodies silting up, less rain water is stored and the water table will stop being sufficiently recharged. Not only that, the fertilizers flowing into the water bodies causes weeds like the water hyacinth to flourish and further chokes the water bodies.' The employee just looked at me and said, 'Ma'am, do you think these people are not aware of these things? But no one appears to care.'

I hope things are better now, and coordination with state authorities has improved and led to better practices since the time when I was posted at Lucknow. But the long and sad neglect of our farm sector and the short-termism that informed many of our actions are now coming home to roost in the form of farm-sector stress. For a long time, bankers had been seeking interest subventions on agricultural term loans that would have enabled more capital formation on the land. But subventions stubbornly remained a part of the crop loans or working capital loans, mainly as a means of keeping food prices in check. There was a whole class of absent landowners who took advantage of these rock-bottom rates, whereas the tenant farmers – in the absence of laws that enabled registration of tenancies – continued to live in the grip of moneylenders, as formal banking channels could not lend to them. The cherry on the pie for the absent landlords is the tax exempt status of their agricultural income. What it did not budget for was that productivity gains were not happening in rural areas, ensuring better margins to farmers. In the absence of productivity gains, the depressed economic state in such areas is merely perpetuated.

Meanwhile, Sukrita had settled into her new school. She was now in class four, but dealing with older children was posing its own challenges. The topper in the class was a girl named Aastha, who almost looked after Sukrita like a mother hen. But there were others whose cruel jibes were hard to ignore. There was no additional teacher in these classes, and keeping up with classwork and homework was becoming an increasing problem for us. The teachers paired her with a very diligent and gentle girl called Vidushi, and her mother took the trouble to photocopy all of Vidushi's notes and send them to me.

I also found a teacher who taught in the same school and stayed close to our place. She offered to tutor Sukrita after school hours. By the time we left Lucknow, she had got so attached to Sukrita (her own children were grown-ups and had left the home) that she offered to keep Sukrita with her till she finished school. But it was still a struggle sending her to school, and I was beginning to have an inkling of what an uphill struggle school would become as she got older.

My travelling was also another challenge. Sukrita would have frequent colds, culminating in breathing difficulties, and perhaps this was brought on by stress as well. Normally, Sulekha, who looked after her, was quite familiar with the routine of steam inhalation and gargling, but when the attack was severe, she herself would panic. In such cases, if I was away, Shree or Jayanti (the spouses of my colleagues) or someone from office would step in immediately. One phone call from Sulekha, or me, and they would organize a visit to the doctor, colour code the medicines, so that Sulekha didn't make a mistake, and sometimes stay back till either I returned or Sukrita felt better. There was never an occasion when within an hour a doctor had not seen her. Once we became familiar with the paediatrician, most times he could resolve issues over the phone. So in the middle of meetings, I may have stepped away to organize the purchase of inhalers or taught Sulekha to administer them, but the job got done as quickly as it would have happened had I been at home.

The bungalow that we stayed in at Mahanagar was a big, sprawling one. Coming from a three-bedroom apartment in Kolkata – large by Kolkata standards but tiny by Lucknow standards – we savoured the space and the garden surrounding the house. We had a gardener who lived in the outhouse for whom every plant was a labour of love. I still remember Sulekha plucking fresh mint, coriander leaves and tomatoes from the vegetable garden for a salad. As she cut and ground the ingredients together, the lovely smell of fresh mint and coriander leaves permeated through the house. It reminded me of the gardens in my childhood and of my mother making salads. I find that fresh aroma sorely missing from market-bought vegetables. The front garden was always a riot of colours, the flower pots beautifully arranged and painted orange. These more than made up for the attractions of Kolkata that we missed.

The top management team at Lucknow comprising the CGM and two GMs (I was one, and B.V. Chaubal was the other) was very cohesive. Our CGM, Shiv Kumar, lived and breathed the bank. I used to think that he even dreamt of how to make the bank better, and the results showed in the improved circle rankings. He would, however, often have to play referee between us GMs, especially when we were competing for human resources. My area comprised such difficult terrain that nobody wanted to be transferred there from Lucknow. I could understand their sentiments, but was helpless as I had offices to manage and people had to be sent to far-off places. It was a big struggle to get manpower to go there. The larger places would claim officers of higher calibre. It was common sense to send well-performing people to areas of potential. It was also a means of rewarding good work. But the more difficult places also needed good people to discover potential and steer performance to greater heights. It was always a struggle to determine whether to post the superior talent in places of more potential or more problems. Finding a good balance was never easy.

Pritimoy would visit every six weeks or so, and stay with us for ten–twelve days at a time. But for most social occasions, I would go alone. I remember requesting Pritimoy to sometimes make an appearance at some of these events, so that my colleagues in Lucknow would not think he was a figment of my imagination. But being a single parent soon became a habit. I would get back home quite late, usually by nine or ten in the night. Sukrita would wait up and we would revise her lessons, often staying up into the night. But I could make out that the burden of studies was becoming too much for her. The amount of work was difficult for her to manage and I worried about what the future held.

I had completed about a year and ten months at the assignment when I received a transfer order out of the blue. I was to be relieved immediately to take up an assignment as GM (new business) at the Corporate Centre, Mumbai. I was to take charge of a new initiative – to set up a new business in the area of custodial services.

I had not yet held a position at the Corporate Centre. While the posting itself was exciting, I had forebodings on two counts. First, I was told that the new initiative I was to head seemed to be an iffy project – not too many people understood what it was trying to achieve – and heading it in lieu of being in direct circle operations probably meant that I was being sidelined. Moreover, our promotion to the next grade of CGM was due in a month and if I was in the running, I would not have been transferred to a GM position so close to the interviews. The second point of concern was on the family front. Mumbai was notorious for housing shortage for our officers. I had known colleagues having to stay in guest houses for almost a year before being allotted housing. How could I manage with Sukrita if no housing was available? Added to this was the task of finding a new school for her. However, I felt sure that a city as large as Mumbai would surely have integrated schools – it was only a question of discovering them. As is often the case in the bank, nobody sought my opinion regarding what suited me. The orders had come with a request for immediate release and so I was on my way to Mumbai within the week.

Immediately after landing, my first visit was to the estate department. I had left Sukrita and Sulekha by themselves in Lucknow. It was a very uncomfortable situation, and I needed to resolve it at the earliest. But wonder of wonders, two three-bedroom apartments were available on the seventh and eighth floors of a building called Harbour Heights in Colaba, which was very close to my office. Without even looking at the apartments, I asked them to allot me the one on the seventh floor. Seven seemed like a lucky number. But I soon received a call that the special secretary to the chairman, who had been recently promoted, wanted that apartment. He couldn't officially book it as his transfer orders were not yet published, but would I mind taking the one on the eighth floor instead? 'No, I would not,' I responded. I just needed a decent place so that my family could move in, and I wasn't fussy about the floor. And eight would turn out to be as lucky as seven, as events showed.

While my housing got sorted out fairly quickly, there were issues on the office front. Mine being a new position, no office space had been allotted. When I asked the CGM heading the department, he smiled and said, 'You are about to set up a new business. So take this as your first job and find a space for yourself. You will face many more onerous challenges. So start with this one.'

Nothing like a challenge, I thought. So I went on a tour of the floor. There was not a single empty cabin or any unoccupied cubicle or work station. The only cabin that had no occupant was a large one marked prominently 'For Audit and Inspection Staff'. Obviously at that point no audits or inspections were underway, and so it was empty. I entered and found it well furnished, equipped with a PC and printer. My next job was to get the password from our CGM's private secretary and a roll of Sellotape. With that, I made out my nameplate on a piece of A4 paper and taped it to the glass door. I then quickly typed a memo to the estate department telling them that I had taken temporary possession of the room, but would move as soon as they allotted me an alternate cabin. For the record, that never happened.

After having got a place to sit, I got down to the job of going through the existing files to determine the next course of action. I found that the bank had already decided to form this initiative as a subsidiary. A decision had been taken to make it a joint venture and Société General (SG) had been chosen as the partner. Talks with SG were to commence next week. They wanted to talk to the person who would be in charge of the project – hence, the hurry to get me to Mumbai.

I found the work quite challenging. Setting up a new business was indeed a great learning experience. But doing it from within a public-sector bank took on a whole new dimension altogether. There were umpteen processes to be followed, stakeholders to be convinced, competition to be checked out, market opportunities to be determined, total available market to be calculated and strategies to be decided. Then there was the task of putting together the team. The many formalities of registering the business proceeded simultaneously. One needed to think about staffing and how many people would come from the two partners, and how many would be market recruited. Technology platforms for the businesses had to be assessed. There were a million questions to be answered and a million decisions to be taken, including the all-important question of how much capital would we need and what returns we could promise and by when. And if we didn't have satisfactory answers to this, we would be unable to convince either our bosses or our board.

Before I knew it, a month had passed. Interviews for promotion to CGM were to take place shortly. A few days before the interview, my deputy managing director told me that I should not anticipate a promotion. There were a number of seniors ahead of me; I was one of the youngest and had just been entrusted with a new role. He felt that should I do well in this assignment. I could hope for a promotion the next time around. This conversation depressed me.

The interviews were a few days away and I had just got into the serious preparation stage. For a few hours, I thought I should give up. 'What is the point?' I asked myself. I had been told that for me, appearing at the interview would be a mere formality. That night I talked to Pritimoy about it. After a patient listen, he told me, 'I still feel you should give it your best shot. If you don't, you will never know whether you didn't get it because you didn't try hard enough or whether it was a foregone decision. Don't take that risk. Try your best and if it doesn't happen, we will face that in due time.' And so my preparations continued.

I did get that promotion, but, from all accounts, the women on the board, Shyamala Gopinath, the then deputy governor of RBI, and Bharti Rao, SBI's chief development officer (CDO - the head of human resources) and the first female deputy managing director in the bank, countered the 'too young' and 'can wait' lobby strongly. Their point was, if I was found to be suitable, I must not be held back just because I was younger and/or a woman. Nudged by their efforts, the board decided that I should be given the promotion.

My scope of work as CGM expanded to cover all new businesses. I continued to head the custodial service initiative while the bank looked around for another GM. I also took over the initiatives for launching the Infrastructure Pvt. Equity Fund with Macquarie, the general insurance company, with IAG of Australia, operationalizing the pension fund management subsidiary, as well as launching the platform for mobile banking and another for financial planning, while also strategizing for creating a payment gateway. What followed was a year and eight months of frenetic activity. I was discussing joint venture (JV) agreements with three international companies. At the same time, I had continuous interactions with all the regulators, RBI and SEBI for the private equity fund and custodial services; with Pension Fund Regulatory and Development Authority (PFRDA) and with Insurance Regulatory and Development Authority (IRDA) for the general insurance company. Moreover, I had regular interactions with lawyers for registering companies and ensuring other compliances. We were simultaneously working on framing the business plan, vision, mission, policies and other process documents. We had to search for suitable premises, as well as for the right kind of talent. Technology solutions had to be assessed in order to decide the right platforms for the various initiatives. On top of that, one had to report progress regularly to the bosses as well as to the board. Never in my wildest imagination had I thought that I would have such an opportunity. We actually worked like start-ups on shoestring budgets, aiming to deliver the maximum impact on minimum spends.

The learning on a daily basis was enormous. Once, when I recruited someone for a very important function and at a competitive salary, the person wondered aloud whether it wasn't difficult for me to recruit someone with a much higher compensation than I myself received. It gave me pause, even as I realized that there could hardly be another assignment where the opportunities to learn would be so great and which I would enjoy as much. I understood then that compensation comes in many forms.

One other incident that took place during this stint highlighted the need for a slightly differential treatment for women. One of our senior female executives suddenly applied for leave for four months. In SBI, one rarely takes leave beyond two weeks except on health grounds, so I called her and asked what the matter was. She told me that her only daughter had just joined an MBA course in the US and was having massive problems adjusting. My colleague felt sure that if she could intervene personally, she could provide the necessary support, but she needed a longish leave for that. She was also quite sure that at that stage this was her priority above all else and the only option if her leave was not granted was to put in her papers. I sanctioned the leave unhesitatingly, though there were some rumblings of discontent from her peers heading other groups, who would have to pull a little extra load until she returned. Her timely intervention worked and her daughter is now well settled in the USA. Our officer returned with a feeling of having done her duty, and went on successfully to deliver some of our most sensitive projects with her usual efficiency and exuberance.

By the time I left after one year and eight months, most of the initiatives were operational or close to being so. To have completed three JV agreements in that period, set up four entities and two technology platforms was indeed extremely satisfying. The main credit, however, belonged completely to the multiple teams I handled, as they all delivered as per mandate. The only initiative which lost traction was the one on financial planning. It would be something that I revived during my chairmanship.

While I was doing well professionally, my personal life was once again seeing trouble. I had come to Mumbai fully convinced that I would be able to locate a good integrated school. But try as I might, I could find none in south Mumbai where I was staying. Travel in Mumbai is a big challenge, and I could not afford to send her to a school that was far away. The kind of support I got from my colleagues in the smaller centres was missing in this big city. Everyone was too busy keeping their own heads above water, and so reaching out to others was rare. As school after school expressed their inability to accept Sukrita, my anxiety mounted. After a lot of running around, one school near Charni Road agreed to admit her. It was then that I realized that a child in class six was expected to study thirteen subjects – English, Hindi, Marathi and Sanskrit, as well as physics, chemistry, environmental science, history, geography, maths and computer science, along with arts and crafts and ethics! For a child who had learning challenges, it seemed an awful lot. But we had no choice. Soon, however, it felt as though both she and I were drowning. I would come back home by 8.30–9 p.m. and we would discuss her homework as I changed into my night clothes – even that little time had to be put to use. A quick dinner, and we would start. Even then, we rarely finished before 12.30–1 a.m. We stayed the course for about ten months before I decided that life couldn't be lived like this. I consulted her principal, who was sympathetic but unable to help. She did tell me about a convent school in our locality that had a section devoted to the National Institute of Open Schools (NIOS) syllabus. I approached the nuns running the school and they agreed to admit Sukrita.

The NIOS offered several advantages. The biggest of these was the option to approach one subject at a time as exams were held every half-year with retests every quarter. A student could start appearing as soon as they attained fourteen years of age and, with a little planning, could graduate at sixteen along with the rest of the batch. While Sukrita found this far more comfortable, she was not very happy with her classmates, who were all much older than her. Most of these girls had attempted the class ten exams a few times and had then taken admission under NIOS. We planned out the subjects she would take the exam for, and began to prepare her for two subjects at a time. She also became quite proficient with a computer at about this time. Though she had problems in writing, the same issues did not manifest in typing. Her natural intuitive ability helped her easily navigate the PC, and she learnt to write small essays, surf the net, open a Facebook account and handle it all on her own. There were some missteps about what could or could not be put online. But then, most children and even adults have these issues, and she quickly learnt from her mistakes. However, I suspect she was bullied by the older girls, because though she was not so harried with her studies, she was quite reluctant to go to school. It was not a happy time for her. We had no choice but to persist, when transfer orders to head the Bengaluru circle arrived. I looked forward with trepidation as well as hope to this change of location again.

# 9

# Bengaluru: The Return of Harmony

Bengaluru was a great posting – both on the professional and personal front. Unlike Mumbai, Bengaluru is a metro with the heart of a small town. My colleagues had to just hear about anything I needed to jump into action. Soon, I was told there was a convent school in Malleswaram that would fulfil my requirements for Sukrita. They ran a NIOS section within the main school where children who could not keep up with the syllabus or who wanted to concentrate on other disciplines, such as arts or sports, were taught. The rest of the school activities were integrated.

They also prepared the kids for a few subjects at a time, though classes were regular and the same timetable of class tests were maintained. For the first time, Sukrita had classmates her age who were similar in their abilities. She also found a great home tutor. Pramilla had worked with kids with disabilities for over thirty years. She did us a big favour by agreeing to become Sukrita's home tutor, thereby reducing my workload to a great extent. Once, Pramilla told me that she had never seen another individual who was as sensitive as Sukrita. She said that whenever she felt low, either physically or mentally, Sukrita would sense it immediately and ask her what was wrong. The two took long walks in the grounds and sometimes went out for visits. She took my daughter to Mass with her sometimes as Sukrita loved the peaceful environment and the choir. One time she came back very excited to tell me: 'Do you know Jesus is Ma Durga in fancy dress?' I didn't know what to say till Pramilla clarified that Sukrita had asked her the difference between Jesus and Ma Durga, and she had explained that they were the same. However, when pressed by Sukrita as to why they looked different, she had replied, 'Probably it's Ma Durga in fancy dress?' That satisfied Sukrita. When we left Bengaluru, Pramilla gave Sukrita a trophy inscribed 'World's Best Pupil'. I don't know anyone else who has received such a prize.

Our residence and office were in a campus spread across 10 acres in the heart of Bengaluru. The house was an old European edifice – reportedly the residence of Mark Cubbon at one time, the famous British commissioner of Mysore. Our research could not prove this. However, the title deed of the house – 'Hopeville' – records that the judicial commissioner of Mysore, C.B. Saunders (later the British Resident of Hyderabad), did stay there. The house was beautiful, though not in the best state of repair and upkeep. I had the Indian National Trust for Art and Cultural Heritage (INTACH) come in and restore the many crumbling balustrades, the curls and curlicues on tops of pillars and other places where seepage had begun to destroy the ceiling or walls. The restoration was done in the traditional way, with mortar mixed into mud, lime jaggery, burnt coconut shells and bits of burnt brick – following the age-old process.

We also had an incident of an electrical fire that was quickly put out, but the electricity surged to such an extent that a few bulbs actually popped. So the whole place had to be rewired, an electrical diagram created and things like miniature circuit breakers put in place. Sulekha's only lament was that she spent much of her time cleaning up after the workers. As luck would have it, I got transferred the moment the renovations were completed, thus leaving this beautifully restored house for the next officer to move into. I consoled her by quoting the unwritten law in SBI – one gets transferred the moment one discovers a good tailor (for our sari blouses) and a good hairdresser.

One of the first emails I received after joining the Bengaluru office was written under a pseudonym, and told me that our campus was the largest free parking lot in town. On enquiry, to my horror, I found that the campus had seven gates, all of which were left wide open through the day. There was no demarcated parking space, and no questions were asked to anyone who came in and parked their vehicles. In fact, we even found a few dust-covered vehicles that seemed to have been left there for a few months! As a first step, I closed all but two gates, one each for entry and exit. We put in security and started recording vehicle numbers, with details about its destination (whether it was a customer, vendor or staff member) as well as the details of the driver. We co-opted an officer with specialization in horticulture to landscape the campus and create a proper garden. Soon, the place became a thing of beauty. The cleaning staff of our campus always came to work very early. So every day at 6 a.m., when I stepped out for my morning walk, the paths had already been cleared and the fallen leaves swept into little mounds. Most mornings, I would find the sun shining, birds singing and the early morning blooms would be swaying in the cool, gentle breeze. I have never had such happy morning walks again.

This circle taught me a lot of things, and though 80 per cent of our business came from Bengaluru metro, the rest of the state could be a challenge. When I took over, the iron ore mining issues had just started. After about a year of my stay, the courts stopped all mining activities. Almost within the month, the bustling towns of Hospet and Bellari began to resemble ghost towns. The truck operators, who had made their living hauling the mined ore, simply parked their vehicles in front of our branches, walked in and left the keys on the officers' tables and disappeared. Hundreds of jobs were lost, families rendered homeless, children taken out of schools and reverse migrations to villages, where possible, took place. The disruption of so many lives is hard to digest, but it is indeed this human suffering that we lose sight of in the pursuit of higher goals. We need to empower our agencies so that they can recognize and nip wrongdoing in the bud instead of allowing them to flourish before initiating action that costs thousands of people their livelihood.

The culture in Bengaluru was also far different from that of the north. In Bengaluru, on receipt of the news of promotion, many of our staff would come in to work with boxes of sweets. These invariably contained just two to four sweets, unlike in the north, where the typical size was a 1 kg box. People appeared to be more into religious observances, and the lifestyles of the typical Kannadigas was quite simple and humble. The people in the north appeared to be more style-conscious. Not so, the Kannadigas. Of course, I speak of people outside Bengaluru. That city is a great melting pot and it would be difficult to characterize its culture. But what I liked best about the city was its hordes of entrepreneurs. It also has a buzzing social sector and the kinds of social entrepreneurs that we met in Bengaluru was in itself a very rewarding experience.

I worked closely with two of these, EnAble India and Agastya Foundation. EnAble India worked with us to identify roles in our work chain for employees who were challenged. They then worked on trainings and aids required to make such work possible. But the programme really came to fruition in the later years, so more on that in a bit. My work in this area, I think, remains one of my best achievements.

Agastya Foundation, on the other hand, worked in the area of science education. They would pack a van with around 200 scientific experiments and equipment, and drive to schools that had no labs, set them up and have the students conduct the experiments. The quality of their equipment was superior. When we donated two such vans on Bank Day, they came and set up the experiments in our head office premises to show us what they were doing. Our staff got so engrossed in doing the experiments that I had a difficult time shooing them back to their desks. They also had a campus in Kuppam, Andhra Pradesh, where they held summer camps for children from municipal schools.

This vibrancy of entrepreneurship in Bengaluru is unparalleled. It is the thing I most remember about the place, along with the fact that Bengaluru is an island in the midst of a state that is otherwise mainly agricultural, and faces huge challenges of water availability and lack of industrialization. There were pockets like Belgaum and Hubballi and the Bellari belt that were more developed, but this was nothing in comparison to Bengaluru. A more balanced growth should be the aim for both the city and the state.

The Bengaluru chapter ended with my promotion to the rank of deputy managing director, and I returned to Mumbai to take up the job of chief development officer. My only true regret was taking Sukrita out of the school where she had settled in so well. She had finished almost the entire curriculum for class ten, had passed in a number of subjects and only needed to appear for a few subjects more. The teachers were very hopeful though and felt that if we could home tutor her till the exams, she would pass quite easily. Of course, it meant going down to the school to take the exams, but I thought that was a doable solution. This worked out for the completion of her class ten, and we continued the same method for her class twelve – we found a home tutor for her in Colaba, and the school provided us with notes and study material. The greatest gift Bengaluru gave Sukrita, and me, was the confidence she got from writing her board exams. It gave her the hope she could graduate from school, and she did!

I won't say that I was especially keen on the CDO's job. It felt as though I was once again being relegated to a platform function, rather than an operational role that allows one to display performance.

I recalled that when I had been posted to Bengaluru circle, I had succeeded another lady as the CGM. As a result, I had heard snide remarks that Bengaluru circle should be renamed as 'Bangle circle'. The derision rose from the fact that Bengaluru was a comparatively smaller and newer circle (having been carved out of Chennai) – though nobody thought of it that way when men got posted there and few took the trouble to compare performance numbers. Was I being given this portfolio of CDO because I was a woman? It seemed to be a direct corollary of ideas such as 'women are more caring, have more empathy.'

What I realized later, though, was that the chairman O.P. Bhatt, who was to retire in three months, had actually given me a great opportunity. I was part of a services organization. Our strengths and weaknesses stemmed from our human resources. Knowing how we were acquiring that talent, developing and training it, meeting their aspirations and how we were communicating with them would provide the bedrock on which I based the most extensive reforms in the performance management area when I became chairman.

My ideas on recruitment, learning, job families, ideas to retain women talent, succession planning, improving our philanthropic outreaches and many others were formed during this time, and would subsequently drive my HR transformation agenda.

One of the things that struck me on joining the department was the sense of power that the personnel department staff seemed to enjoy. It was power over people's lives – their transfers and promotions. And I realized again the basic pain points of our employees – transfers and promotions, as well as insufficient attention to individual growth.

Let's take the transfers first. SBI has operations across the nation and executives could be transferred anywhere. Junior executives stayed within the state, but seniors could be moved anywhere in the country. Clerical staff were transferred only when they opted for higher in-cadre assignments or when they got promoted to the officers' ranks.

This was an area where I knew the organizational interests would need to come first. But did that mean that personal goals need not be considered at all? What if we could merge the two – would that not maximize both productivity and employee morale?

We decided to experiment by allowing a newly promoted list of around eighty deputy general managers to put in three choices for their posting. There were a lot of naysayers who felt we were unnecessarily raising people's hopes, as we would not be able to position people as per their requests. Wonder of wonders, we managed to get 97 per cent of the people posted as per their choices (though only about 24 per cent got their first choice). But I thought it was a great first attempt. My aim then was to create an organization that laid out for its people the road map of their career and then asked them how they would like to attain their goals. Utopian? Sure, but it also showed me the need to get people to participate in their own movements and career development, and not leave it to the whims and fancies of the personnel department.

In cases where rules needed interpretation, my single-point directive was that if allowed by the spirit of the regulation, the ruling should be in favour of the employee. I felt that the abuse of power by a few, for many generations in the personnel department, had led to unions gaining strength. Delving into the roots of power yielded by unions, I came up with three distinct employee needs:

They need their grievances to be heard. Any grievance needed to be routed through 'proper authority' – which meant your manager – and if they didn't think it worth forwarding, the matter never got heard. Yes, we had a whistle-blower policy, but that was not meant for personal matters.

Transfers were a major pain point, and a lot of employees approached the union bosses and swore allegiance to them to get help on this count. There were genuine cases amongst these – some provable and some not. For instance, there was the case of a recently married woman who claimed that her in-laws had threatened divorce if she got transferred. We couldn't ascertain the truth of this and while I gave her the benefit of the doubt, we did tell her she would need to tell her in-laws that her career would entail transfers at some point.

The last and most powerful reason for allegiance to the unions was that these were the people who acted as the defence counsel in internal disciplinary and vigilance proceedings. While a number of wrongdoers were charged, so were many innocents. The bank proceeded with the belief that should a loan go bad, staff accountability had to be assessed and the guilty booked. I believe what needs to be established is whether any staff member had personally benefitted from giving or administering the loan. Other than personal gain, one could blame them for incompetence, bad judgement and unsuitability for the job, but not start vigilance processes against them. That however, did not necessarily happen and the staff felt obligated to stay on the right side of those who they could turn to for defence.

I decided to tackle these issues one by one. For the first, I had a grievance portal created with a hierarchy of people looking into the issue. The case could only be closed by the complainant and if within a period of time, the complaint didn't get handled, it would automatically migrate to the next higher authority and so on, till it reached me. For the first time this gave each employee a voice so they did not need to go and request either union or personnel department functionaries for redress.

With respect to the second issue of transfers, we cascaded the 'option seeking' down to the region level. SBI in those days was transferring more than 37,000 people a year (that was the staff strength of Bank of Baroda in those days). Imagine the numbers of families broken up, the disruption of lives and, on the bank's side, the costs incurred in transferring employees, the amount of business lost in ramping up people to become truly productive. On one occasion, when an officer came directly to me to plead for cancellation of his transfer order, I asked him what the problem was. He said the biggest issue was getting his two children admitted to a good school, as hefty donations are sought by most schools these days. I had never really thought of this problem from that angle. I therefore proposed a generous transfer allowance to cover this exigency.

Normally, all staff benefits were proposed by the unions and negotiated with the management. When the management agreed to any such welfare measures, the circular always stated that this was done at the behest of the unions. So when the circular for the transfer allowance increase came to me for approval, it came in the standard format. I, however, struck out the reference to the unions, as this had not happened at their behest. They were quite peeved at the development, but couldn't do anything about it. The department began to understand what was required – that is, to think proactively about our employees' welfare, instead of thinking of it only when the associations and unions arm-twisted us. The fear is always that if we are proactive the demands would increase multifold, but this was quite unfounded and we managed to prove it so.

As for transfers, I used to tell my colleagues to embrace it and take their families along because every transfer meant getting exposed to new cultures, new ways of working and new challenges. It meant the kids had to make new friends, learn new languages, learn new ways of thinking and have new experiences. When we were young, the disposable income of most middle-class families was far lower. With limited resources, we faced many challenges as we grew up. Today's kids, by comparison, are a cosseted lot – especially kids in families such as mine. Transfers were like 'synthetic' challenges that taught kids essential survival skills. I think it's for that reason that most banker's kids are outstanding achievers.

As for the last point regarding disciplinary actions – I took up that agenda for rationalization only later during my chairmanship, when I tried to ensure that if there was no undue enrichment, the matter would be dealt with as breach of discipline, rather than breach of ethics.

Having provided a grievance portal, I also wanted to create a platform for multi-point communication. There was little support for this project, as IT seemed to have taken a back seat, and new initiatives on that front were few and far between. But we still managed to get an IBM platform to begin creating internal blogs and for communication amongst all staff. The results weren't great as it was done without sufficient fanfare, and somehow the initiatives that don't have the chairman's backing don't get enough time in the sun. But at least some staff started writing about their experiences and their suggestions. We had made a start on the collaboration and communication platform. The single channel of communication only from the top had been broken in a 210-year-old, command-and-control organization and that was indeed a huge step.

The concept of continuous self-learning on the digital platform was seeded during this time. This was an area that truly worried me because of the swift evolution of both technology and regulations, as well as the environment. As most of our officers were not recruited from management schools, we decided to offer the Harvard ManageMentor programme, which had forty-four online self-learning modules on management, at the end of which they would get a joint certification from Harvard ManageMentor and SBI. We calculated that even if we could get 2,000 of our people to go through the course, it would pay for itself. It took a little time to gain traction, but it became so popular that to date SBI continues to offer it to its employees. Alongside, I exhorted Anupam Dureha, DGM of the Human Resources Management System (HRMS) implementation, for getting it together in spite of the technical challenges. My dream was to ensure that we could source posting recommendations from the system. This meant feeding in the requirements for each role into the system, creating a database of the experience and capabilities of each employee and inserting other posting parameters such as years at a centre or branch, the need to complete line assignments or requisite postings, such as rural or independent assignments, to qualify for promotions. Though the implementation was completed, this was not an ambition that I could realize as CDO, but it would happen much later.

The project we had started with EnAble India gained pace now. As per government directives, 2.5 per cent of a company's employee base should comprise people with disabilities (This has now been raised to 4%). We complied with the requirements, but these employees were rarely fitted into proper roles and many of them could hardly participate. It was a lose-lose situation for the organization and the employee. The organization paid salaries but got insufficient output, whereas for the employees it meant a dissatisfying career that left them uninspired and did nothing for their self-esteem. The project had started earlier, but was languishing for lack of prioritization. We decided to proceed with this with full force. Over the years, it has yielded great results.

This stint actually convinced me that HR was one area that was crying out for reforms. Our customers were our employees. But were we identifying with their hopes and goals? Were we enabling them to confront their fears and inhibitions? Were we empowering them to overcome their shortcomings and bet on their dreams? Were we helping them develop as per their potential? Did we even know what their aspirations were? Or what they could reasonably aspire for? What about feedback from managers to their reportees? There was no system in place for that at all. I tried bringing this in by instituting a process whereby all annual appraisal numbers would need to be communicated to the employee. This resulted in huge pushback as managers felt this would put them under tremendous pressure to rate everyone well. To ensure that a bad rating did not come as a surprise, we initiated a feedback system on a quarterly basis. Once again, there was much complaining with people saying they didn't have time for it. We increased the periodicity to half-yearly feedbacks, and even allowed verbal communication and self-certification by the managers that they had indeed talked to their reportees. As for allowing the employees access to their own reports, we decided to do them grade by grade, and so started from the junior-most grade. In all fairness, if someone was going to be rated poorly, the employee had to know about it well in advance so that they could improve. But this was an uphill battle as very few people were capable of having the kind of open conversations that this required.

My clear assessment was that being a services organization, managers were spending about a minute and a half each year on completing annual appraisal forms, and that was the sum total of their intervention. As a corollary, 85 per cent employees received 100 marks out of 100 (that way, managers pass their responsibility on to someone else for the career progression of their subordinates), and promotions become dependent on corridor/water-cooler talk and a ten-minute interview.

All of this I knew would take time to evolve and change, but the agenda had formed in my mind. In the meanwhile, the then chairman, Pratip Chaudhuri, had started a direct confrontation with the Officer's Association. I really thought this was not required as we were disintermediating them quite steadily through the grievance portal, the transfer option initiative, the communication platform and proactively determining the benefits that our people required. I felt we could better use our energies elsewhere. However, it did give me the experience of approaching a vacation judge at her home in order to get an injunction for a strike call – again, a first for the bank. Mr Chaudhuri's idea worked well here. It brought the association back to the negotiating table and the management regained the upper hand, as had been the chairman's plan. But as matters intensified, he probably felt that he needed someone far more supportive of his agenda which he wanted to pursue with greater energy.

At this time, one of the MD positions fell vacant and some of us were called for the interview. There were about seven of us in the running and I was one of the junior-most. I knew my chances were slim, more so because a platform role in the bank, no matter how important, was not accorded its due weightage. For the first time in my career, I did not succeed in an interview. In a way, it was good to have experienced the setback. It taught me to overcome disappointment and keep functioning without missing a beat. It brought home how one felt on missing promotions, and strengthened my resolve to make our processes more transparent and fair.

By this time I had spent a year and a half at the role when I got a call from Mr Chaudhuri suggesting that I choose between becoming the MD of State Bank of Mysore and the MD of SBICaps. The latter position had opened up as the person who headed it was now going to become the MD of the bank. I chose the former for two reasons. One, I could return to Bengaluru and that would be great for Sukrita, and second, the experience of running a bank would surely help me, should I get a shot at the chairmanship.

However, when the orders came, I found that I had been given SBICaps. In hindsight, I can only thank Mr Chaudhuri for his foresight, because this experience too proved to be invaluable going forward.

## SBI CAPS

The difference between being a member of the senior management of the country's largest bank and that of heading an institution in the private sector (albeit carrying the SBI name) was realized by me quite sharply within a few days after I joined.

When I was at SBI, I rarely needed to make any appointments at the Department of Financial Services (DFS) beforehand. A message sent even a few hours in advance usually got me a slot with the required official. The day after I joined SBICaps, I travelled to Delhi to attend to some meetings at various ministries. In one of them, I got delayed as conversations spilt over, and with senior officials present, I couldn't excuse myself in a timely manner. As a result, I was delayed by ten minutes. When I went to the next ministry and presented my card, I was flatly told that I was late and so the official could not see me any more as she had other commitments. My pleading that I came from SBICaps and that I had got held up at another ministry cut little ice. The bald answer was: 'Well, you are from SBICaps, not SBI. Sorry, we can't make an exception.'

But the private sector had its own rewards too. I was working with a workforce where the average age was the early thirties, compared to SBI where it was the late forties. I loved the energy of the younger lot, but missed the solid experience of my parent company. We just held walk-in interviews on a regular basis for recruitment – we didn't need to initiate a nine-month-long process. We didn't need to follow the Central Vigilance Commission (CVC) mandated guidelines (though we voluntarily did so). But there is a great difference in doing something of your own accord and being forced to do it. We had a choice and it meant something.

My biggest gain was getting back in touch with corporate banking that I had last done thirty years back. It was like swimming – one doesn't forget swimming just because you haven't swum in the last so many years. But I had never done project finance before and that was a new area of learning. What concerned me though were the aggressive repayment programmes that had been put in place. Take for instance a road project – the concession was for thirty years, but project repayment was due in an average weighted period of eight years! The projection itself was based on two premises – i) the economy was galloping at 8 per cent plus annually and was expected to reach double figures; so with increasing economic activity, adequate cash generation was expected; and ii) the lenders were banks (most infrastructure/project-lending bodies having been done away with) and banks had ten-year money and could not run heavy asset–liability mismatches. This was like staring at a yawning abyss.

If the thin bridge of GDP growth didn't materialize, there was no other way but down. I wondered why we couldn't do a model where repayments would be small in the beginning (as should be the case in infrastructure and large core-sector projects, where usage and cash flows need to be built up), and do a bullet repayment at the end of five years that could be refinanced. I knew this is how it was done in other countries. Our own clients got such terms in foreign lands where they did projects, but not in India as the regulators here would not allow this. And this was because it was a fact that the refinancing would have to be done mostly by banks in India, unlike in other markets (because in India the other segments of lenders, such as debt markets and long-term fixed income instrument markets, were very shallow). Moreover, participation by funds, such as the pension and endowment funds, that could afford such long-term investments, was not deep and vibrant enough in India.

We sought details on the infra refinancing models from various countries, and decided to present our ideas to the regulator, given that we could see the problems that lay ahead. Nothing much happened initially, but the regulators did ultimately come up with two dispensations (I make no claim that this resulted from our representations) – one was for raising long-term liabilities by issuing infra bonds and the other was the introduction of flexible structuring of long-term project loans. This was commonly known as the '5×25 refinancing model', where the loan could be structured for payment over 80 per cent of the life of the asset. The repayment could be aligned with the cash flows and the outstanding amounts could be refinanced every five years for a maximum of five times. The latter, however, didn't work because internationally, the whole debt could be considered for refinancing, but in India the regulators allowed only the expenditure on actual capex.

In most organizations, the problem really was the interest accrued during construction (IDC). The delays had not been factored in and the resulting IDC was met with short-term corporate loans. Therefore, not allowing repayments to be aligned with cash flows proved to be an insufficient measure, as there was still a large sum to be repaid within a short period (the corporate loans) and the cash flows just couldn't support it. Remember, by this time the country's GDP had halved – so the assumptions for usage had gone totally awry.

When I joined SBICaps, most large projects had already started showing stress. There have been reams written about the corruption of borrowers and the inefficiency of lenders that led to this stress that threatened to swamp the banking industry. But this high-decibel discussion was all directed at trying to affix blame and finding the wrongdoers. Sadly, there has been little attempt at proper analysis of the many attendant contributory issues from which important lessons have to be drawn.

Let me name some: project design, misallocation of risks, changing rules and regulations, judicial pronouncements that changed the entire premise of projects, multistep approvals which took much longer than anticipated, incomplete appreciation of risks by bankers, overly optimistic projections on timelines, public interest litigations and writ petitions impacting land acquisition or environmental clearances, lack of collaboration between departments and ministries, withdrawal of in-principle approvals, promoters pumping in debt taken at the holding company level as equity thereby skewing the entire financial structure. The list is long.

Let me give a small example. Consider a power project that's nearly completed. All it needs to do now is to finish up the transmission line for evacuation of power. Unfortunately, the transmission lines pass through 28 kms of land designated as forest. Suddenly, the in-principle, or stage one, clearance from the environment ministry is recalled. What happens to such projects? Who is at fault? The borrowers or the lenders? It drags on while the borrowers and lenders run from door to door and ministry to ministry seeking a solution, while the interest on the debt keeps mounting.

Let's take another example. A road has been built, but a patch of land could not be vacated as it has a place of worship there and is being litigated. Although the road is mostly built, because it is not complete and because 80 per cent contiguous road is not available, tolling cannot start. So while the money is stuck, the cash flows cannot begin either. In yet another case, the road is built and tolling begins. The locals are unhappy and the candidate standing for election promises the removal of the toll if he and his party come to power. Both happen, and the party keeps its promise. In such a case, the government is required to pay as per the contract to make good on the loss of cash flow. Years go by, but the payment doesn't come. The account turns into a non-performing asset (NPA). Many such examples can be given. What bothers me is that none of these are insurmountable issues. It needed a single empowered authority to look into these cases and resolve them.

While the pursuit of the wrongdoers and the corrupt can and should continue, we also need to put in place the solutions that will enable us to get on with our core industry and infrabuild. Confidence must be re-established between lenders and borrowers. Many countries have gone through phases similar to ours. We can choose solutions that suit the Indian situation. We can even create India-specific solutions. But they need to be holistic, not patchwork answers. I sincerely feel that time is of the essence. Our demographic dividend will not last beyond two more decades, and unless we can provide the infrastructure and the right environment of growth, our potential will remain unrealized.

The other area where I got excellent exposure and understanding was in the area of raising equity/capital. This was an area that I had had no experience in. Actually, we were unsuccessful in the first three pitches I led. I developed a complex and even told my team that I seemed to have only brought them bad luck. But my young team was highly supportive. They wouldn't allow me to take the easy way out of not accompanying them to pitches. I learnt to make bids in a manner that slowly began to show results. I learnt first-hand how to create investor pitches, the due diligence that goes behind it, how to choose the right investor set to pitch to, and also enjoy our successes and critique our failures in order to learn, but never to give up. Later when I was raising capital for the bank or interacting with the investor communities, I was reminded of my young colleagues at SBICaps and sent them my silent good wishes for the knowledge they shared with me.

Another MD position was opening up, and this time, there were only two contenders – myself, and an equally dedicated and passionate officer with a solid background in credit and with the experience of running one of our associate banks. It would be a difficult choice for the interview board. Also, three months after that the chairman's position would fall vacant and, as per the rules existing at that point, MDs in position on that day with two years or more residual service would be eligible for consideration. As none of the other MDs would have two years of residual service, whoever amongst the two of us became MD would be the only contender for the chairman's position. The same thing had happened with O.P. Bhatt, who too became MD and then, as the only eligible candidate, went on to become the chairman of the bank. It really seemed like a winner-take-all situation. Both of us were well-balanced in respect of assignments – my competitor had more of an IT and credit background, whereas my credit exposure was less but I was more well-rounded with my recent exposure to investment banking. I also had treasury experience – which I felt was a must for the top job – as well as experience in launching new businesses. But in every other way, we were well-matched contenders. He had joined the bank a year earlier, but along the way he must have missed a promotion, so I was senior. In this respect, too, we were neck and neck.

I don't remember much about the interview except that the secretary, DFS, who headed the board, found it strange that a person who had joined earlier could become junior, reminding me that in bureaucracy, promotion was a function of time spent at the job. Another bit of interaction that I do remember was a query posed by the director of one of the IIMs, who was there as the management expert. He asked me what I would have been had I not been a banker. After the grilling I had been through, I thought a little comic relief was in order and so I answered that I would have been a museologist. 'A *what*?' The expert was truly stumped. 'Well, you know, a museologist – someone who manages museums, works with ancient artefacts, discovers lost knowledge and presents it to the current generation in the most attractive way,' I responded.

The professor was too surprised to continue his line of questioning. And that concluded my interaction with the promotion board. (I was speaking the truth, though – among my many ambitions, this had been one. Old things have always held a special place in my heart.)

I have always disliked the period after an interview when one goes through a phase of self-criticism. I would run the interaction over and over in my head, and dissect every answer I gave. I would agonize and wonder whether I had conveyed what I wanted to say clearly and I would worry endlessly trying to remember the body language of the board, and if anyone appeared hostile. But thankfully, these thoughts get drowned out soon enough as one snaps back to reality, especially at the sight of the heap of files on one's table.

In July 2013, I returned to the main bank as MD and chief financial officer (CFO). Once I got a hang of the role, I realized the difference between being part of the top management and that of being the CFO. It was like possessing the blood reports of the institution to which no one else had access. It provided me with not only the vital parameters but also the nuances that were of great help at later times.

One thing I realized almost immediately was the short-termism that informed most of the bank's actions. In fact, in my first interview with the *Economic Times*, I strongly put forth my reservation on what I called QSQT, or the 'quarter se quarter tak' policy. I felt that quarterly performance pressures took away our strategic long-term focus – something that was of great importance if one wanted to create and grow sustainably. The thought later found a lot of resonance from eminent bankers across the Western world, including Jamie

Dimon of JP Morgan Chase and others of his ilk. I still believe this is important, though I also know that it is a demand that is unlikely to be met. The only solution, therefore, is to create a balance between the short- and long-term goals, and the one who navigates that path well can bring true success.

One other really important initiative that had been taken up by my predecessor, Diwakar Gupta, was to do with data cleansing. The quality of data was terrible, to say the least. If one went through the date-of-birth data of SBI's customers, one could probably locate customers who were 230 years old or some who had not been born yet. I decided that where we found significant data entry issues, we should impose a summary cash penalty on the person entering the data. This had the union up in arms, but when I showed them printouts of people who through the entire day had fed in every customer's PAN number as 9999abcd999, they retreated. The task felt almost like we were clearing out the Augean stables, but we were determined to get it done. Ultimately, we came to an agreement that if deliberate or repeated mistakes were observed by any staff member in data entry, they would be given two written warnings, after which cash penalties would be levied. I won't say that this solved the entire problem, but awareness had been created and the quality did begin to improve.

The other important initiative I launched almost immediately was to bring in better collaboration between the internal inspection and audit (I&A) department, the compliance department and the risk department. The I&A acted as our eyes and ears on the ground. How well were they covering compliance issues or risk parameters? Were these parameters dynamic or static? Did they reflect current concerns? Were they forward looking enough? These collaborative efforts resulted in far better appreciation on how to use our resources with minimum overlap and maximum impact.

Pratip Chaudhuri was to retire in September, and there were rumblings that a new policy was being framed. Under the existing policy, I was the only eligible candidate. This was soon revised, stating that all four MDs in position at the time of the chairman's retirement would be eligible, regardless of residual service and would be given a fixed tenure of three years. This meant that I would now be competing with all three existing MDs who had been in their position for periods far longer than mine, and had solid track records to boot. I, therefore, needed to be strategic and paint a vision of where I would take the bank if given a chance to run it. Of course, the policy changes meant a further period of uncertainty but I welcomed it. I prefer a competition to a walkover, and the three years fixed term was a small step in the right direction.

As I prepared for another gruelling interview, my main focus was on creating a credible road map for vaulting the bank into its next avatar. Considering the stress and the challenges that SBI was facing in the face of swift tech advances and evolving regulations – and the fact its asset quality was worsened by a slowing economy – I determined a six-pronged line of action. They consisted of overhauling the risk function, controlling the cost-to-income ratio, creating customer experiences of a superior order, collaboration within and with subsidiaries, NPA resolution and overhauling HR practices, and all of this running on a strong technology backbone. The RBI representative on the board was a little upset that I had not mentioned NPA resolution as my main priority. My logic was that I first needed to stem the flood to allow waters to recede. My priority should certainly aim for better asset quality in the future – the past is a reality and would be tackled in all seriousness.

The incumbent chairman retired on 30 September, but there was no news from the ministry about who would be taking over. We all went about our work, unsure of what would happen and even more unsure of when. On the morning of 7 October, a top journalist covering the banking sector called me to say that the orders for my taking over as the next chairman was on the way. Like so many other matters, I took that with a pinch of salt. At around 4 p.m. that evening, the much-awaited fax arrived, appointing me as chairman for a fixed three-year term. I just happened to find enough time for one call to Sukrita and Pritimoy before my room filled up with my colleagues stepping in to congratulate me, even as a wave of nostalgia for my father and mother engulfed me. I remembered my brother, who had passed away in 2012, telling his friends that his sister would be the first woman chair of SBI. A journey that had started thirty-six years ago had now entered its last lap.

# 10

# The Eighteenth Floor

*(The first woman probationary officer joined SBI in 1960. This chapter is a tribute to all those women who trod the path before me, and all those women and men who extended their hand to me whenever I stumbled.)*

The SBI Corporate Centre building at Nariman Point is an imposing structure. The chairman's suite on the eighteenth floor even more so. The doors open on to a longish corridor. As one steps in, there is a door on the right leading to a lunch room – on one side of which is a comfortable seating arrangement of sofas upholstered in pristine white and, on the other side, a small four-seater dining table for intimate lunches.

On the left side of the corridor is a door leading to the restroom. The only person in the Corporate Centre to have his or her own personal restroom is the chairman. Though, in most branches even the branch manager has this facility. I used to joke that having one's own private facilities was a powerful incentive to everyone aspiring for the chairman's position.

Straight ahead, at the end of the corridor is the door leading to the chairman's room. It's a large room with floor to ceiling windows overlooking Mumbai's famed Marine Drive. The chairman's desk is placed diagonally at one corner, with the chair facing the door and its back to the windows. A person sitting in the chair would be facing the door and looking at a wall with an outsized TV.

The walk to the chairman's desk can be an intimidating one. Was it with that intention that the farthest corner of the room was chosen for the desk? And was this the reason the chair faced the door, rather than the lovely sky and sea just outside?

The room had never been refurbished in the last forty years, except for the occasional coats of paint. The walls were rough, some indifferent paintings adorned them, probably fashionable when it was last redesigned. The floor was wooden, laid on top of the original flooring, probably because no chairman had so far agreed to sit in some other room for the two or three months required to refurbish the room. While the desk appeared fine at first sight, the drawers were almost falling apart and not functional. I knew that I would have to get the room redesigned – if anything, because I hated staring at that massive TV. It entailed sitting in my MD's room for the next three months, but it was completely worth it as I changed my desk position to enable me to see the sky and the sea and the imposing Reserve Bank of India building every time I looked up from my work.

I looked around, marvelling how just a few days ago, I had come here in response to a summons by the previous chairman. Light was streaming in from the windows and fell on the desk, casting a warm glow. It was 8 October, the fourth day of Navratri, the most auspicious nine days in the Hindu calendar. As I walked down to the other side of the desk for the first time, it felt surreal. I wanted to pinch myself, but there were too many people around for me to do so even surreptitiously.

As soon as the crowds thinned out, I took on my first big job, which was to visit the three MDs in their rooms. All three were senior to me. I also knew from personal experience how painful not getting through an interview could feel. In spite of that, my experience told me that in SBI we still show up and operate. I wanted to clearly reassure them that I would highly value their contributions. I wanted to create a workplace filled with positive energy. Our jobs are stressful, but I wanted it to feel like constructive tension; like a workplace with moments of fun and joy and celebrations whenever we overcame a challenge. A workplace where people would want to get up in the morning and joyfully return to. And it had to start at the top.

Unfortunately, the eighteenth floor of SBI building, where the chairman and MDs had their chambers, didn't have a great reputation for collaboration, or being a seat of collective positive energy – not even during our most illustrious chairman R.K. Talwar's time. I was determined to change that reputation. I had adopted 'collaboration' as a major theme of my tenure and I felt it needed to start with me. So I had to take that first step.

Not surprisingly, all the MDs were uniformly welcoming, and promised cooperation and help. On my part, I followed a few protocols invariably, and consistently. I continued to address them as 'sir' (the common SBI appellation for a senior male colleague) as I had till just a day before. I also ensured that whatever changes I made in their area of operations, I did it in consultation with them and with their participation. We very soon evolved into quite a cohesive team. The atmosphere of collaboration, transparency and mutual respect continued when they retired and new MDs, junior to me, joined in their place. I think I can take pride in changing the culture on the eighteenth floor because it has persisted beyond my tenure.

I had set myself a large agenda and had only three years to complete it. In an interview shortly after taking over, a journalist asked what legacy I wanted to leave behind. It took me by surprise –

wasn't it too early in my tenure to talk of legacies? And when I asked myself this question, I just knew that I must leave the bank better and stronger than when I joined it. That is what all my predecessors had done. Beginning with the venerated R. K. Talwar, the first SBI staffer to head the bank (till then the Government of India used to depute someone from the bureaucracy to head it), who laid the foundations by clearly delineating the values that the bank would embody; to my recent predecessors – all had left their mark.

D.N. Ghosh, in the mid-eighties, had the foresight to begin customer segmentation and launched the commercial and industrial (C&I) segment – the most profitable segment of the bank. He also set up subsidiaries like SBICaps and SBI Asset Management Co., as well as set up the first project for total computerization. He was the first to get the bank rated, thus giving us access to the US markets. D. Basu followed his lead, and became the architect of the organizational restructuring and also contributed towards strengthening the bank's capital structure by conducting the first rights-cum-public equity issue. M.S. Verma set up SBI Cards, another successful subsidiary (which was listed recently). Janki Ballabh started SBI Life Insurance – the first subsidiary from the SBI stable to list during my time. He also kicked off the core banking system (CBS) project by signing an agreement with TCS for the core banking implementation. A.K. Purwar, who followed him, carried on the core banking initiative and began the bank's retail banking focus, as well as initiated the business process re-engineering (BPR).

His successor, O.P. Bhatt, completed the core banking transformation, while strengthening retail focus through various custom offerings like the 'salary package'. His continuation of the BPR journey and innovative mortgage products helped SBI become the largest home loan lender. He also conducted the first two mergers of associate banks – the State Bank of Saurashtra and State Bank of Indore, which provided us with multiple learnings. He also incorporated SBI General Insurance Co. and our Pension Fund

Management Co. Pratip Chaudhuri, from whom I took over, had reset the equation between the management and the Officers' Association.

Now, it was my turn.

Within a day of my taking over, I was due to leave for the International Monetary Fund meeting held in Washington, D.C.. The first day and a half was a whirlwind of activity. I had asked for my visiting cards to be printed as 'Chairperson, State Bank of India'. However, as soon as the sample card arrived, our legal department nixed it by commenting that the SBI Act (by virtue of which the then Imperial Bank had been converted to State Bank of India in 1955) had no such designation, and that I should stick to the title of chairman. So, my very first decision was summarily dismissed (and here I had thought that the number one at SBI was very powerful!), and the cards now read, 'Chairman, State Bank of India'. I had to sit through briefing after briefing till Pradeep Rao, my private secretary – and my most valued resource at SBI – almost shooed me out so that I could pack and take a 2 a.m. flight.

Unfortunately, I didn't have a spouse who would do my packing; I almost envied my male colleagues, most of whom had this advantage over me. In spite of my hurry, I remembered a cardinal rule of packing: always have one set of formal clothes in my hand luggage should my check-in luggage get lost. It was lucky that I did, because we had the SBI reception that evening and my luggage did get lost. Unluckily, though, I had forgotten to pack formal shoes in my hurry. So I had the option of wearing a beautiful sari with sneakers or buying a pair of shoes. My schedule didn't give me any option to go shopping, so I requested one of our staff members pick up a pair in my size. It all went as per plan, except that at the SBI reception even as I smiled as guests arrived (including the RBI governor, finance secretary and many others) my feet were absolutely killing me. Wonderful training for a job that would often need me to keep smiling even though I may have been wanting to scream murder!

The flight back from Washington gave me a well-earned respite (on the way to the IMF meet, I was busy reviewing the notes for the umpteen meetings that had been lined up). As I absorbed the facts of the last few days, it dawned on me that I now had the chance of actually bringing to life the many initiatives I had wanted to undertake but couldn't on account of lack of authority or opportunity. The realization was accompanied by a crushing sense of responsibility, which almost took my breath away. The banking sector of any economy is always important, and the SBI chairman is considered the first among equals in India, mainly because of the bank's size, its ability to influence any banking initiative as well as its illustrious past.

The position exuded an aura of authority, but equally, it imposed a great responsibility of adding to its reputation, not detracting from it. On top of that, I was the first woman chair of this 210-year-old institution. Would this entail having to prove that I deserved to wear the mantle? Would there be heightened expectations from the women in the institution, and even from those in the industry? As all of this sank in, I didn't know whether to be elated or worried. I had to pursue my vision, but also take it one day at a time. In some areas, baby steps would be required, and in others, I would need to pole vault. But more than anything else, I had to get every member of the team excited and willing to pull their weight.

I had first felt like this when I took over SBICaps – going over the monthly numbers, I felt the weight of the expectations of nearly 3,000 employees whose salaries had to be paid and we needed to be able to earn enough to do so. That number had gone up to 2,70,000 now! There were the other stakeholders, too – the customers, the investors and shareholders, the service providers and the very large ecosystem we supported.

I went back to the six broad plans I had detailed while appearing for the interview for the chairman's position. Since then I had spent quite some time elaborating what each of these initiatives could look like and whom I could depend on to lead and deliver on this agenda.

The time to implement the plans had arrived and I needed to determine the order of priority. But when I looked at the points, I knew I would not have the luxury of highlighting one area over the other. Each of them needed immediate action, especially if I was to raise the morale of the SBI staff and change the perception of the broader market, which felt that the bank was losing the plot. I needed multiple teams delivering various initiatives, the sum of which would show the ecosystem what we were really worth and the value we could create. But to do all of this together involved collaborative effort on a massive scale. I had to find the best way of achieving that and unleashing the constructive energies of our team.

# 11

# Sabka Saath: The Key Is Collaboration

It was collaboration amongst the top management that I tried very hard to inculcate in every project. I knew that many initiatives started by one chairman got reversed when a new chairman took over. My efforts were to minimize this to the extent possible. The chairman has a short tenure as it is. What is the point of undoing earlier initiatives rather than building on what is left behind? As a result, every initiative was thoroughly discussed by the Central Management Committee (CENMAC), and unless we could convince the majority, the plan could be amended, changed or even dropped. The rule was simple. Once an initiative got launched, we would all pull together, even the dissenters.

CENMAC sometimes had a number of people talking simultaneously, each passionately trying to get their point across. It initially appeared disorderly, but I made sure that we stuck to the agenda and ended with clear action points, something which I remembered from one of the noted management guru Ram Charan's sessions that I had attended. One of the DMDs once told me, 'Earlier, we were told to only open our mouths at such meetings to eat cashews, and we had to do that to stop ourselves from yawning. Its far more fun these days.' But V.G. Kannan, a junior colleague who became MD shortly after my taking over, had this advice to give: 'Ma'am, if you don't mind, could you speak on an issue after everyone else?' I asked him why. Sometimes, when an initiative excited me, I would barge in right at the beginning and I saw nothing wrong in that. But Kannan thought differently. 'The moment you speak, the dissenting voices stop, and that's not what you want, is it?' So much for my efforts to do away with the traditional feudal ways of behaviour!

I wanted to hear others' views and thought it extremely important to surround myself with people who had more knowledge and insight in areas I was not an expert in and held different perspectives. It was something that I had actively done, and it had always benefitted me. When I became the chairman, the DMD interviews were due in a few months. The number of vacancies were relatively large. Compared to that, the number of candidates were too few to give us much choice. So I decided to include the next batch in the interviews as well. This batch had just about completed a year and some months as CGM (usually officers served in the post for four years), but there were quite a few talented candidates there, and I wanted them in my top team at the earliest. This gave us more choice and the opportunity to find the right fit for the right role. I consider one of my strong points my ability to find round pegs for the round holes, and no role demanded this more than the current one. Once I found someone suitable for a role, I considered it important to obtain their buy-in of my vision and goals, and then give them enough space to lay out their plans to operate.

The other day, Sunil Srivastava, one of my retired colleagues who had been DMD of corporate banking recalled the considerable freedom I allowed employees to operate within their portfolios. 'Operationally, we did not have to ask you for any permission, as long as we were within the policies and the framework defined by the bank,' he said. However, in some cases, where larger relationships were involved, I expected to be kept in the loop, either post the event or, in some cases, before any action was taken. There was one particular case he brought up. 'Having sanctioned around ₹2,000 crores to a large Indian corporate based on terms which had been discussed and finalized, we were approached by their officials to revise the rate of interest as a competing bank was offering better rates. We were quite surprised as the process was nearly complete, and certainly didn't behove the status of this corporate. I decided to call back all our loans to the corporate aggregating approximately ₹15,000 crores and instructed our branch to ask them when we should send our people to collect the cheque for the entire amount and close their account.' He was sure that with this escalation there would be a resolution. However, he did not inform me before conveying his decision to the corporate. He believed I would throw a fit or at least advise him to restrain himself from taking such spontaneous decisions regarding such a large corporate. 'But to my surprise,' he said, 'you said you supported a decision taken in the best interest of the bank. You also said that you knew that their senior officials would reach out to you and that you would take care of it.'

And so it happened. Within the next hour or so, the company's CFO reached out to me and I had an opportunity to convey that what they had done was not acceptable to any bank, and that they couldn't force banks to revise decisions taken by the board and accepted by the company. 'You reiterated that SBI never went back on its commitments and you didn't expect a corporate of their stature to do that either,' he added. 'This only strengthened our relationship because they came back to us for perhaps the highest-ever syndication in the domestic market and ₹35,000 crores was sanctioned for them. While the corporate found in you a resolute person who stuck by her words but was willing to help out in case of genuine requirements,

I became aware of the extent to which you had empowered us and were willing to back us up.'

If asked for the recipe of my secret sauce, I would say it was this – getting the right people in the right place, obtaining their buy-in, empowering them and then backing them up when they took courageous calls with the right intent. It was what enabled us to do so many things in the span of four years.

As I had mentioned earlier, the collaboration I was seeking was not only with people in the Corporate Centre. I wanted the rank and file to participate as well. We revived the internal blogging platform that we had set up when I was CDO. As one part of my agenda was to decrease costs, the first blog post I wrote sought suggestions from our employees about how costs could be reduced and controlled. That generated a lot of interest and useful responses. For example, one of our staff wrote that while returning home from the airport late at night, he had found all our glow signs on and wondered why they could not be switched off at 10 p.m. We implemented this by putting timers on all our signs so that they would turn off automatically at night. Another pointed out that we had no standardization of generator hiring or usage costs. While fixing these charges, we also decided to do energy audits, resulting in appreciable savings in our energy bills. This helped us focus our attention on initiatives for renewable energy by using the rooftops of our large buildings, and ensuring that all our large complexes got green certifications.

The movement to shave off costs gained purchase throughout the bank. We curtailed expenditure on travel by video conferencing more; lease payments of all our branches were centralized and we adopted a policy of starting discussions on renewals eighteen months ahead of time, so that we could seek reductions. If that was not acceptable, we would still have time to seek alternate premises. I felt that I needed to show a personal commitment to this initiative, and so started travelling in economy class on domestic flights. This was a most unpopular decision, especially amongst senior colleagues and I don't blame them. We had little by way of compensation, and sometimes I would meet defaulting borrowers travelling in business class with Louis Vuitton luggage, and it did pinch. But when there are delays and a lounge is required to have a little privacy to complete some work or when one is late and needs to go through security quickly, travelling economy does become difficult. It also means arriving at the airport well ahead of time, thereby wasting precious hours. So I made it optional, but stuck to my guns for a year and a half. Unluckily, in one of the flights, I had a person sitting beside me who was coughing and sneezing throughout the flight. I remarked about it to my office staff, as at that time H1N1 flu cases were on the rise. Soon after, I was diagnosed with H1N1. After that, my office prevailed on me to revert to travelling in business class. Lots of people, including my liaison officer, Hemant Vyada, and his successor, Deepak Thakkar, heaved a sigh of relief as they had had to pull in personal favours to get me past security super quickly as I mostly arrived in the nick of time. The initiative for cost control, however, continued unabated.

While I was trying to reduce costs, there was the need to increase income as well. Fee income is what we needed to look at, as I felt it had tremendous potential, untapped mainly because of lack of cooperation and coordination amongst departments. Let me give an example. Our supply chain finance people were in talks with a car-hire company to finance driver–owners under a tie-up with us. As a driver registered with the company, they would check whether the driver was open to a loan for purchase of a new car, and if so, would send his data to us. Loans of this nature were processed within seconds. We got the cross-selling department to work out a tie-up with our general insurance subsidiary to offer car insurance at very competitive rates. As a goodwill gesture, the company also bought a personal accident insurance cover, which could be made really reasonable if the driver happened to be a savings account customer due to a group policy being available. The company also offered to reimburse the drivers should they opt for a health policy from SBI's general insurance arm. Instead of just a car loan, we also acquired a customer for a savings account, car insurance, health insurance and accident insurance. This was a win-win because the customer got the best of pricing and unified service, while we also increased our wallet share of the business from the customer. For every single line of business, this lens was used.

B. Sriram, MD of National Banking Group (NBG), also came up with an initiative we called Griha Tara. It was an attempt to increase participation in bringing in leads for sales (from teams other than sales). The idea was that whoever brought in a lead for a home loan that got disbursed would be eligible to be called a Griha Tara and would be given a star-shaped lapel/sari pin. I thought it a great idea, but agreed to launch it only after the top management had earned their stars. Luckily, I got a star pretty soon as one of our customers, who had come to discuss a new project, admitted to me that he was looking to shift his housing loan as his current bank's rates were quite high. When we launched the initiative pan-India over video conferencing, each of us at the Corporate Centre wore our stars with pride. This turned out to be the most successful home loan campaign ever, in which nearly 75,000 employees of the bank actively participated. Apart from creating collaborative spirit and inculcating the habit of marketing/sales amongst employees, both from front and back office, the bank was also able to mobilize over one and a half lakh new home loans, amounting to over ₹31,000 crores under the campaign. This also resulted in process improvements, leading to improved turn around times.

When I had first joined the Corporate Centre as GM, I sometimes got invited to meetings of the credit committees. When proposals were being discussed, the then MD of corporate banking, T.S. Bhattacharya, would invariably ask how many credit cards had been issued to the employees of the corporates and how many salary accounts were with us. I also remember the guys from the credit department and their disdain at such questions. Their attitude told its own story – that they were here to answer questions on the credit decisions, not on petty retail matters. It was this lack of understanding at the ground level and a narrow understanding of the customer wallet that we needed to fight and change. While we lent thousands of crores to large companies, a private-sector bank would come in with a working capital loan of ₹10 crores and walk away with all the high-margin retail business as well as other fee-generating lines such as transaction banking and investment banking opportunities – anything that generated good fee income. I had had enough of that. We made collaboration across silos mandatory. If transaction banking could not get a proportionate amount of the fee generating income because the corporate refused to use our cash management product and would not allow our salary package as an option for their employees, I was willing to call up the loan. I remember that in the case of one very well performing unit where we had an exposure of ₹8,000 crores, and they refused to give us our proportionate share of fee income generating business I gave permission to recall the loan with a suggestion that they get it from the bank to whom they were giving all of the non-interest generating business. That worked. But I started this only after ensuring that each of our products were at par or better than competition, as it had to be a win-win for our customers as well. The MDs of both national banking and corporate banking took up as their priority the task of ensuring that our products and service levels were the best.

SBI was opening almost 50,000 new savings accounts daily. But most of these were in urban and semi-urban areas and of low value. There was no real concept of canvassing for account opening. Deposit mobilization was mainly in the form of fixed deposits, where costs were far higher. Also, market share/customer share in metro areas was low. SBI had a good salary account franchise, created by O.P. Bhatt, which was mostly focused on employees of the defence, central and state governments, and public sector undertakings' employees, apart from teachers of central schools, etc. On the other hand, the mainstay of customer acquisition drives by the three large private banks was focused on salary accounts of the private sector, including our corporate accounts group (CAG)/mid corporate group (MCG) borrowers. We set out to get a share of the private sector, borrower and non-borrower salary accounts, especially in the IT sector.

To do that, we had to create customized salary packages, ensure coordinated efforts by branches focused on employee sets. Whereas we had earlier expected employees to come to the branch to open accounts and for transactions, we now set up camps at employees' workspaces, especially at the time of their joining. Once a customer opens a salary account with one bank, they stay on with that bank and account even if they change jobs as all their utility payments/ EMIs are linked to that account. So the opportunity to acquire a customer existed mostly at their first job.

Companies had a set of approved banks and allowed the new joinees to open salary accounts during their induction. Either one bank was invited per day or all three or four banks would be present at the company premises daily during this period to ensure people signed up to open accounts. After detailed study of competitor modus operandi, we identified certain branches as salary account branches near large employers. We created account opening teams, instituted key account managers (KAMs) whose job was to acquire employers and keep their HR departments satisfied, by answering the needs of their employees and creating salary account variants consisting of a full package with insurance and loans – with variants based on employer status rather than employee status alone. Comprehensive presentations were prepared for use by KAMs. A multi-locational employer had to be acquired only once and was given a unique code. All other locations could open salary accounts linked to the employer code. With daily monitoring of salary account acquisition, sharing of credit with the relationship managers of CAG/MCG, in one and a half years, SBI acquired a 20–25 per cent market share in private sector salary accounts and was overall a leader in salary accounts.

We also adopted the 'customer first' approach in all circumstances. For example, during the Chennai floods in 2015 where many other banks could do little to support their salary or other customers as connectivity had failed totally, SBI employees went around in boats with point-of-sales machines, so that ATM cards could be swiped and amounts up to ₹2,000 could be offered as we could not check balances. In many cases, we provided mobile ATMs and cash dispensers at various campuses. SBI was proactive in extending Xpress Credit loan tenors by two months. The contrast between the responses of SBI and other banks finally brought some hard nuts to our fold for salary accounts.

With the principle of 'collaboration inside and competition outside' firmly in place, I challenged people to set out their own goals. Gita Narasimhan, who was heading cross-selling when I took over, recalled the other day how in our first meeting I told her that I wouldn't give her a budget for cross-selling. 'I had to fix it for myself,' she said. 'The only goal you set for me was to make cross-selling a core function instead of a peripheral afterthought. And you reassured me that you would always be available for any enablement should I need it. Because of the importance you gave to "other income", we grew cross-selling income substantially, which continued to snowball in later years. In 2013, the income was a mere ₹208 crores. By 2017, it had quadrupled to ₹914 crores, and it has doubled to ₹2,025 crores in the last three years.'

There were murmurs of abuse and mis-selling. One of my batchmates, Atanu Sen, (the first batchmate I had met on the railway platform on the way to joining SBI), at that time was heading SBI Life Insurance. Along with the collaboration ideas, I requested him to put in place a call-back from his HQ for every new business involving premiums above ₹5,000 (which was to be recorded) to determine correct understanding of the risk and reward by the customer before closing the deal. He was to retire in July, and I requested him to ensure to put in place the processes for this activity before his retirement. He kept his word and got it done. Later when we revisited the entire performance management system, we worked on a principle where there would be equivalent weightage for regular banking activities as well as cross-selling, and that every member of a branch had to contribute to both.

The other initiative that we created on the liabilities side was wealth management. I had always thought that there was a great need for this – to cater to the people with rising disposable incomes, especially Young India. Once at a top technical institute I had commented that the students were 'illiterate', which immediately raised the hackles of the audience till I qualified the term as 'financially illiterate'. It is true that most found it difficult to understand how to invest in order to secure their future. Though they theoretically understood the power of 'compounding', most youngsters still don't start saving from the day they start earning, not realizing that they will have to save much more at a later stage to make up for the lost time. In fact, it was Arun Jaitley, the then finance minister, who had personally encouraged me to start this initiative. I had failed once in launching a platform for this purpose when I was CGM of new business. Though the platform got launched it was abandoned soon after.

So I took up the task again. We branded the initiative as SBI Exclusif (currently rebranded as SBI Wealth). The leader and relationship managers were market recruited. What differentiated us from current offerings in the market was our reliance on technology. We created hubs that could act as service centres for centralized handling of all client requests. The road map indicated the use of bots, artificial intelligence and machine learning for servicing, for communicating as well as predicting and understanding the risk profile, the risk appetite and needs of our customers. It was a one-to-many model because the aim was not to cater to the ultra-high net worth individuals (UHNI), but rather the masses who would form UHNIs in the future. 'Mass with class' was what I called my mission. My vision extended to making this a one-stop shop for wealth management, estate management, tax advisory – in fact, creating a holistic experience, which I know is yet to happen. But the growth of India makes this imperative. As more and more people witness rising income levels, which they will, I firmly believe that the need for such advisory and services will increase, and I am hopeful that the initiative will be enriched and made more comprehensive.

# 12

# The Future Is Digital

All of my initiatives as chairman needed a strong technology backbone to enable us to differentiate and scale up. Therefore, the very first project I initiated was the one to improve our network. Our branches were like bricks strewn helter-skelter. Unless one connected them with a network to act as the cement binding these bricks together, they wouldn't form a house. How strong the structure would be depended on the quality of the network. One customer grouse I heard constantly was the failure of connectivity at branches, or the time taken for pages to load and how slow the service seemed. At that point, the branches were networked to city aggregation points (CAP) from where data would flow into our IT centre at Mumbai. Not only did this cause frequent disruptions because there could be local cable cuts on account of road construction, etc., but also increasing bandwidth was not possible. It was thus decided to move to multi-protocol label switching (MPLS) technology and do away with CAPs.

This was an intelligent networking technology, which directed traffic through the most optimal route to improve efficiency of the network. CAP, on the other hand, had all traffic following a predefined path. With the new technology, increasing bandwidth for a branch became easier too. Many branches were on 128 Kbps, so one can imagine the time the systems took to perform a single action. It was decided to raise the bandwidth to at least 2 Mbps at every branch, and it was raised further at bigger branches. Automatically, the customer experience began improving. We followed this up by implementing thin client technology, getting all of our local servers, desktops and ATMs on active directory – and subsequently, by the 'branch virtualization' programme – to reduce the time lag, and improve speed and stability of service. One of the path-breaking networking experiences that we experimented with during this time was the seamless working of multiple technologies and multiple service providers in the last mile. Certain branches had to continue working with very small aperture terminals (VSAT), radio frequency (RF) and leased line because of our sheer geographical spread. In addition to BSNL, we also roped in private providers and RailTel to minimize the single point of failure risk, thereby improving uptime and customer experience.

Now, merely listing down everything we achieved on the technology front makes it sound very simple, but at every stage these projects had huge challenges. Chief information officers, N. Jambunathan and Mrutyunjay Mahapatra, along with chief technology officer, S.K. Bhasin, and various other officers such as Sunny George and D.A. Tambe could write a separate book on the subject. Suffice it to say that there were hardly any projects of this scale, scope and size that got implemented globally.

Another area that we worked on was the establishment of the biggest private cloud, and starting the journey towards a virtual private network (VPN) – a must-have now for the work-from-anywhere world. But at that time, all this in the public sector space was uncommon.

When I got promoted, one of my cousins had told me that he would consider me a success if I could appreciably improve the customer-service levels at the branches. I knew how difficult it could be. Chairman after chairman had tried it. And I am sure each of my successors will do the same. We were dealing with human beings, after all, and it was difficult to ensure uniform cookie-cutter behaviour from them. People came with their own troubles, their own attitudes, their own experiences. On top of that, there was very little that could be done to incentivize great service and penalize bad behaviour. Changing anything in the bank was like turning a battleship.

What we did was embark on a Customer Experience Excellence Programme, once again supported by technology. The key initiative was to simplify and improve customer experience. With the help of a consultancy agency, 40,000 customers were surveyed across all segments and geographies. Based on the findings, a six-part action plan was created. Technology elements were worked in, such as usage of cash deposit machines (CDM) by using ATM debit cards, cheque deposit kiosks (CDK), self-service passbook printers and queue management systems. It also envisaged changing the layout of the branch by placing the back-office functions to the rear of the branch, and creating a service desk at the entrance. We also planned on dynamic manning of counters based on wait times, as determined by introducing the queue management system or historical data – such as on salary days, days before festivals, etc. Daily huddles at the start of the day were introduced to track service and sales metrics.

The initiative was piloted in fifty branches and showed great promise as customer wait times dropped to below ten minutes on an average; processing times dropped, service quality scores as well as migration and sales parameters improved.

However, when we started rolling the initiative across branches, there was a lot of resistance. Front-line employees were used to arriving a minute or two before customer hours (late arrival was also common), and doing a daily huddle before start of business became a problem. Even when branch timings were changed so that they were required to arrive fifteen minutes before customer hours, branch managers of smaller branches, who had never communicated in this manner before, found it difficult to conduct this meeting.

The tech initiatives, however, made an impact and service did improve, though definitely not to the extent that we had aspired for. We instituted training programmes, did motivational interventions, but I also realized that in order to better service levels in a sustainable manner, it was imperative to bring in more technology, more digitization and more do-it-yourself (DIY) channels for our customers. This led us to ultimately start a user-experience lab to embed customer experience into every product and service by default. This was a pioneering effort in the banking industry in those days.

An assessment of our customer base also revealed that while we claimed to be the 'banker to every Indian', we surely were not so for Young India – and India is a young country. The younger generation viewed SBI as their grandfather's bank or the bank for staid government 'babus'. It did not bode well for us. We were absent from all social media – it was said that it had been tried a few years ago, but the experience had not been good (we probably got trolled badly). I was determined to change that narrative. We forayed into all social media platforms. To create interesting content, we asked for applications from our younger staff members and got enough talent to form a team. Before I left the chairman's position, we were number one or two in India on every social media platform amongst banks (globally, we were number one on Facebook – thanks to our demography and our northern neighbour banning the website).

We started by creating self-service e-corners as a tech initiative by putting up CDMs (Cash Deposit Machines), ATMs, CDKs (Cheque Deposit Kiosks) and passbook printers, multi-function kiosks, etc., which could remain open 24×7 and thereby give the customer the choice to take care of their banking needs by themselves at a time of their choice.

We knew we had to hasten our digital agenda. There are always a few sceptics, and some of them had asked why we needed to think digital as we already had an internet banking application and offered mobile banking services as well. An initiative of this size needs a groundswell of support or else half our energies would get spent on merely fighting the resistance. So I came up with the idea of our 'in touch' branches. We branded these branches so because they mostly worked on touchscreens and it was meant to get us in touch with the young generation.

This in a way was counterintuitive. I was trying to push people into adopting processes that are virtual, but at the same time, I wanted to create physical branches to convince them about it! I felt though that unless our people could see and feel the vision, it would be difficult to get them excited about it.

We chose seven metro/large cities to launch the branches, and we placed them in the best-located shopping malls in these cities. The idea was that both staff and customers would visit with families, and find that banking had changed from being a drab and sometimes painful activity to a fun one. What did I want these new-age branches to look like? They had to have bright, unconventional décor, manned by a few employees dressed in smart casuals. Lots of touchscreens, a desk like the one from *Star Trek*, little private cubicles and a system for opening accounts instantaneously with digital KYC, plus a machine to create a personalized debit card in a few minutes.

Ultimately, the branches had a lobby like an e-corner with ATMs, CDMs, CDKs, multi-function kiosks and passbook printers that could be separated from the rest of the branch by a shutter, so it could remain operational round the clock. Inside the branch was a large touchscreen on which one could look up various products. For example, to buy a car, one could touch 'auto' – the screen would ask whether you are looking to buy a new car or a used one and your budget. Depending on what you indicated, it would show all the models and makes available. One could drill down to what the manufacturer had stated regarding the model or what social media was saying about it. The screen then asked whether the customer would like a loan and if yes was indicated, it would ask a few more questions to determine an approximate disposable income and then suggest a loan. This came with a slider to enable one to increase/decrease the EMI or loan tenure. The whole family could participate and the idea could be extended to home loans or study loans with virtual walk-throughs of proposed apartments or campuses. And finally, one could even generate an in-principle approval letter for a loan, and take it to a branch for quick processing.

The branch also had smart tables with in-built screens to play around with investment goals and programmes. There were cubicles where one could virtually meet investment or loan experts on one screen, while they could view or print documents being shown or sent by experts from another desktop. There were teller counters manned remotely, with tellers sitting at a central point and appearing on screens, for encashing large-value cheques – the customer would place the cheque on a scanner and the image would travel to the teller for necessary action.

The branches were also equipped with systems on which by merely scanning one's fingerprint and typing in one's Aadhaar number, accounts could be opened and even a personalized debit/ATM card could be printed and delivered, all in twenty minutes. In the larger in-touch branches, there was even a small amphitheatre with tiers of steps, with brightly coloured cushions strewn around, where we could hold launches of new products or events on financial planning, investment advice or the like. The branches were showcasing cutting-edge technology and were unlike anything else in India at the time.

The point of this experiment was to act as a myth-buster – the myth that we were an old, outdated organization – and to that end, the experiment was a great success because it started changing the perception of SBI as a technologically backward bank. It brought to the fore our employees' sense of pride of belonging to an institution that had the ability to evolve swiftly and reinvent itself as required.

Not that this initiative did not result in some terribly embarrassing moments! Once we had stabilized the branches, we requested the RBI governor to visit the Mumbai branch and open his account with us using our instant account opening system. We tested the system repeatedly to make sure that everything was working smoothly as our intention was that he should walk out of the branch with his personalized SBI debit card. On D-Day, the walkthrough went smoothly and he was indeed impressed. The finale was supposed to be his opening an account, but when we asked him to scan his fingerprint and input his Aadhaar number, there was no response from the Aadhaar server. Desperate calls were put through to our IT centre, only to be told that while our systems were working fine, the government's Aadhaar server was not responding. The account couldn't be opened. Sometimes, I think technology has a wicked sense of humour – it refuses to put on a show just when we want it to.

However, the branches were proving to be ROI negative as some of the features were way ahead of its time. Therefore, we took a call to carve out those initiatives that were working best in the seven branches, and roll out a simpler and more economic version at other centres. But it was important to get a full buy-in from all of our top management. In order to do this, I took our team of MDs and DMDs for an off-site at the L&T training centre at Lonavala, where we had all the tech and consultancy majors such as IBM, Oracle, Amazon, Microsoft, McKinsey and BCG presenting the latest solutions and their views on the future of banking and technology. The group then split into smaller teams to decide what should be the bank's priorities. A few days later, we flew down to Bengaluru for a meeting we had asked iSprit – a voluntary organization that mentored start-ups – to arrange, in order to get a look at the disruptive solutions that were being worked on by the fintech industry. It was an aha moment for a number of us. The new world of fintech and the application programming index (API) led method of consumption, the use of cloud technology and the speed of change made me realize how far behind we were. But it also gave me the strength to know that the means to leapfrog existed and the sense of urgency the meeting created hastened our actions.

One direct result of this off-site was the creation, with the approval of the board, of a ₹200-crore corpus for collaborating with fintechs. The collaboration could work in three ways – we could form a joint venture, become strategic investors or agree to pay on the basis of the number of transactions done through them. A panel including external experts was created to vet the proposals of potential fintech companies that we found interesting or those that applied to work with us. Again, this was a first in the PSU space, but I must acknowledge the wisdom and enthusiasm of the SBI board that extended its complete support to us in our endeavours.

The bank's digitization journey accelerated. We, however, realized that now the next step was to provide a mobile application that would enable people, especially our young customers, to take care of their banking needs from the comfort of their homes. During discussions, Sriram, MD of NBG, suggested that we should also aim to have a marketplace and not only an app. On consideration, I thought his idea to be absolutely on point and so the scope was expanded. We wanted to have an application that would enable our customers to seamlessly conduct banking as well as allow them to do all other activities, such as shopping, booking shows, surfing, connecting to social media platforms – that is, doing everything through a single application. And thus 'You Only Need One', or YONO, was born.

YONO was expected to be launched in early 2017, but on account of implementation delays, it was actually launched a month after I retired, in October 2017, by my successor Rajnish Kumar – which, in a way, was fitting, for in his then capacity as the head of the NBG for the past year, he had been heading the YONO implementation committee.

While the digitization proceeded apace, we undertook many other initiatives such as implementing the customer relationship management systems, loan origination systems, loan life management systems, as well as the creation of API libraries and exposing them to possible partners. We also progressed our analytics platform and recruited a team of analysts from the market. Security was another area where we made huge strides. A 24×7×365 security operations centre was set up, outfitted with the ability to both detect and respond should an emergency occur, and prevent possible attacks and breaches. This was done along with setting down the procedure for creating a response task force.

For all of these initiatives, we had to follow rigorous processes, implement price discovery mechanisms, assess capability and then, after determining the vendor, undertake relentless follow-up to get the implementations done and the initiative delivered.

There were projects backed by technology in every vertical. Prioritization was a huge challenge but our CIOs – first Mr Jambunathan and then Mrutyunjay Mahapatra, as well as the CTO Mr Bhasin (who was market-recruited on contract), ably supported by our chief general managers Sonny George and Mr Tambe, rose brilliantly to the occasion.

# 13

# Risks and Rewards

In my interview for chairmanship I had indicated that I would put the maximum emphasis on risk – its measurement and mitigation. Yet, this had always been considered as a non-core function at SBI. In a way, I could relate to that. Take, for instance, the risk scenarios we used to review to assess our readiness to tackle them. If I remember correctly, there were sixty-two scenarios. And the pandemic is the sixty-third. Was this not a risk that had been called out at various forums? So the best of preparations may still leave some risks exposed, but that is no excuse to not make a sincere effort.

In order to ensure that risk was given its due importance, it was necessary that the person handling it had a presence at all board meetings. I decided to give additional charge to the chief credit officer (CCO), Varsha Purandhare, who ran the highest committee for sanctioning of credit proposals, oversaw the bank's entire credit process and was also a DMD, and, therefore, a permanent invitee to the board. We rechristened the role as chief credit and risk officer

(CCRO). However, very soon, two things became apparent – first, that to drive the risk agenda and bring about a true transformation, we needed someone at the MD level to ensure that the initiative carried enough weight; and second, the workload on the CCRO was untenable. The RBI too felt that the two roles were in conflict, and they had a point. So we created an MD position for risk and compliance. I had a tough time convincing Praveen Gupta, the MD I thought would best fit the role, that I was not doing this to sideline him (this had happened in one of my predecessor's time). It was not easy selling the agenda to him, but when I shared my vision and all that I wanted done, he agreed to give it a try.

I really wanted this MD to be more powerful than all the rest, and for his department to have the authority to say no to loans or new initiatives if the perceived risk was too high, not well understood and could not be mitigated. We already had a comprehensive structure at the Corporate Centre, with separate groups looking at credit, operations, marketing and group risks. The idea was to enable them further with technology tools, pool in data and knowledge from all available resources, cascade awareness down through rank and file, and make process changes to provide a platform for risk to have its say. Risk was a tick-the-box function. I wanted it to be far more dynamic and central to our decision-making process.

We started with the implementation of an early warning system (EWS). There was so much information out there – some structured, some unstructured. But we were stuck to the age-old Tandon-Chore Committee norms, and based our decisions on ratios that didn't capture what was most important: cash flows and the ability to repay when it was due. We got top-quadrant vendors to design a system that would give us an early warning of imminent stress based on financial performance, turnover in accounts, cheque returns, devolvement of letters of credit, invocation of guarantees, delays in payments of wages or workers dues to the Employee Provident Fund Organization, adverse media reports, high-profile exits from the company, pledging of promoters shares, etc. The system had built in escalation matrix to ensure action. This also helped us kick off a dynamic credit rating activity, which earlier was only done at stipulated intervals regardless of triggers indicating the need for review.

The independent risk advisory (IRA) was simultaneously implemented. While we had a well-defined system of credit process and sanctions, the senior executives who were members of various credit committees had to go through the full proposals, without an independent agency vetting the proposals – effectively the proposals were only being seen by people in the business verticals who had business targets to meet. Imagine going through twenty-five proposals of 200 pages each, week after week, over and above one's allocated work. Someone other than the business owner needed to have an independent look. The important question before us was whether the risk department would have the power to decline any credit proposals not found suitable by them, and consequently, take responsibility for all the sanctions. It was felt then that asking the risk department to give a final yes or no to all large credit proposals could be too drastic a change. I believe that this has been implemented now. In the event that the risk department adopted a risk-averse approach resulting in declining most of the proposals or imposing conditions which couldn't be fulfilled, the entire process could come to a halt – particularly at a time when the bank was already grappling with a lot of stress. Prudence dictated that we ease into the process in stages.

The risk department began vetting all credit proposals and submitted their observations in the form of an independent credit assessment report, leaving the final call to be taken by the appropriate credit committees. A number of external data sources were made available to help them arrive at a well-informed opinion. The whole process was digitized, so that all proposals and their observations could flow online, from and to the originating branches. The branch responses on the observations were included in the proposals sent to the credit committee for their decision. A timeline of three days was stipulated to prevent delays.

The next step was the creation of a loan life cycle management system (LLMS) which completely digitized the credit process in the bank for all high-value proposals. All proposals were processed in the system, at various levels, including at the highest sanctioning committee, completely eliminating the printing of voluminous documents. The system was strengthened further by rolling out more aspects of post-sanction monitoring, including standardized calculation and monitoring of drawing power (DP), as well as mobile apps for officers conducting unit inspections to help record their observations.

While these operational measures were coming into existence, the credit policy needed a revamp to stay in sync with these modifications. A separate team overhauled the loan policy to bring greater clarity to the various aspects of the lending activity of the bank. A risk appetite framework was introduced, and both quantitative and qualitative parameters were identified and drilled down to business groups.

On joining as chairman, I had gone around the country meeting all of our regional managers in groups to determine their perception of the bank's biggest opportunities and challenges. Only a handful of them had flagged capital as one of the challenges. I was a little taken aback by the lack of appreciation of how difficult raising capital was, and the need for it for us to expand and grow. Our employees needed to realize how scarce and costly capital was. Consequently, risk-based budgeting, which tracked returns generated by the business units on the basis of risk weighted assets of the unit, was introduced.

A customer one view (COV) facility was put in place to track the bank's exposure to large customers on a number of systems such as core banking, treasury, foreign offices, etc. This helped us determine where we needed to scale up or down. A new department called credit performance and monitoring was started, to keep an eye on the credit portfolio at the bank level (this was earlier done by the business vertical), and allowed pre-emptive action as required.

## Assets: The Challenge and the Opportunity

The most imminent threat to the banking system was the burgeoning NPAs. While several actions needed to be taken to stem the flood, the stagnant pool already created required immediate attention. I aimed to rebalance the portfolio from 54 per cent corporate and 43 per cent retail exposure to precisely the opposite. At the end of my four years, it had reversed to 46 per cent corporate and 51 per cent retail.

We realized that NPAs in different segments had to be treated differently. The biggest problem was in the large corporate sector, followed by small and medium enterprises (SMEs), and agriculture and the personal – or P – segments. The solutions would have to be differentiated for each segment. The mission communicated to each of our groups was simple: formulate the steps to be initiated for ensuring better asset quality in the future, along with cleaning up the mess from the past. I didn't believe that we could do only one and not the other, as it was like repairing a running car. We couldn't stop it completely for repairs.

In the P segment, though we were doing well, I knew we could do much better. I remembered a conversation I had with a client when I was in SBICaps. I had asked him that if he had two housing loans, one from SBI and the other from a private bank, and only enough money to pay one EMI, which bank would he pay? The unhesitating reply was: 'The private bank.' 'Why?' I had asked. 'SBI is more tolerant and lenient. The private bank would immediately levy huge penalties, claw back any discounts given for processing and could even call up the loan. SBI would never do that,' he told me.

It was a lesson learnt. Our supportive or considerate behaviour was perceived as a weakness at its best and inefficiency at its worst. That would have to end immediately. We began sending SMS notifications a week before EMIs were due, and follow-up started at midnight the day after the due date in case of default. Our technology initiatives helped us get this right.

I had also noticed one other lacuna. Whenever we launched a product, we did not provide a comprehensive standard operating process (SOP) that covered the product cycle from birth to death. For example, the SOP for the gold loan product did not have instructions on marking the value of the security to market. Nothing was prescribed as to what warranted auction of the securities, the periodicity and processes to be followed, the outcomes to be achieved, and so on. I made it mandatory that product committees did not approve any product that did not encompass the entire life cycle, including disposal of the asset, reconciliation and reporting requirements. We also commenced product reviews on a quarterly basis. We had not sunset any product for as long as I could remember. There was no metrics for determining which products were giving what kind of returns and deserved to continue, and which ones should be withdrawn.

The focus on retail started by Mr Purwar had been brought to fruition by Mr Bhatt. To his credit, he had understood the potential, the margins in it and, along with the business process re-engineering that created centralized processing cells, had revolutionized this segment. Over time, SBI became the largest mortgage lender in the market, but the processes needed refurbishing. For instance, the process of storing title deeds of the properties mortgaged, retrieving them for inspection and then replacing them in the right place had become a challenge given the sheer volumes we handled.

The result was misplaced title deeds that caused our customers and us endless grief. The answer was to retain soft copies in a document handling system to obviate the need for physical handling. Similarly, follow-up processes needed digital enablement. We started tying up with the builders we were lending to for our rightful share of the retail loans and properly monitoring the cash flows from bookings, so that these flows were not diverted to create land banks, instead of being used to complete the projects for which the advances were given. Many builders had a propensity to do so, with the aim of maximizing their margins by buying the land for future projects at the earliest, little realizing that they were locking up precious liquidity. Moreover, land banks would prove useless in a slowdown, which is exactly what happened. The entire effort was led by G. Vaijnath, one of the most efficient and good-hearted officers I have ever met. In my entire career, he was the only one who once met me and requested me to recommend a colleague for promotion instead of himself, as I could send in only one recommendation. He explained that he had age on his side and could be recommended the next year, but for his colleague this would be the last chance. This kind of generosity is rare in a workplace.

In order to create competitive pressure, we launched a slew of new home loan products, of which 'SBI Her Ghar' (the name was a play on the word 'her' because written in Hindi, it means 'every', whereas in English it is a feminine pronoun) was my favourite. It was an exclusive home loan product for women, where we promised a .05 per cent lower rate of interest should the house be bought in the name of a woman or if she was the first holder of the title.

It was launched in December 2013, a first in the banking industry and a step towards empowering women. Some newspapers mocked the rebate as too little, saying it would be just enough to buy a box of sweets – but the response was phenomenal, and almost one third of our home loans started getting sourced under this.

Similarly, we launched 'SBI Shourya' – an exclusive home loan for defence personnel, again a first in the industry and as a way of us appreciating the work they put in. The other innovative products were 'SBI FlexiPay', which offered flexible EMI options to the customer to suit their varying income levels during the entire home loan tenure and an 'Insta Home Top-up' loan – a paperless product, offered on the bank's internet banking platform.

Home loans had already been established as a core portfolio. In fact, it had become the second most important source of new customer acquisition. In contrast, auto loans suffered from a low market share – we were the fourth largest player. Our problems lay in the poor and erratic delivery quality across branches. It was also a fraud-prone portfolio with high NPAs, indicating poor customer selection and follow-up. We needed to treat vehicle finance as a single portfolio, encompassing dealer finance, finance for commercial vehicles and finance for individual passenger cars. This model cut across many silos in SBI, and required an iron fist to implement it. I challenged Anuradha Rao, CGM of personal banking, to bring about a material change.

We introduced a lead management system (OCAS), created exclusive in-house teams for auto loans and supplemented it by outsourcing both lead origination and follow-up to our brokerage subsidiary. We also revived and nurtured close relations with the leading auto makers (OEMs) – Maruti, Hyundai, Tata – from the Corporate Centre, and started structured monthly meetings in which we measured OEM-wise penetration and asset quality. Frauds were controlled by feeding dealer details in the loan origination system (LOS).

Automatically populating OCAS details into LOS and to the core banking system (CBS) to open accounts cut multiple hours of processing time. In case of default, timely seizures of vehicles was enforced, and quick sale by the auction agents at designated spots, time and dates became a popular event in several circles. For instance, in Kolkata where this used to take place on a street called Auction Gully, some of our staff almost became professional auctioneers!

We constantly used LOS data to minutely correlate credit quality to credit approval parameters. For example, we found different vehicle models attracted different customer segments with different results for asset quality. Pricing and follow-up was modulated accordingly. The net result was that we became the number one originator of car loans overall, as well as for the top four auto manufacturers by the end of 2015, with an asset quality comparable to the best in class.

With respect of the SME segment, I knew that we needed to work hard on reducing the stressed assets, but I also wanted to ensure that the credit flow to the segment didn't get choked up on account of risk aversion.

D.P. Mazumdar, CGM of SME, worked on identifying areas of low risk by undertaking portfolio analysis. We had created a data warehouse, but had no analytics team. We began our foray into this by setting up an analytics team and recruiting analysts from the market, and we initiated various risk-modelling efforts with help from IIM Bangalore and IIM Calcutta, as well as IIT Kharagpur and IIT Mumbai. We hired laterally from the market for a leader for this team. The idea was to bring analytical rigour that aligned people, processes, technology and governance for the bank's data journey. Some of the early use cases were to do with customer churn, product traction, and, of course, underwriting principles and risk modelling.

Simultaneously, we began improving appraisal methods to prevent adverse selection. With the help of consultants, we implemented a tool that used various data points and bank account statements to prepare our own profit and loss and cash flow statements, obviating the need to depend on the ones submitted to us by borrowers. We also started shifting our products to cash flow–based ones rather than depend on balance sheets, which provided only snapshots (which, incidentally, could be photoshopped) of a business at a point of time, whereas for a business to sustain and repay loans, continuing liquidity and cash flows were key. Tie-ups with industry majors were pursued to do supply chain and dealer network lending. Templates were designed for lending to micro businesses, based on detailed market surveys.

Obtaining proper valuations of collaterals offered was key. We often found that the value of collaterals, especially land and buildings, decreased dramatically when we tried to dispose them. While some amount of value erosion was expected as these were distress sales, strange problems tended to crop up here. In one case, the land had no access road, reducing its value drastically. In another case, the unit was built on a land a part of which belonged to someone else, thus preventing its sale. We tightened the rules for empanelling valuers and recorded their performance history to enable us to weed out the undesirable ones. But there was very little else we could do. Any wrongdoing by a valuer or a lawyer or an accountant had no consequences. In respect to the last two, at least they were part of professional bodies and we could lodge complaints against them (though strict action was rarely taken); for valuers, even that was absent.

We had also noticed huge gaps in post-disbursal monitoring and supervision. It was alleged that inspection routines were not followed and sometimes reports were filled up without visits. To counter this, GPS monitoring of inspection officials as per system-generated inspection schedules was introduced to ensure actual visits. Inspecting officials fed data directly into analytical tools to reduce subjectivity. Let's take the example of an inspection of a pipe manufacturing unit. The systems would show how much finished goods of various qualities and dimensions are available. But how would one determine whether part of the stock is damaged and unusable or whether the pipes are of the dimensions mentioned?

There was a case, for instance, where an edible oil unit was storing its finished goods in hoppers. Our inspectors would climb to the top of the hoppers and do a dipstick test to check if the volumes of stock declared in the statement were actually present and would come back satisfied. When the account started showing signs of stress, a more thorough inspection was ordered. When the dipstick test was done from top the results were fine. But when samples were drawn from the tap at the bottom, what came out was water! The company was falsifying stocks by leaving a layer of oil on top and filling the rest with water. The quality of inspections therefore needed improvement. While we allocated accounts to professional stock auditors based on value and complexity, we also introduced an escalation matrix of calling in specialist stock auditors if any unusual signals were observed.

Improving skill levels and the enablement of our officers was a priority. Online courses were introduced and made mandatory. Over the course of four years, we created three levels of certification. Officers handing SME accounts needed to be certified at the first level. Those handling large, complex accounts had to have the second-level certification, while people handling project finance or complex, stressed accounts needed the highest level of certification. Most of these courses were online with advanced levels buttressed by in-class sessions. Intensive courses were created for those handling credit for the first time.

As a last level of check, we created a concurrent audit of sanctions done and a compliance audit after disbursement, to ensure that pre-disbursement terms and conditions had been met.

On the agriculture front, the steps required for controlling and reducing NPAs were different. When I went in as chairman, NPAs in this segment were over 10 per cent, and trending upwards due to a debt waiver announced by two state governments, where elections had just concluded and where debt waiver had been an electoral promise.

The issue of agricultural debt waiver is a fraught one. I got cited for breach of privilege by a state legislature as I had publicly opined on it while it was still under discussion. These did give me a few anxious moments. What I was unable to convey was that I never felt or said that our farmers do not need or deserve more support. But I also truly felt that debt waiver was not the solution. Even if debt is waived, at the time of the next planting the farmer will have to avail of debt again. What is required is to increase his repaying capacity.

If the same amount of money spent on debt waiver is instead spent on helping the farmer raise productivity, it would create a far greater and long-lasting impact. Farmers needed modern ways to support sustainable farming, better market access, more information and better techniques, more scientific inputs, better crop management, an increase of non-farm income and creation of a steady income stream to help them remain debt-free during the period between sowing and harvesting. None of these is unknown, and yet there is little progress.

We started on a daily monitoring routine of account renewals in a campaign mode. Dr M.G. Vaidyan, CGM of rural banking, started focused campaigns in areas of high NPAs to create maximum impact. Extensive churning of data threw up details of borrowers where a single account was overdue and was pulling down this individual's all other accounts to NPA status. A little monitoring by the branches ensured that most of these accounts could be upgraded, thereby upgrading the borrower's entire portfolio of accounts. Special schemes were launched for one-time settlement of dues, and Lok Adalats and Bank Adalats were extensively leveraged. Despite the debt waivers announced by several states, we reduced the NPAs to below 9 per cent, a level never seen in the past three years.

There was a need to increase the asset base in this segment. The idea was to do it in a more risk mitigated and sustainable manner. Innovation and new products were the call of the hour. We started focusing on lending under corporate tie-ups, for entities such as dairies, water pump suppliers and drip-irrigation equipment manufacturers.

We started lending to Farmers Producer Organizations for the first time. This is now a common product across the banking sector. To my horror, I found that SBI's tractor loan product had a 40 per cent–plus NPA, and we were still continuing with it with no thoughts on how to improve it. Under our system, the repayment of the loan was linked to harvests after a moratorium of one year. This meant that if we were giving a loan to a farmer raising sugarcane (an annual crop), the first payment would be due after two years! No wonder we had such high NPAs. A retail, small-exposure customer whom we don't touch at least once a month is already partly lost to us. Retail, by nature, is a high-touch activity. We scrapped the existing product and launched a new one with monthly EMIs – as tractors are used in rural areas through the year for haulage. We further gave a rebate if the spouse was made a co-borrower, as research indicated that women were less likely to default. A third step was to offer a far more attractive rate of interest if further collateral of gold was offered. In fact, over a period of time, 34 per cent of the agriculture portfolio was collateralized. The gold loan push had started during Pratip Chaudhuri's time and we continued with it. We also implemented and improved the technology backbone for origination, monitoring and follow-up of agricultural loans. Dashboards indicating actions required were created for the use of the various branches.

The business correspondent channels were expanded rapidly, but with due care. They were then trained and certified to do activities pertaining to follow-up and collection. Monitoring their activities to prevent frauds, by using dashboards and exception reports, was stepped up. If a business correspondent showed no activity for three days or reported sudden spikes or fall in business, the hub branch was instructed to visit and check on it immediately. Overall, the results were encouraging.

The most difficult problem was presented by the corporate segment – where it was clear that new laws and regulations were required. After the global financial crisis of 2008 the country saw an immense opportunity to break the shackles of a Hindu rate of growth. The GDP was expected to grow at a compounded annual growth rate (CAGR) of 8 per cent or higher. To sustain this, estimates of our future requirements of goods and services indicated substantial investment in infrastructure sectors and basic industries. The planning for all such investments factored in a contribution of 75 per cent from the financial sector. In the absence of developmental financial institutions like the erstwhile ICICI and IDBI, which had converted into universal banks, and any alternative financial markets, much of these investments were expected to come from the banking sector. Within the banking sector, SBI was expected to take the lead, which it did.

As is usual, even the best planned efforts have their pitfalls, and most of the banking sector exposure in the power; roads; engineering, procurement and construction; and steel sectors became stressed. Public sector banks were blamed, berated and pilloried by all, and undue comparisons were made with those private-sector banks, who had very wisely stayed away from such exposures. It also appeared that an undue share of the blame was being apportioned to SBI.

Other banks, including some private-sector ones, looked up to SBI to take charge of resolving the issues so as to optimize recoveries. As chairman of SBI, I was expected to take up this mantle and represent the banking sector. These were trying times, and required extensive internal and external discussions – some fruitful, some not so much. As the new government came into power, consultations began for the budget. In the first consultation held by the new finance minister, we were told that each of us could put forth one demand. As the representative of the largest bank, I was asked to speak first. I remember making a fervent plea for a bankruptcy law. Having served in New York, I knew how important such a law was and it was of the utmost importance to give lenders more power to resolve asset-quality issues through a proper legal framework. Suffice it to say that as difficult a law as this got drafted by the government and promulgated in a record time of twenty-four months.

It was clear to us from the very beginning that each of these corporates needed different solutions and a cookie-cutter approach would not work. Where the promoters cooperated sincerely, we could turn around some units. In one case, the family stepped in to help and pieces were carved out between different parts of the family, thus ensuring the inflow of more equity and the lowering of debt. Similarly, in another case, one of the state governments agreed to step aside in favour of a private partner so that fresh equity could be infused and the management would stabilize. It was not an easy job to convince the state. But I pointed out that in the absence of a clear and responsible management, the bank would not be able to help further and we would be forced to call up the account. The unit was a fulcrum in its area, and our estimate was that in the extended ecosystem it supported 2,00,000 livelihoods. The government acceded eventually, and the unit stabilized and did well. About two years later, I happened to meet the finance minister of the state at an airport lounge. He thanked me for the help with the unit, and ended with the words 'Ma'am, you estimated that about 2,00,000 livelihoods would be lost; it's more like 5,00,000.' That was the impact that could be created by timely and correct action.

But there were borrowers asking for the impossible as well. I remember the head of one such unit approaching me with a proposal that was just not doable. And I told him as much. I recalled that about four years ago, when I was with SBICaps, I had gone to see him with a prior appointment. The company was in its heydays then. After an hour of waiting, his office informed me that he would not be able to make the meeting that day. I told him that I respected his company much more that day than this one, and wished that his company would see those days again – but it wouldn't happen in the manner he was proposing.

In one case, the borrower came with a one-time settlement offer. The money to be paid to the bank was all contingent on some extraneous event happening – such as a case being decided in his favour, or some damage claims coming through or him receiving some settlements. I explained that all of these would, in any case, accrue to the lenders and one cannot do settlements on the basis of possibilities of receipts of money. I wanted him to commit cash. Knowing fully well that he was about to throw a lavish birthday bash, I asked why he could not defer that and put the money on the table as a token of his good intent? His answer stumped me: 'One is sixty only once.' He then went on to say that if we didn't accept his proposal, he would keep us in the courts forever, and that his friends had assured him that this could be done. My response was unequivocal: 'With such friends, you don't need enemies.' While I said that, I also knew that what he was saying could actually be true. In his case alone, we had already attended seventy five court dates – with little progress. The law was really crying out for a change. My contention is not that all borrowers were of this nature, or were to blame for the stress in their units, but we surely encountered quite a few. With each such encounter, I realized how much the lenders – that is, the banks – needed to be empowered.

The power sector was one of the main contributors to the stress in the banking industry. Power for all was a clarion call of the Planning Commission. Private-sector participation in power generation was encouraged to augment capacity to meet this requirement. From a deficit power producing country – which saw frequent load-shedding, even in urban areas and metros – we have almost tripled our generating capacity and now supply uninterrupted power to most areas contributing to growth in the economy. In this process, however, while the installed capacity has increased to almost 360 GW, the capacity utilization has reduced to below 55 per cent or so. Surely, there may have been some errors in demand estimation.

The other mistake we did was privatizing generation without first privatizing distribution and transmission. Many successful countries that have privatized the power sector did so by first privatizing distribution, then transmission and generation, so that the efficiencies ensure the right returns to the generators. At that stage, we had thirty-four projects with an aggregate exposure of almost ₹1,70,000 crores (₹1.7 trillion) that were stalled. Some of these had been completed, but their coal allocations had been cancelled or were yet to be firmed up or their power purchase agreements with state-run distribution companies were not being honoured or were being revised unilaterally. Some had cost escalations on account of revisions in original assumptions arising out of policy reversions. Delayed clearances, including for environment, had led to both time and cost escalations. This led to overruns on account of application of interest during construction (IDC).

The promoters had run out of equity and, in a couple of cases, large private equity players, daunted by the uncertainties, had just abandoned their investments and the remaining promoters did not have the wherewithal. In most of the cases, the per MW cost had increased much beyond what had been originally projected in the detailed project report prepared by eminent consultants. In one case, we had invoked the counter-guarantee of a bank of a northern neighbouring country on behalf of one of our customers for deficiencies in supply by one of their equipment suppliers. This invocation was never honoured by the foreign bank, despite interventions at the highest level. Banks had made their mistakes and taken approvals/allocations from the concerned authorities for granted, based on in-principle clearances, relied on the technical expertise of engineering consultants, and, perhaps, were not at that point equipped and trained to handle project exposures. Haircuts needed to be considered for restructuring the accounts, but with the capital inadequacy in the system, the option of writing off of the exposures was not available. There were only a few buyers of these assets who also demanded huge discounts. In this situation, the attempt was to sort out fuel supply and power purchase issues wherever possible, and try and operationalize some projects, apart from completing those which could be completed within their defined time schedules with minimum capital infusion. In essence, preserve, create and recover value to the extent possible was our chosen line of action.

This process involved numerous interactions at both the central and state government levels, trying to get the various stakeholders – including the coal suppliers, the railways, the electricity regulators – besides our own regulators – to find workable solutions. At most of these interactions, I tried to do as much of the heavy lifting as I could. A few of these met with some success and got resolved – the SHAKTI scheme of the coal ministry and the pooling of the generated power to ensure off-take were helpful initiatives.

We had also contemplated to rightsize the debt, convert part of it into equity and invite the large public sector behemoths to takeover and operate these assets on behalf of the banks till these found appropriate value. While a lot of effort was put into all these initiatives, a large number of projects still remain in limbo – at least as far as the banks are concerned, despite the efforts made at the National Company Law Tribunal, and other legal bodies. I feel that much more could have been achieved if we had a single body to resolve these differences among the stakeholders, perhaps as is being endeavoured now through the National Infrastructure Projects Pipeline monitoring. The banks, though, are hopefully now wiser to the risks of project financing and are not likely to repeat these mistakes going forward.

The engineering, procurement and construction sector also comes to mind for the sheer time and effort it required from all of us. With a large number of projects initiated simultaneously, like most other sectors, there was a clear case of inadequate planning, insufficient capital, misallocation of risks (all risks were passed on to the developer and lender, with the government not taking any responsibility for land procurement, issuance of approvals on time, among others), and limited capacity and capability. Road projects accounted for most of the travails of this sector. Payments had not been made as their receivables had been stuck in various stages of arbitration, appeals and then courts. The projects had stalled and guarantees had been invoked, rendering the accounts irregular. The promoters did not have enough equity either to regularize their accounts or complete the projects. The entire sector was stuck and a majority were on the verge of default, which would have rendered them ineligible to bid for future projects. This would have seriously jeopardized the future infrastructure programmes of the government. More importantly, projects would not be completed and our dues would become unrealizable. I had raised this issue at the highest levels, as had the industry, for a need to find a solution to a large number of claims being held up in arbitration and in appeals by the government post-award to the courts, though the arbitrators were appointed by them. A meeting of all stakeholders was convened where, on behalf of all banks, I supported the industry suggestion to release 75 per cent of the arbitral award against a bank guarantee as long as the money was used to regularize the account.

This would enable the developers to operate their accounts, thus allowing the completion of the projects. The banking sector exposure would not increase as fresh infusion of funds by promoters would go towards completing projects and the various authorities could be exhorted to expedite payments on performance. This found favour with all and, thanks to NITI Aayog, the relevant order was also issued immediately. We were in awe of the speed of the government action, and were quite sanguine that eventually the other issues would also be sorted out. However, that was not to be. One of the authorities wanted to know who would be responsible for the interest on the 75 per cent of the award amount in case the company lost the appeal or the court case, preferred by the concerned authority against the award. This was a valid observation, but no one questioned them as to how many cases had they actually won in such appeals and court cases, and how much interest was payable by them. Besides, who was held responsible for the legal costs and delays, mainly resulting from indecision?

Attempts to ensure the survival of this sector failed, and the tribunal also has not been able to provide a solution yet. This made the banks wiser, but funding for this sector can only become more difficult going foward. Thankfully, the operating and, business models for the roads sector has been revisited and hopefully, the allocation of risks would be more equitable in future. The bane of this sector has been the unequal equation between various stakeholders, leading to each optimizing for itself, which in turn results in overall sub-optimal results for the nation.

Another sector which required serious intervention was the steel sector. Besides the cancellation of coal blocks and closure of iron ore mines impacting a few of them, the sector was also suffering from low demand coupled with dumping by some countries. Most steel companies were showing negative results quarter on quarter, and operating margins had eroded substantially. The banking sector had a huge exposure and could not afford any further stress. Again, I really had no option other than to lead the banking sector in their efforts to prevent stress in another sector, and had to represent the banks at various forums stressing on the need for immediate action.

While the steel industry was making their own representations, the banking sector was also pitching in to prevent further closures. At this point, some economists asked why we needed this sector at all as it would be cheaper to import our requirements. Such suggestions were largely ignored though and the concerned ministries – steel and commerce – acted with alacrity and initiated corrective action. The health of the steel industry after that has been pretty good and most of them have deleveraged substantially. The outcomes were quite satisfying. In conclusion, it can be said that we saw mixed results despite our best efforts to conserve and preserve value. Some we were able to resolve, some we were able to preserve and the balance had to be referred to the tribunal post asset-quality reviews by RBI.

In respect to the accounts where we did succeed, we learnt that two or three things are essential for revival. First, speed of action helped preserve value. Second, the lifeblood of any business is liquidity and it needs to be pumped in more as equity rather than debt because the former can wait patiently for repayment, which the latter can't. The interest on debt is like a taximeter – once switched on, it will keep piling up, pulling companies into an irreversible debt trap. Debt doesn't wait for a bad or good time to get paid; it needs regular consistent payment. Also, the entire financial structure was skewed to debt – what we found was that many borrowers had pumped in their portion of equity by taking loans at the holding company level by pledging their shares. The entire project had become debt-funded and, therefore, a delay in cash flows meant a death knell for the project. And third, the management needs to be one that can be relied on by stakeholders and lenders. For this, high standards of corporate governance and a board with enough expertise and independence are prerequisites.

As for solutions, if we look at the macro level, the economy and the banking sector needed to have all three 'Rs' happening simultaneously: recognition, resolution and recapitalization. For the public sector banks, the fourth 'R' of reform also applied. The banking sector had pointed this out as early as 2014. There were no effective laws for resolution, but work had begun on the bankruptcy law. Bank reforms were initiated, as was recognition and recapitalization. But as recapitalization happened in bite-sized pieces, recognition too could only be done piecemeal.

What was the need of the hour? Swift action to reduce debt, and either take write-downs (which brought in questions of availability of capital and fixing accountability, even in cases of genuine business failure) or convert debt to equity (which would need change of management control, whereas most managements were resistant), provision of liquidity (to keep the business going, but difficult to accede to unless one was assured that more good money was not being thrown after bad), coordination between all stakeholders to resolve the roadblocks of getting approvals and finding solutions to what caused the slowdown and time overruns in the first place.

In the absence of a bankruptcy law, we had been referring stressed accounts to the Board for Industrial and Financial Reconstruction, but the process yielded little result. A complete overhaul was necessary. There was also a corporate debt restructuring mechanism, but this had also been weakened over time, making the exercise ineffective.

Banks made several representations to the regulators about this, leading the RBI to notify three initiatives. The first was the flexible structuring of existing long-term project loans – popularly known as 5×25, which I have described earlier. The second was the strategic debt restructuring framework that allowed debt to equity conversion up to 30 per cent, but with the proviso that such equity be disposed off within eighteen months completely – thereby making the scheme impossible to implement. We could think of no entity that could exit with a gain in such a short span, especially when those who may be interested in buying would know about the compulsion to dispose so that prices would get driven down further. The last framework was called sustainable structuring of stressed assets, or S4A. This stipulated that loans could be restructured if 50 per cent of the debt could be found to be serviceable. There was no logic given for why the 50 per cent level was decided, but mostly large projects did not qualify for this, and hence it was a non-starter as well.

There were a number of other solutions suggested, such as nationalization of these assets, creation of a 'Bad Bank', and so on. Of course, the hesitation was natural and may even be called for as there is indeed a huge moral hazard here as well as lack of trust (and not always without cause). I feel that these were the two things and the lack of a bankruptcy law that did not allow something like Trobled Assets Relief Programme (TARP) of the USA to take place. The common refrain was that TARP represented 'privatization of profit and socialization of losses', though it was not mentioned that every single tax dollar used for TARP was paid back with interest and the effort kicked off the longest ever streak of expansion in the US economy.

There was also the consideration of fiscal prudence – and the path India chose to control fiscal deficit to the extent possible. No one can fault that. My only submission in this matter is that the more we delay, the more the erosion of asset value. Every day matters. Therefore, now that the banking system has made substantially higher provisions, the time for creating a separate 'Bad Bank' is being reconsidered (This book was written before the budget declaration of the ARC and AMC for stressed assets). Let me however mention that a lot of coordination with and between government departments will need to be mandated to remove roadblocks and ensure support for the turnaround of many of these incomplete projects. The sloughing off of bad loans into a separate entity will allow undivided attention for getting the bad assets resolved, and also enable banks to concentrate on other challenges in the fast-evolving technology and regulations space.

There is no doubt that the bankruptcy law is a game changer in the Indian landscape. But like any other law, it is evolving. Starting from increasing resources, improving infrastructure, ensuring equivalency of judgements across various forums and fast disposal of cases that get referred to superior courts, a lot of effort is being made to ensure that it becomes a stable and effective forum. It may be good to take forward the idea of separate forums for restructuring/bankruptcy cases and other issues under company law, such as mergers and acquisitions. It would reduce volumes as also make for more specialization and reduce delays, which could bring substantial benefits.

# 14

# The Banker to Every Indian

*'Poverty is the worst form of violence'* – *Mahatma Gandhi*

While stressed assets continued to take the centre stage, the need to respond to the other challenges facing the banking system and the broader economy could not be kept aside either. It was imperative to bring about an economic revival and put an end to the financial exclusion that had led to the stymieing of the hopes of millions for a better standard of living.

The government was cognizant of this, and this was driven home to us on 15 August 2014 when the prime minister declared the country's, and probably the world's, largest financial inclusion initiative – the Prime Minister's Jan Dhan Yojana (PMJDY) – from the ramparts of the Red Fort during his Independence Day speech. PMJDY is perhaps the most successful financial inclusion programme the world has ever seen in terms of numbers and impact. It has been one of the most important schemes of the present government to showcase their resolve to enable every citizen to participate in mainstream banking and improve their living standards.

The idea was that every household would have a bank account, with the most necessary and toughest obstacle of 'know your customer' (KYC) for opening an account being taken care of by the Aadhaar card (issued by the Unique Identification Authority of India on the basis of biometrics) and the communication channels created by the expansion of mobile networks. The intention here was that the accounts would be accessible through mobiles. This formed the JAM (Jan Dhan, Aadhaar, mobile) trinity, which brought about transformational changes in the structures of government-sponsored schemes. As a comprehensive financial inclusion programme, its six pillars were:

i. Universal access to banking facilities
ii. Bank account with overdraft facility and a RuPay debit card
iii. Financial literacy
iv. Creation of a credit-guarantee fund
v. Micro insurance
vi. Pension for the unorganized sector

All the above were attempted and delivered, except for the creation of a credit-guarantee fund, which is yet to be done.

What contributed to the PMJDY's success was the project mode in which it was executed. Not enough has been said about this. While the coordination and project oversight were undertaken by the Department of Financial Services (DFS) in the Ministry of Finance, the work on the ground was done mainly by the public sector banks, over and above their regular work. The entire project cost was borne by the banks.

All the earlier attempts at financial inclusion only addressed the supply side issue, that is, making available a bank or a bank agent within a reasonable distance to provide banking services. What was not addressed was the demand side of the issue, that is, the customer should see benefit from the bank account and other related services, and should be able to access it easily. PMJDY addressed these issues very well.

The entire country was divided into sub-service areas (SSAs), and distributed to the dominant bank in that area. The lead bank was the nodal agency to ensure that their area was fully covered. It was incumbent on the banks to survey the SSAs allotted to them and list out all the households without a bank account.

The next step was to set up customer service points (CSPs) in all SSAs so that all households had banking services within a radius of 5 kms. Some relaxations were permitted in difficult and hilly terrains. The banks were asked to ensure that CSPs stayed operational and delivered services. They were geotagged, and their locations were displayed on banks' websites for public notice. It was also our responsibility to ensure that the CSPs earned enough to continue operations. Services were free for the customers. The CSPs had to be paid by the banks on the basis of transactions. As the number of transactions were expected to be low in difficult areas, banks decided to pay fixed sums to these CSPs so that they did not discontinue their services. This was challenging, as some CSPs decided that no work was necessary as income was assured. Over time, non-performers had to be weeded out. The other challenge was to ensure connectivity – we had to put up VSATs at many places – and also train the CSP operator to use a desktop/laptop.

The CSPs were made interoperable. They were given micro ATMS for RuPay cards and were also onboarded on Aadhaar Enabled Payment Services (AEPS). This gave customers a wider choice. Moreover, the customer need not necessarily visit the CSP in their own village. They could avail of banking services anywhere.

Further, all customers were issued RuPay cards which offered an accident insurance cover of ₹1 lakh at no additional cost, as long as the card was swiped at least once a quarter. This was a big pull factor. Issuing RuPay cards to all customers did pose a huge challenge as the vendors did not have enough plastic and issuance facilities. Delivery of RuPay cards and PINs to customers was difficult, as many had no fixed address. It also increased our cost of opening the accounts which ended up around ₹260-plus per person. And this amount was borne by the banks. We had to arrange special camps near all CSPs to ensure that RuPay cards remained active. To enable this, all CSPs needed to be provided with micro ATMs. There were only two vendors globally who provide point-of-sales machines and their capacity was limited. Also, buying so many machines was an expensive proposition for the bank. But this infrastructure was extremely helpful both at the time of demonetization and the pandemic.

Because of the broad remit of PMJDY and the fact that many people did not have any idea of how to use the CSP services or swipe their cards, financial literacy was made an integral part of the project. All banks were expected to hold camps/events for disseminating financial know-how.

Customers were also offered two insurance covers at a nominal premium. The settlement of claims was made hassle-free. One was the Pradhan Mantri Suraksha Bima Yojana (PMSBY) – accident insurance cover of ₹2 lakh on an annual premium of ₹12 – and the other was the Pradhan Mantri Jeevan Jyoti Bima Yojana (PMJJBY) – life insurance cover of ₹2 lakh on an annual premium of ₹334. Both products were extremely successful.

A pension product, Atal Pension Yojana, was also launched with a contribution amount for drawing a monthly pension up to ₹5,000, being stated upfront.

There was close monitoring by the Department of Financial Services (DFS) of the Government which prompted everyone to rise to the occasion and open more than 300 million accounts in just about six months.

PMJDY was not the first attempt or programme to achieve financial inclusion, but what differentiated it from the earlier attempts was its comprehensiveness. It attempted to bring banking, investment, credit, insurance, financial literacy and easy access to the financially excluded.

As mentioned earlier, besides getting the data, DFS did a weekly monitoring of progress and MDs of most banks were required to attend this meeting. The person delivering this for SBI was Manju Agarwal – I had sanctioned her four months of leave previously when I was in the new business department (She went on to become DMD of digital, and substantially contributed to our efforts there). At the time of PMJDY she was a CGM heading rural banking. Courtesy her efficiency and performance, I never had to attend a single DFS meeting. At the end of the programme (the time for which had been curtailed from twelve to seven months), 98.3 per cent of families had been covered. SBI alone had opened 110 million accounts. We had also informally advised our functionaries that an attempt should be made to open the accounts for the senior women in the family. Approximately, 51 per cent of the accounts were opened for women. It is true that when all the PMJDY accounts were opened, 97 per cent had zero balance. However, as per the latest numbers given by SBI on its site, the number of financial inclusion accounts has swollen to 129 million with a balance of ₹330 billion ($4.52 billion) in a matter of six years!

The opening of these accounts enabled the government to target direct benefits transfer (DBT) to the population below poverty line (BPL) without leakage and duplication. For example, when the Centre decided that it would sell cooking gas (LPG) at market rates and credit the subsidy into bank accounts, the number of connections dropped from 150 to 130 million, proving that over 20 million commercial customers were posing as individuals and abusing the system. When this was taken a step further, and it was decided to link Aadhaar to the accounts in which the subsidy was being credited, the numbers further shrunk by another 10 million. The figures may not be strictly accurate as they are from memory. The savings from prevention of subsidy leakage was a tidy sum. But the bank did have to make investment to handle the LPG subsidy for all the subscribers. We had to upgrade our IT infrastructure so that we could handle more than 5 million transactions only on this account on a single day. This was undertaken because financial inclusion was an article of faith for us.

In order to actually assess the impact of the PMJDY and DBT, SBI's economic research department decided to undertake a study in two districts, where the bank had more accounts of women than men. The results were quite revealing. Expenses in these districts increased the most towards the purchase of medicines and tuition fees, and decreased in the amount spent on the purchase of intoxicants. We felt vindicated that we had lived up to the spirit of our bank – validating the faith that lawmakers had reposed in us while taking over the Imperial Bank in 1955.

## Demonetization

If PMJDY posed a very large challenge to the banking system, demonetization was no less.

On 8 November 2016 at 2.30 p.m., I received a call from the RBI deputy governor's office requesting I attend a meeting at 6.30 p.m. When I asked what the agenda was or whether I should come prepared to discuss any particular area, I was told to come without any preparation. That didn't seem to bode well, but by then I had schooled myself not to worry unnecessarily (easier said than done).

On arrival, I found a number of other bank CEOs already assembled and the rest trickled in soon after. None of us knew the agenda, but it was obvious something big was in the offing. Soon all the deputy governors other than R. Gandhi walked in. The conversation started with stressed assets as usual, and went on to other areas such as capital raising, technology, etc. At about 7.50 p.m., a number of other

RBI officials walked in and the TV was switched on. At 8 p.m. sharp, the prime minister came on and we heard about demonetization along with the rest of the nation. For a few minutes, there was stunned silence as we tried to digest what we were hearing. In about four hours, all the ₹1,000 and ₹500 notes – comprising 86 per cent by value of notes in circulation in an economy where 12 per cent was in cash – would no longer be legal tender! Banks would be closed for one day to receive the new notes in their branches, and would have to start exchanging the old notes for the new notes from the day after. Thirty-six hours! That's all we had to supply the new notes to our branches, work out the processes for the exchange, change the IT system so that cashiers get a new screen with additional columns for the new ₹2,000 and ₹500 notes and for accounting purposes. Imagine the logistics required merely for supplying the new notes, and for collecting and returning the old notes to RBI, the daily data that would be required, the customer education that would need to happen ... It was mind-boggling. It appeared that the new currency had already been supplied to the currency chests maintained by banks on behalf of RBI. But those in-charge of these chests had been instructed not to share this information with the banks, as a result of which we didn't even know how much stock of new notes we had and where it was available.

But there was an even bigger challenge looming. As the new notes were displayed to us by RBI officials, we realized that they were smaller and thinner in dimension, meaning that all ATMs would have to be recalibrated manually to dispense these notes. The recalibration would need the cash trays to be fitted with a small part – and of this part there was limited supply locally, and the rest would probably need to be imported. Till the recalibration was done, ATMs would be useless, increasing the crowds at the branches.

The biggest challenge would be, however, the logistics of getting the new notes out to the branches. Currency notes cannot be stuffed into pockets and taken across to branches or ATMs. The supply of notes required concurrence of the police, and could be moved only if they cleared routes for us and there was sufficient security accompanying us. To get it done in a single day was one of the biggest logistical operation the banking industry had ever undertaken until then, and it was many times more onerous for us in SBI, given that we had over 24,000 branches as well as other banks and post offices linked to us. The cash distribution on the first day ended on a tragic note. One of our vehicles returning from supplying notes to distant branches overturned in the wee hours of 10 November on the road between Kanpur and Lucknow, and all eight members travelling in the vehicle were instantly killed. I console myself that an accident can happen anywhere and not necessarily for a particular reason, but it added to my sombre frame of mind.

As soon as the meeting at RBI ended at 9.15 p.m., all the CEOs rushed out. We had no time to talk to each other – all were busy on their mobiles, calling up their teams to assemble at once. I called my team over to my place as the senior executives lived in a building close to my residence. We started by working out first how we could communicate what we needed done right down to the grassroots. WhatsApp groups were created by all of us covering our next two tiers, such that a message that originated at the leadership level could be cascaded down to the frontline within half an hour.

People in charge of currency supply were asked to work through the night to determine the amounts that would need to be supplied to branches connected to them, based on the size and type of branch. Emphasis was on retail because it was expected that corporates could manage payments through cheques or digital channels.

The processes of obtaining permission from the local police for undertaking the remittance of new notes, recording of currency exchanged, details of the persons presenting the cash, segregated storage, changes required in the IT applications and the cashier's screens were noted and conveyed. It was decided that Rajnish Kumar,

MD of NBG, would start holding video conferences at 6 a.m. to pass on the instructions. We ended the meeting at around 2 a.m. with the list of actions completed. Teams, however, worked through the night to flesh out the action points required to be conveyed to our various regional managements, so that they could not only begin the process of obtaining the new notes but also make all necessary arrangements for the pandemonium that would inevitably ensue when we opened for business the next day.

The next sixty days tested our skills for negotiating the unknown and uncertain in ways that we had never imagined. During this period, as many as seventy-two patches were applied to our IT systems (remember that it was a real-time online system) to take care of the changing requirements stipulated by the government and regulators. Changes to processes were made on the go and disseminated through the internal communication platforms on a daily basis, with intimations being sent through the WhatsApp groups. Branches forgot all about the 4 p.m. closing time. The enormous queues outside had them working till late at night, when they had to perforce close in order to do end-of-day operations. Within three days, we understood the number of customers each staff could handle per day. Based on that, tokens were issued for the next day when the number of people in the queue exceeded the number that we could handle within the day. As a result, we only asked people who could be served to wait and the rest were issued tokens for subsequent days, solving, to some extent, the horrific sight of queues stretching on for kilometres and customers braving the elements – it was winter in some parts of India, and scorching hot in some, while it poured with rain in yet others – for hours together.

The ATMs started getting recalibrated and pushed into service. But they ran dry within an hour, and keeping them supplied was a challenge. The ATM at the Delhi airport created a record when it had to be refilled nineteen times in the course of a single day. When I visited Delhi in early December, I was proud to note that out of the eleven banks' ATMs at the airport, ours was the only one dispensing cash that day.

The response from the customers was overwhelming. After the initial chaos, and barring scattered incidents, for the first time in my career, I received more complimentary letters than complaints. In various places, we got reports of the customers coming with food for our staffers as those serving at the counters couldn't even find time to eat. A chartered accountant in Chennai, who came to deposit cash into his account, was so moved by what he saw that he volunteered to work the queues and make sure all had their forms properly filled out, so that minimum time was taken at the counter. From the next day, he sent in his wife and daughter to work the queues, and they continued to return every day till things stabilized. An old lady living alone in Bengaluru bought a bunch of rosebuds and distributed them to the staff of her branch. Someone took a video clip of the distribution and forwarded it to me. It made my day.

From day one, I had started sending a WhatsApp message each night that got communicated down the line to every single employee. In the messages, I thanked our staff, and exhorted them time and again to remain polite and calm. I knew that there would be impatient or even rude customers. I reminded our staff that much of the anger stemmed from fear or a sense of helplessness, and the customers were not against us personally. But for them, we were the face of the authorities, and so it was up to us to reassure them that no value was lost and they would get an equivalent amount of notes soon.

There was no dearth of attempts to circumvent the rules, though. We had reports of truckloads of people being brought in to metro branches from the suburbs. Often, they would be family members of employees of various small units. Each person was told to bring all varieties of identification (Aadhaar card, voter's ID card, PAN card) and line up using a different ID each time, as each person could exchange only ₹4,000 at a time for new notes. To prevent this abuse, the government suggested we ink the fingers of people with indelible ink. The Election Commission immediately raised an objection saying that some states had elections forthcoming, to which it was suggested that we ink the forefinger of the right hand and not the left, as is done at the time of elections. But then where would we get the ink supplies? The Mysore Security Press that manufactures the ink threw up its hands, saying it didn't have enough stock. So we turned to online platforms, and found them there. The problem of delivering this ink to the branches also got solved as each branch ordered its own.

There were many more such challenges. People who had marriages scheduled were in real trouble for ₹4,000 would not be enough even for tips. The government relented and announced that per marriage ₹2,00,000 would be released. Our bank decided we would release the sum if a wedding card was produced as evidence. Some other banks refused outright. They asked how it could be ensured that a wedding was going to take place – and it wasn't a case of someone fraudulently getting a card printed to get the cash – or how it was to be ensured that both the bride and groom didn't avail of the facility from different banks?

Along with such problems, which were of a social nature, some situations made me lose sleep at night. We kept pleading for more supplies as stocks of the new currency ran low, fearing that the crowds could run amok at our branches if we ran out. Distribution was uneven. In certain hard-to-reach places, military helicopters were pressed into service. We knew that the mint was being run in three shifts around the clock. It was rumoured that the army was helping by providing its personnel to facilitate continuous printing. But the supply chain, despite working at its optimal best, still took time. There were remote villages where inhabitants thought that they were being scammed as the new notes were so colourful and small that they didn't look like real currency. They had no TV and had not heard the PM's speech. We had to procure video equipment and a recording of the PM's speech and play it for them to convince them. There were some hair-raising incidents as well. One afternoon, when the supply of currency was running low, a CGM called in utter panic to say that the police force guarding one of our branches in a border district was being withdrawn. There were huge, agitated crowds outside the branch as it had run out of new notes. The branch manager was trying to pacify the crowds on the one hand, and pleading with the forces to stay on the other. They, however, cited their orders and were adamant on leaving. The CGM had been desperately trying to contact the state authorities, but was not able to. He felt the situation may slip out of control. There was real panic in his voice. I knew the fallout should there be rioting in any place – it was my worst fears coming true.

I quickly called the secretary DFS, only to be told that she was deposing before a Parliamentary Standing Committee and I knew nobody could disturb her there. I had no option but to go higher, because I knew how rapidly the situation could escalate. I called the highest authorities accessible, who, to my relief, assured me that they would initiate necessary steps immediately. As soon as I got off the phone, the CGM called me to tell me that the staff had barricaded themselves inside the branch and the situation was getting worse by the minute – the crowd had started pelting stones at the branch. I reassured him that I had been promised help and it was forthcoming. Half an hour later, the CGM called to tell me that the police had returned and the state authorities had got back in touch with him. They said that there was some miscommunication, and they would help maintain law and order. By 8 p.m., the branch staff had been rescued and escorted home. For those sixty days, I prayed every morning as soon as I got up that we would go through the day smoothly and thanked God every night that there had been no major incidents.

I started appearing regularly on TV to reassure people, to convey that there was no need to panic. There might be delays, but we would fulfil the needs of the people. I sought cooperation from the public, acknowledged their understanding and help, and reassured them that all possible steps would be taken to speed up the currency exchange. Whenever any abuses came to light, the strictest of actions were taken. A few innocents amongst the bank staff got unnecessarily entangled as well. I remember a case where a corporate was allowed their weekly cash withdrawal as soon as we reopened on Thursday, because they were a good customer and this was their routine for the past many years. But we had no way other than to suspend the person who authorized it.

I had been reassuring the people that the entire programme would get done by February. We ended up exceeding that time frame, but not by much. By mid-March, the crowds thinned, more ATMs became functional and we began returning to our regular banking activities.

## A Forty-Year-Old Expectation Gets Realized

I had heard sometime soon after entering the bank that the merger of SBI with its seven associate banks was on the agenda – it was only a question of when. It took forty years for the expectation of our people to be completed. I had asked the finance ministry about it immediately after I took over as chairman, but found no traction there. The matter was raised again by the ministry sometime in 2015, and I expressed my interest in it. But there was a condition attached: the centre would allow it only if I merged *all* the banks simultaneously. All the banks put together would form an entity bigger than the second-largest bank after SBI. Not only that, each one had its own culture, challenges and ways of doing things. Putting them together was definitely my plan – but to do it simultaneously? It gave me pause. I tried to assess the pros and cons – why had I asked for the merger in the first place? Because it would take away the duplication: of licenses, roll-outs, departments, branches, etc. Also, we undercut each other in various markets. But more than anything else, I felt that there was no way of ensuring governance levels with merely chairing the board and having a representative thereon. There was a clear conflict with the parent bank and we needed to clean up the structure.

I called in the top team and laid out the proposition. I remembered Kannan's advice and remained mum as others weighed in. The sentiment seemed to be positive for a merger, in spite of the difficulties. At that point, I told them that I was in favour of the merger and the die was cast.

We appointed Neeraj Vyas – a DMD who had worked with me earlier and who I knew would be able to do the job – to head the task force. He partnered with Dinesh Khara who was the MD looking after the associate banks department. Both had the right mix: methodical minds coupled with the tenacity and willingness to tackle issues head on. We created seven teams under Neeraj, each looking at different areas like IT, asset book, policy and procedures, accounting and balance sheet, communication, HR and operations and branch network. Every team would have members from each bank.

One would imagine that in the area of IT, our job would be easy. Not so at all. Though we were running the same core banking system, different versions and other peripheral systems existed. Something like 272 such differences were identified. Prior to the merger the IT department ran sixty-plus mock runs before we undertook the actual job. There were numerous migrations from the peripheral systems that had to be done. In the State Bank of Bikaner and Jaipur, we found blocks of accounts that had the same number as the ones in the parent bank. Solutions to work around such issues were put in place. Customers' cheque books had to be replaced, but more than that they needed to be reassured that their friendly neighbourhood bank would remain their friendly neighbourhood bank, only better. There were a million such details that had to be ironed out.

The way we decided to do this was to merge the balance sheets of all the banks on a particular date. We would then wait for three weeks for the auditors to certify the merged balance sheet. Thereafter, every weekend, we would take up the merger of the databases one bank at a time, completing the job in six weeks.

The government gave its final approval on 17 May 2016. My retirement was due on 6 October 2016. However, in view of the merger, the centre granted me a one-year extension; the third time such an extension had been granted after being given earlier to Mr V T Dehejia and Mr R K Talwar. We were targeting the beginning of the calendar year, but all our plans changed in a trice when demonetization was announced. We ultimately put it through on 1 April 2017, giving me just six months to stabilize the initiative before I retired.

In any merger, HR is always a major issue. This stems probably from a 'victor–vanquished' kind of mindset, though it is nothing of the kind. Technology made it possible for me to address letters to each employee of the six banks. We undertook a lot of internal and external communication as well. I also took this opportunity to rebrand the parent entity. We didn't want to deviate too far from the existing logo, which had such wide and deep recognition. We merely changed the colour from cyan blue to a brighter purple-blue and shortened the name to SBI. It was a brand refresh that I hoped would be liked by the youth – many of whom had now become our customers, courtesy our digital initiatives and social media presence.

I continued the pursuit of bringing the merged banks' staff on board. I appointed a DMD as mentor for each bank, and they conducted several town halls to reassure the employees. A portal was built for them to address their concerns, and there were times when we answered more than 200 queries a day. Mostly, the concerns pertained to transfers, pay fitments, allowances that SBI didn't have and the like. The majority of the staff were in favour of the merger, though some feared the loss of their heritage or traditions. We agreed to preserve as much of the heritage as possible, and reassured them that whatever we did, it would be done in a transparent manner. There were tricky issues, wherein smaller banks had undertaken rapid promotions – such that persons joining in the same year in the parent bank were at lower levels of seniority. These issues had to be carefully handled.

There were concerns on the asset-quality front. When we applied our yardstick, the NPA numbers mounted. But I preferred to have things out in the open. Unless we knew the extent of the disease, we couldn't nurse ourselves back to health.

Ultimately, the day dawned. The IT department had put in place dynamic real-time dashboards that monitored the progress of the merger. I went to our IT centre for the final consolidation and when the last file had merged, we all got up and applauded ourselves, as a long, unfinished agenda had finally reached its logical conclusion. I do not believe that such an exercise of merging six banks with one entity in one go has ever been attempted and completed so smoothly anywhere else in the world. Kudos to my team and especially the IT department, led so ably by Mrutyunjay Mahapatra, for pulling it off. It somehow underlined again the strength of our bank in overcoming obstacles that appear insurmountable.

My two best accolades were from two different sources. The then secretary DFS called to congratulate us. Tongue in cheek, she added that we probably should have created a little more of a ruckus and some more problems and unrest, as now such a large merger was being viewed as a very easy job. The other person who sent a letter to congratulate us was Prof. S. Sadagopan, director of IIIT Bangalore. He had been a long-time customer of State Bank of Mysore. On 2 April, with some trepidation, he had accessed his internet banking account. He was very impressed that it worked seamlessly and he could access his accounts as easily as before, with the same ID and password. The only difference he noted was the name and logo of the bank.

With that, another of our notable ventures passed into history.

# 15

# Employees First: Managing a Diverse Workforce

My stint as CDO had given me an understanding of how little attention we had paid to the pains and developmental needs of our own people. It was the only area in the bank where no consultant had ever done a transformation project, and neither had the bank tried it on its own. The first set of changes were introduced in the early part of the decade, by the then CDO Bharti Rao, a long-time mentor of mine. I was determined to give this area it's due importance, and prioritize the hopes and aspirations of SBI employees.

The two major pains of our people and what led to them getting demotivated was the promotion process and the lack of direction for career development. For instance, 85 per cent of our employees scored above ninety in the annual performance appraisal reports. One had to be off-the-charts terrible in order to get any lesser. Only 10 per cent of the roles had budgetary targets.

A branch manager would be the only person in a branch with a budgetary target. There was no formal appraisal of our clerical employees, nor any targets or budgets. What can be expected of an organization when two thirds of their employees have no targets and assessments? Target setting was arithmetical and cascaded from the top with no relationship to potential or performance. If Bengaluru had to increase its loan portfolio by 25 per cent, so did Berhampur Ganjam. If Nagpur had to raise its deposits by 30 per cent, so did Nainital. As everyone got similar marks, and performance based on data was available only for 10 per cent of the staff, promotions depended on a ten-minute interview if you were lucky, or corridor talk if you were not.

There was no laid-out career development plan. One trusted God and one's own reputation to get into the right positions. The manual process of transferring people took a huge amount of time and we were still moving around 40,000 people a year causing enormous personal hardship and expenses.

Were we getting the right people for the right roles? There were a number of restrictions on compensation, incentives/disincentives and recruitment. We were required to do an all-India search for every single role – no campus recruitments into permanent positions were allowed, not even from the National Institute of Bank Management set up with RBI and public sector bank equity. This was despite the fact our private-sector competitors recruited from there!

And another, more essential question – were we a learning organization?

As one of the first steps, we decided to create self-learning modules on our learning platform for every role – be it for someone opening accounts or for someone operating a locker. As soon as a person got posted, an email would go to them asking them to complete the modules. Certain modules on anti-money laundering and sexual harassment were made mandatory for all. To ensure compliance, I suggested that five marks in the annual appraisal be allocated to completing the recommended modules. There was immediate pushback from the unions, but once I could convince them that employees would benefit hugely by making fewer mistakes – thus protecting them from probable disciplinary actions – they decided to support the change.

The next thing I did was to go back to my notes as CDO and complete the actions I couldn't take then. The communication platform was relaunched and activated, making way for channels of communication that had never existed earlier.

But the biggest initiative that we launched was Project Saksham, one of the world's largest data-driven and tech-enabled career development system (CDS). This was delivered by the then CDO Ashwini Mehra and, after his retirement, by Prashant Kumar (currently the CEO of Yes Bank). As a first step, we redesigned employees' key result areas (KRAs) across all roles (more than 900-plus, from a Hindi officer to a pharmacist). I wanted to ensure the autofilling of data with no subjectivity in the assessment of measurable KRAs, and so a unified database was created by drawing from 50-plus data systems. We managed to create measurable, or budgetary, targets for 90 per cent of the roles. In order to ensure that the budgets and targets were reasonable and realistic, the budgetary process was entirely amended to roll up from micro-market studies from the bottom, rather than a uniform top-down method. To prevent comparing apples and oranges (Bengaluru with Berhampur Ganjam), a cohort-based grading system was created. The cohorts comprised employees in similar roles, tenures/geographies.

Once again, there was resistance from the unions and associations because they too understood that the creation of such documentation and data would enable us to put in place a proper back-up on performance of individuals. This would give the management the ability to not only incentivize but also disincentivize – use the carrot-and-stick method, so to say – neither of which we had objective data to base our actions on at that point.

The CDS system enabled continuous evaluation with monthly scores on each KRA. We could create a transparent and meaningful differentiation of 65 per cent employees in the top two grades, and link them accordingly to promotion eligibility and incentives. It also enabled the initiation of a feedback culture, which is so important for personal learning and growth.

A data-driven manpower assessment system based on over eighty parameters was created to determine manpower requirements by scale and cadre for every branch. Something that had long been done intuitively at last got replaced.

Similarly, a digital tool called PROSPER was created for automatic generation of vacancies and postings. Forecasting these would enable us to seek options from our employee base to help them to plan ahead and take away the uncertainties of postings. For the first time, a succession-planning tool was also launched for critical senior positions.

SBI had traditionally only had generalists. But the need now was also for specialists, given the fast-changing environment. Therefore, unique career paths were defined for key job families, such as credit, risk, treasury, IT, to balance the need for specialization and still provide an all-round experience to those who we rated as 'stars'.

With respect to recruitment, we tried the new tagline 'grow every day' to focus on the growth prospects within the bank. Social media platforms were used to disseminate knowledge about careers in SBI. We also created campaigns for college campuses, where we started recruiting for specialized roles on contract. A new state-of-the-art career portal highlighting the journeys of top bank officials was launched. It explained the career paths and the bank's HR policies in a visual, employee-friendly manner. To take care of the requirements of our young joinees, a Facebook page was launched to facilitate their interactions.

During my time as chairman, both the bank and I received numerous awards, but the two that I cherished the most were in the area of human resources. The first was conferred on us by the president of India for integrating the maximum number of employees with disabilities into full-time, productive roles. The second pertained to SBI being adjudged one of the 'Top Three Best Places to Work in India' based on 15 million reviews for overall employee experience by a leading global job site.

It reaffirmed my belief that I had, with the help of my team, created a culture of change within the personnel department that made them perceive our employees as their customers, and who therefore needed to be looked after in the same way that we expected our frontline staffers to look after our consumers.

**But That's Not All We Did**

SBI's international banking group (IBG) was an important vertical. When I took over, though the bank was present in thirty-six countries, 80 per cent of the assets held were India-related. As the corporate sector in India came under stress, IBG numbers soon showed signs of pressure. Another challenge we faced in this area was that there were ongoing regulatory issues in fourteen of the countries in which the bank was operating.

As a first step, the DMD of IBG, Siddharth Sengupta, and I decided that we would reduce India-based assets to 60 per cent as a risk mitigation measure. The team far outdid my expectations, and by the time I retired, India-based assets had reduced to 40 per cent of the portfolio. Not only that, all of the regulatory fires had also been put out.

The way we worked the transformation was by quickly grasping the complexities of the issues, and enabling changes in the way we operated in foreign locations. We focused on hiring local talent for the areas of compliance, risk, credit and marketing. We concentrated on enhancing governance standards and improving transparency, transforming even our most chronically troubled subsidiary – SBI

California – into a profitable, well-run bank in one of the most challenging regulatory environments.

In 2013, all the US offices were facing regulatory action. SBI New York and Chicago had accepted a memorandum of understanding on corrective actions required, and SBI California had a 'troubled' status. We selected Padmaja Chunduru, CGM at the time (who had just retired as MD of Indian Bank), as the country head, US, in 2014. She had worked in Los Angeles and possessed a deep understanding of the US regulatory environment, which stood her in good stead in tackling all the regulatory challenges we faced.

The SBI New York and Chicago branches were staring at a possible payment of substantial Federal Deposit Insurance Corporation (FDIC) premium for certain transactions undertaken, which we believed were permitted. With continuous communication with the regulators, the possibility of the premium payment was rolled back.

It was SBI California that posed the biggest challenge – regulators felt that we needed to improve everything: the board, the management, asset quality, internal controls. We responded by thoroughly overhauling the board and bringing in new directors in the place of those who had been serving for over fifteen years, causing much ire and heartburn. As governance was the biggest issue, we brought in a new CEO by transferring Ram Mohan Rao (currently heading SBI Cards), who had proved his mettle in running the Chicago branch, and by taking a few exceptions from the board and the Government of India. The change of board members and CEO, under the guidance of Padmaja who frequently met the regulators to update them and seek their guidance, was the magic bullet that quickly sorted out issues, resulting in the bank moving to a 'well run' status in two years. SBI California has been making profits ever since, and even repatriated profits to the parent holding – a first in its history of twenty-two years.

On my visits to various countries, I tried my best to act as a brand ambassador for India, and all the CEOs of our foreign operations were expected to do the same. I recall a meeting with the FDIC chairman in 2015, when I explained how India and SBI achieved financial inclusion. He shared with me how the poor in certain parts of the US were still excluded from mainstream banking. I believe that our story must have struck a chord, since FDIC called us shortly thereafter and collected a lot of information from us on the PMJDY initiative.

On one of my US trips in 2016, I met the erstwhile treasury secretary, Timothy Geithner, who had overseen TARP. We hit it off so well that when we invited him to address the SBI Economic Conclave in Mumbai that year, he immediately accepted.

I continued to build relationships through continuous communication in as transparent and candid a manner as possible with investors, merchant bankers and other key stakeholders. I addressed all sensitive issues directly, but would steer the conversation towards the strengths of SBI – diversification of portfolio, income streams, the strength of our retail franchise, digital initiatives, among others. I felt it best to not stand on ceremony and visited the offices of many investment firms in the US, such as Morgan Stanley, Neuberger Berman, Charles Schwab, JP Morgan and Citigroup, to pitch for my bank and country.

Many times, it was suggested that we hold the meetings at our own offices in New York, Singapore or Hong Kong, and invite the analysts there. But I felt that if we went to their offices, the main partners would come for the meetings as well, whereas if we have it in our office, they would only send their junior analysts. I wanted to talk to those who made the decisions because I knew that investors put a huge discount on our value on account of our public sector ownership, and I needed to change that perception to ensure we were correctly valued.

This lesson was learnt from a bitter experience. As CFO, I had realized that the bank needed to raise capital at the earliest. The outgoing chairman was of the view that it was an agenda for the incoming person. So, we decided to launch a qualified institutional placement of ₹9,600 crores. It took about three months to get the approval from the government. We appointed the best merchant bankers, and though I sat in on the steering committee meetings, I delegated the work to the CFO and some of our senior executives. Work began immediately and we started visiting investors, our first stop was Life Insurance Corporation.

The book building went well. We had more or less decided to launch it by the end of January 2014 when global trends suddenly started turning adverse. On 24 January, the Argentinian peso devalued by 12.5 per cent. On 28 January, Central Bank of Turkey raised its overnight lending rate by a massive 450 basis points. I was deeply concerned and repeatedly consulted the merchant bankers, but they kept reassuring me that there was no need to worry. A Monetary Policy Committee meeting of the RBI was scheduled on 29 January. I had more or less decided that if the RBI raised rates, we would call off the issue. My apprehensions did come true, and the RBI did raise the rates by 25 basis points. We had called the merchant bankers for a final meeting. I went in with my mind made up to call it off, but at the meeting the lead banker repeated that there should be no cause for concern, and with the amount committed by various investors, getting to our number would not be difficult.

We launched the issue the next day, but by 2 p.m. it was apparent that we would fall far short. The international book had melted away, and even domestic investors had turned wary. I decided that I couldn't depend on anyone any more. I started working the phones, and called any and every one of the qualified domestic investors (to whom we had made our pitches) to persuade them that the investment at the suggested price band would be absolutely worth making. I was to fly to Delhi in the night. I pushed the flight back to the last one that day so that I could continue calling. It was probably one of the budget airlines which I was to travel by. As they didn't have lounge facilities, I found myself standing beside the charging dock in the waiting area with my phone plugged in, continuing to call till the very last minute. We decided to aim for ₹8,000 crores as the rest could be allocated as an employee share purchase offer.

Many have asked me what was the worst day during my term as chairman. This was definitely one of them. We did manage to raise the targeted sum, saving ourselves the blushes. We also managed to give good returns to our investors within a short period of time. But the lesson had been well learnt. We had to convey the value proposition of the bank and take the calls ourselves. Merchant bankers can be relied on in good times as they have the experience, but in bad times it would inevitably be our responsibility to make the decisions. There was no getting away from that. I created an investor relations department, and market-recruited an executive to head it. When the CFO position fell vacant, I brought in one of the DMDs, Anshula Kant. She was an economics major (and a batchmate of Subir Gokarn – the erstwhile deputy governor of the RBI). She was reluctant initially to fill the role, but later, as we took up several initiatives, it became a great partnership. Currently, she is the CFO of the World Bank. In a way, my choice has been vindicated by the World Bank itself.

One of the other bad days was when I got called out of a morning meeting and was handed a note sent in by the chief vigilance officer (CVO). What he told me made my hair stand on end. It appeared that one of the enforcement agencies had just raided a senior functionary's room and had found two unopened gift boxes inside. The executive had also been in the meeting. I recalled him having left the meeting, probably on the summons of the enforcement agency. On opening the packages, two expensive watches were found. The executive claimed that he had a visitor just before he left the room for the meeting and had no knowledge of the gifts found inside.

It is well-nigh impossible to determine the truth in such matters, and nor do I want to opine on it as the matter is still sub judice. But what it did do was bring to front and centre certain issues that needed to be resolved at once. One was receiving visitors in our rooms. I decided we would stop that practice immediately. I had a room that could be used as a meeting room, but what about the other executives?

The eleventh floor of our building was the only one accessible by both banks of elevators. One lot was meant for floors one to eleven, and the other from eleven to nineteen. But since the inception – that is, for the last forty years – that floor had housed the union and association offices, along with the staff canteen. A few years ago, nobody would have even thought of taking on these bodies to get them to vacate space. But it was the most accessible floor. So if we had to create a floor for meeting rooms, it had to be the eleventh floor.

I conferred with the bank's estate people and came up with a strategy to make this happen. They located possible areas where we could ask the union and association people to shift. We decided on the first floor, which allowed easy access. It was then a question of explaining the necessity from the point of view of the safety of our employees as well as the security of our customer data.

We approached the unions and association, and, to their immense credit and that of the real estate team led by Brahma Rao, GM, and R.L. Singh, chief engineer, we were able to convince them to move to the first floor. In fact, they agreed to move to the basement temporarily, while the floors got done up. Soon, the eleventh floor housed a set of meeting rooms and we made it mandatory for all visitors to be met there.

We further barred all packages, other than papers, from entering our office buildings. We also decreed that these packages could not be sent to official residences without permission. Even flower bouquets were banned, including any Diwali, New Year's hampers or anything that represented gifts. It actually proved to be a great morale booster for our people, except that a few items ordered by Sukrita and Pritimoy from e-shopping websites and required to be delivered at my residence also got returned in the bargain – earning me a few scoldings from my daughter.

To take forward the agenda of creating an atmosphere of integrity and trust, I had been toying with the idea of creating a position for a chief ethics officer. The role of the person would be to create an explicit environment of integrity. We already had a code of conduct in place, but employees looked at it only at the time of joining. I wanted continuous discussions and trainings in this area because there were many situations where one could be confused as to how to react or behave. Our disciplinary action cells were also very dispersed and didn't have centralized control to ensure that similar penalties were imposed for similar offences. Though there is no such position in any other PSU, I put this forward to the board and, understanding the aim of the initiative, they agreed.

Of course, there were questions as to why we needed this when we had disciplinary and vigilance cells. My contention was simple – those cells did post-mortem work. I wanted something that would work in the ante-mortem stage itself. The experiment was a great success in raising awareness and helping us live up to our values. Another initiative that I began with Atul Kumar, chief ethics officer, was creating courses on ethics sensitization for SME borrowers. Most customers who attended these sessions lauded the effort. I don't know whether this has been attempted elsewhere or whether this is still something being done only by SBI. I felt, however, that across society a clear articulation of values was necessary and if we could help our borrowers by providing guidance on this, and maybe even share the materials for them to disseminate within their organizations, it would have a good impact.

At that time, I also felt that we needed to rearticulate our vision, mission and values (VMVs). These had been drafted almost ten years earlier, and needed to be brought in line with the modern and progressive institution we had evolved into. The MD of risk and compliance suggested engaging one of the big four, but Atul volunteered to lead the effort instead. I too wanted it to come from within, so he was given the responsibility. I launched an in-house initiative on our communication platform with a blog post inviting our employees to reflect on the present and share their dreams, hopes and aspirations for the future, so that we could incorporate these into our new VMVs. Nearly 30,000 employees participated with enthusiasm, and I was glad to see the kind of organizational energy it unleashed. A high-powered committee sifted the feedback and came back with five sets of new VMVs. By the time this got ready, my successor, Rajnish Kumar, had already been named. So I decided that it would be right to leave the completion of this exercise to him, which he did and the outcome of that initiative is rooted in and being lived by the organization.

## Giving Back

SBI has always tried to live by certain values – giving back is one of those. As far back as I can remember, SBI used 1 per cent of its profits to engage with the community. However, the efforts were very fragmented. We could not measure impact nor ensure sustainability. For example, on Teacher's Day, it was decided that each branch should donate ten fans to a school in its locality. In its own way, it was a laudable initiative. It served a felt need, was pan-India based and helped connect with the local community. But we couldn't measure impact, ensure the quality of fans delivered or that they didn't get misused elsewhere after a while.

Thus, I wanted to set up a foundation so that we could put the bank's welfare initiatives in the hands of professionals, collaborate with other organizations on bigger projects, and make them impactful and sustainable. After three refusals by the RBI because there was no provision for such a foundation in the Banking Regulation Act of 1949, we finally received permission and started work through the foundation. There were many initiatives of note that we undertook, but let me talk of one that was close to my heart called 'Youth for India' (YFI). This had been started by Mr Bhatt, but had been discontinued after his retirement.

It was such a worthwhile initiative that I was keen to restart it. It was a gap-year programme developed by Geeta Verghese, one of our retired executives. It provided a framework through which young people could join YFI for thirteen months and undertake a project in a rural area outside of their home state. This gave them the opportunity to learn a new language, new customs and a new culture. The project was done in collaboration with one of the seven NGOs that we were partnering with. Some of the projects yielded fantastic results. Not only did we have applicants from IITs and IIMs, but also from the legal profession and medical doctors. One project, for instance, worked on creating no-emission, low-cost mobile toilets for use in the salt pans for workers who were otherwise not allowed to drink water during work hours for fear of contaminating the salt, leading to severe health issues on account of dehydration. I have myself seen the abject poverty of some of these people. They work barefoot, standing in the salt water for ten hours a day, such that it is said that after their demise when their bodies are cremated, their feet are so desiccated that they don't burn.

An IIT Chennai alumnus created a set of tools for tribal bamboo workers who had been using almost stone-age tools, thus improving the quality of their produce. Another project involved empowering an all-women panchayat. Whereas earlier everything was done by the panchayat 'pati' (husband), by the end of the project the women were sourcing money under several government schemes for which their village was eligible – and about which their husbands had no knowledge of – thus bringing a lot of assistance to the poor and the needy. It also helped establish the authority of the women as the actual panchayat leaders. The YFI programme created leaders out of its fellows. Many of them continued their projects even after the stipulated thirteen months, at their own cost.

At one graduation ceremony, many of the fellows opined that the programme should have been for two years. When I asked them whether they would have been able to continue during the first three months had they known this was a two-year programme, they agreed that they may not have stayed on. Every year we chose around a hundred fellows, but only about sixty-five completed it. It was not easy for them – coming from air-conditioned homes to mosquito-infested, dusty villages that didn't have electricity, running water and proper toilets. But they all agreed that the warmth of the villagers made up for all of the physical discomforts. Most learnt new languages, some even learnt the local songs and dances, but all came back with a renewed sense of purpose, commitment and confidence. The last batch, I am told, has received 32,000 applications for the hundred fellowships, attesting to the popularity of the programme.

During the two years before the foundation came into existence, we continued supporting various NGOs, and I must mention one such initiative that showed both the best and the basest of human nature. I had gone for a visit to Shirdi, and expressed my request to the circle that I would like to meet some of our local employees and conduct CSR activities during my visit.

One of the NGOs that SBI had chosen wanted to make a small presentation. They said they were a young couple practising homeopathy. On their way back one night from their chambers, they noticed a woman scrounging in a garbage bin and stuffing what she could into her mouth. She appeared to have mental health problems, but they couldn't bear to see her eating garbage. So they went home, packed some food, returned and fed her. For the next few days, they continued to feed the woman twice a day. One of their fathers, who lived with the couple, noticed this and asked them about it. On hearing of the plight of the woman, he offered them a piece of fallow land he owned and the money to put up a shed to house her. That was the beginning. They began rescuing destitute women off the streets. Most of them were pregnant, having been raped as they were easy to prey on. But the image that stuck in my mind was the picture of one such pregnant woman with one ear lopped off and a huge open wound in its place. I could not imagine the mentality of the person or persons who could have displayed such cruelty.

Thanks to the care and attention showered on them, many women were able to recover. They said that there was a woman who was a nuclear physicist whose brother had cheated her out of her share of their paternal property, and then taken her to an unknown town and abandoned her with no money at a bus stop. She never slept, awaiting her brother's return. When she was nursed back to health, she refused to return and stayed back to run the centre. They were providing shelter to around 114 women, and seventy children all born at the centre. They had requested us for an industrial-capacity washing machine and that was what we were providing them. I was so shaken after seeing their presentation and the pictures of the women that I requested our employees to keep supporting them, one way or the other. Coincidentally, on my next visit to Davos, at one of the networking events, I heard a group from Switzerland discussing the fate of such women and the studies they were doing across countries. I joined the group and offered to connect them to this NGO. The last I heard was that the young homeopath couple had been invited to Switzerland to present their case. There were many such heroes I came across. Every time I could do a little to help, I was filled with gratitude that my position enabled me to meet such wonderful people. They reminded me of the inherent nobility and goodness in human beings, and how much they were contributing to make this world a kinder and saner place.

One other area in which we made good progress was putting sustainability on the agenda of the bank. During Chairman Bhatt's time, the bank had bought a few windmills in order to reduce its carbon footprint. But the regulator was refusing to give permission for more as the Banking Regulation Act didn't allow us to be a generator of electricity! We concentrated on creating awareness across the bank and initiated a sustainability report as per GRI standards, along with our annual reports. We were the first public sector bank, and probably the first PSU in the country, to do so.

## Aesthetics: The Softer Side of Things

The brand of SBI was due for a refresh. One way to do this was to establish thought leadership, and I turned to the economics research department for that. My predecessor Pratip Chaudhuri had recruited an excellent economist, Dr Soumya Ghosh, just before he left office. Luckily for me, Dr Ghosh's ideas and the initiatives I wanted undertaken resonated with one another. The research department started authoring several publications – a daily report, reports on countries and industries as well as on notable happenings. These reports steadily gained popularity as the quality of research was excellent and Dr Ghosh's calls were quite accurate.

Officials from Moody's, during one of our interactions, told me that they invariably read his reports. He also started publishing articles in newspapers, and was frequently on TV whenever there were any developments that needed an economist's point of view. It was also his idea to start an annual Economics and Banking Conclave, to which I enthusiastically agreed. These became signature events, and of the three that were held during my tenure, the finance minister addressed all of them, the RBI governor delivered the keynote address in one and did a fireside chat with me in the next, and several important ministers including those for roads, power, commerce and railways were gracious enough to address sessions as well. Nobel laureate Paul Krugman and Timothy Geithner, former treasury secretary of the US, addressed two of the conclaves. We invited some of the leading lights of our industry and reputed economists to come, discuss topics that were otherwise not often talked about. I remember two in particular. One was on the role of media in society, and the other on the reforms required in the judicial system. In both, we had eminent people from their respective fields come and give their views, so that the sessions would be unbiased and relevant. The economics research department also launched the SBI Monthly and Yearly Composite Index to gauge future economic activity, the first by a bank in India. All in all, we established thought leadership quite comprehensively.

While this was something I took pride in, I felt that our physical image too needed a lift. The Corporate Centre building was more than forty years old. The exterior was covered with small mosaic tiles that kept falling off – leading the building looking pockmarked – and required costly maintenance. It also posed a health hazard as the falling chips could hurt people, or dent cars at the very least. We had to put up ugly nets to prevent that. The real estate department came up with a smart solution. We simply decided to cement in the mosaics, and cover the whole thing with aluminium cladding. This was low maintenance (just needed the occasional washing) and was recyclable, so that when it was changed again in fifteen or twenty years, we would still get value for the metal sheets. On completion, the pristine lines of our building were restored. We replaced the forty-year-old doddering lifts and built vertical gardens on the pillars of the building's portico to create green spaces within. The auditorium too was in a state of disrepair. In fact, during one of the quarterly result press meets, a chunk of plaster fell off the ceiling. Thankfully, we didn't see a headline the next day saying 'SBI caves in'. One of the last ceremonies I presided over before retirement was to inaugurate the renovated auditorium.

The lack of any form of art in the Corporate Centre had always bothered me. I felt that somehow we were disdainful towards the softer and more beautiful aspects of life. As CDO, I had gone to Pratip Chaudhuri with a suggestion that we put aside some amount from the CSR fund to buy one masterpiece each year. This way we could promote art, support artists and also create a work environment that would incorporate creativity and beauty helping employees destress. The chairman asked me, 'You want to sleep well at night, don't you?' When I replied in the affirmative, he said, 'Well, then forget about this hare-brained plan.' I pressed the issue and he said, 'In case one of those paintings turn out to be a forgery, at some point you will lose your sleep for sure!' He had a point. Even if we appointed an external panel of experts, they could still make mistakes. So the plan was shelved for the time being.

After becoming chairman, I had an opportunity of visiting Jamshedpur to deliver the convocation address at XLRI. It was a great trip. Not only did I meet a group of bright young people, but the MD of Tata Steel was gracious enough to personally drive and provide me my first ride in a Jaguar. But the highlight was a visit to their Centre of Excellence. They had not only laid out beautifully the history of Tata Steel and Jamshedpur (we have a similar heritage museum in Kolkata, showcasing where it all started for SBI), but they also had a remarkable collection of paintings by the who's who of the Indian art world. When I checked, they said that they held art camps regularly and invited artists of repute to come and engage with each other, guide young artists and visit places that may inspire them. The artists left behind the beautiful artworks that were created at the camp. The concept appealed to me, and I decided to ask Prashant Kumar to study the model and replicate it. We did it, and I can say that today we have a small but exclusive collection of current masters and upcoming artists. Plus, our walls no longer look bare and forlorn.

Another initiative that I am particularly proud of was publishing two coffee-table books. The first was called *SBI's Living Heritage* (written and compiled by Abhik Ray), and told the story of our bank's origins and evolution through thirty-three heritage properties, each 100-plus years old and in two of which I have had the good fortune to reside. It covered other buildings such as Tarawali Kothi, which was the Nawab of Awadh's planetarium and in which we had the

Lucknow main branch and the CGM's residence, the Chennai CGM's residence on the banks of the Adyar River and the Chandni Chowk branch where the bullet holes dating back to the Uprising of 1857 are still preserved.

The other book is *Flow: India Through Water* (conceived and executed by Sunjoy Monga). The prime minister was kind enough to laud the effort in a message with the words: 'Jal hai to kal hai' (there's future only because of water). The book covered the various water resources of our nation, how they had been degraded, and what could be done to preserve and regenerate this precious source of life.

## The Subsidiaries

SBI had subsidiaries in most areas of financial services such as insurance, asset management, credit card and investment banking. Each of our earlier chairmen had a vision for how the group should grow. Most of these were well-run, board-managed companies, but seemed to lack ambition. One reason could be that SBI did not wholeheartedly support them, and maybe they felt that they were burdens rather than value creators. We had also often seen that the people who got posted as the CEOs of these companies were sometimes those who – though they were good performers – had differences with the then chairman, and so qualified for what was internally referred to as 'export quality'. This didn't make for a good story, and none of our subsidiaries was in the top three in their area of operations. I determined that this would change. I chose younger and really bright officers as CEOs, hoping to give them a long enough stint at the top job to really make a difference. I also chose some of our best performers, as I wanted them to transform their organizations, make it one of the top three in their area and create value for the parent company.

The recipe was sprucing up the organizations and bringing in the right talent. It meant getting in experienced and committed board members. It also meant far more collaboration with the parent organization, but with full compliance and firewalls in place. I wanted both sides to feel like they were in a win-win initiative. However, from the bank's side, we were quite clear that we would not be recommending their products unless they met the needs of our customers and showed superior performance, as in the fund performance in our asset management subsidiary. We laid a lot of emphasis on preventing mis-selling, including taking strong action if it came to our attention. But more than that we created processes that made mis-selling difficult. From rechecking with buyers to creating little handy booklets (also made available digitally) to check out and rate the SBI customer's risk appetite and suggestions on the right kinds of products for each risk category, to continuously upgrading employees' skills and dynamically rating the bank's offerings – we tried to take all the steps for these companies to view us as trusted partners.

The results became apparent soon. SBILife, led by Arijit Basu, became one of the leading life insurance companies, going on to become the first SBI subsidiary to list on the public markets in twenty-five years. Our asset management company, which was set on the path of growth by Dinesh Khara – the current SBI chairman – climbed to the third position when I retired from the six, where it had languished for ten long years (it has since gone on to become number one in India). Our SBI Cards, which had languished at the bottom of the pile since its inception, similarly strategized under the leadership of Pallav Mahapatra (recently retired from the position of MD of Central Bank) and rose to the second position. Most of the other companies showed far improved performances as well.

# 16

# Leading a Banking Behemoth

As the head of the largest bank in India, I got plenty of opportunities to meet with dignitaries in every walk of life. Be it in the government, regulators, business leaders or economists, I was able to meet many great minds of our time, listen and learn from them, share my experiences, and, in general, obtain a better understanding of the Indian economy, macroeconomic trends as well as industry trends.

When I became the chairman, the banking sector too was quite fragmented. The public sector bankers hardly ever pulled together with their peers in the private sector. Even within the public sector, the small and large banks had their differences. In a way, this was normal. There was bound to be competition within the industry, but there had to be a united face to push for reforms required in the sector. I tried my best to pull several groups together by articulating the issues that we faced collectively in the forums that I had the opportunity to attend. For example, at the first gathering of the public sector banks with the new government, I had the honour of presenting our views in favour of a level playing field and more enablement to the prime minister.

It was also at this forum that the prime minister promised the government wouldn't interfere in the workings of banks, while emphasizing the need for financial inclusion. The quarterly meetings with the finance ministry gave us an equally powerful forum to present our issues. We had frequent interactions with the regulators as well. The RBI governor would host a lunch before each Monetary Policy Committee meeting, and also had a summit of bankers and the media, which allowed for us to contribute to policymaking. He used to often joke about the frequency with which I sought various dispensations, but I think he meant it kindly as I did try to represent banking sector issues and asked for only those measures that I believed the sector needed to do well.

Being on the list of Fortune 500 Banks had its advantages. So did the fact that we had operations in thirty-six countries. The opportunity to meet regulators of various countries provided me with ideas and experiences that enriched my vision.

One of the instances that I remember was being surprised that a vibrant economy in South East Asia had a banking regulator that housed a business development unit. It was not only that they had this department, but that they would go out of their way to ensure ease of business. This country gave licenses for both banking and investment banking together. We wanted it separate, as in India these two activities were conducted in two separate entities, SBI and SBICaps. Once they understood our need, they pulled out all the stops to make sure we got separate licenses so that we could set up separate entities.

Similarly, I was full of admiration for the lady who headed one of the central banks in Europe. She was the first female governor of a central bank I'd ever met, and her unassuming manner coupled with her depth of knowledge and understanding impressed me hugely. It was also a learning for me to find that while some regulators wanted us to inform them of every single incident that may have a regulatory impact, others preferred us to wait till they called us.

The learnings from my interactions with some Nobel laureates, academicians and economists of international repute were exhilarating. Meetings with the leaders of the largest international banks and hearing their vision opened my mind to many new opportunities. The IMF and the World Bank meetings as well as the Davos meetings were excellent forums. While the IMF and the World Bank provided a meeting point for bankers globally, Davos was a meeting point for business and industry leaders.

Davos is a one-of-a-kind experience. While the panels had some of the foremost thinkers in the world participating in them, the beauty of the snow-covered slopes surrounding the tiny place were of picture-postcard quality. The place got so crowded during the meet that one had to book a room a whole year in advance. The rooms were quite tiny by developed world standards, and had furniture that seemed hewed out of rough logs. The first year I went, the room I was allotted had a large window beside the bed that faced a hill covered with pristine snow. The slope was dotted with skiers dressed in brilliant colours. A small ski lift went up and down, ferrying the skiers to the top of the slope. It looked like one of the pictures in the storybooks I had pored over as a child. The bathroom, however, was a whole other matter. One had to get into the bathtub to take a shower, which is the system in smaller hotels, but what I couldn't make out was how to operate the shower. There was only the one faucet and one set of knobs to set the temperature, but I couldn't find the one that operated the shower.

After trying everything I could think of, I rang the front desk and asked (feeling quite idiotic). One of the attendants came up immediately. He just pulled the faucet away from the wall and – lo and behold! – the shower began spewing water. I felt even more stupid for not thinking of doing that. I have been to numerous hotels but never had to ask for help to turn on the shower anywhere else. Though once in a while, I have sought help to find the hair dryer, which hotels seem to love to hide in the most unlikely places.

While the slopes surrounding Davos are beautiful, the streets turn slippery and slushy with melting snow on account of the heavy traffic. The Indian attire of a sari is quite unsuitable, as the ends get wet in the slush. Plus, it is bitterly cold and the sari is designed for warm, humid places. I learnt my lesson the first time and from the next time, stuck to western wear. On registering, one is given a pair of crampons to slip over one's footwear to prevent from slipping and falling. I was scared of precisely that happening, and breaking a bone or two. Having once broken my arm after slipping on ice, I detested the walk over ice to the venue after getting out of the car. But the worst was taking off the winterwear – of which one had to put on several layers in order to not turn into an icicle – going through security, putting it all on again to walk across the open courtyard within the inner perimeter, in the bitter cold, and then shucking them off again to enter the venue.

I longed for my warm country, where one could throw on a short-sleeved dress and a pair of slippers before stepping out. But the people I met at the event made up for these small inconveniences. One met and heard and exchanged views with the who's who of the world. One bumped into celebrities at every corner, and the opportunity one could create by talking on panels at the event did raise one's profile. I often found, however, an attitude about emerging markets that distressed me. Understanding about our country remains low and, in my mind, I would often classify the people I met into three categories – those who thought of us as a land of snake charmers and gurus, those who consider us a nation of software engineers, and those who were better informed, though the numbers were minimal in this category.

I also found an ambivalent attitude to initiatives like financial inclusion (FI). While many paid lip service to it, few were really willing to put their money where their mouth was. I especially remember a conference organized by Bloomberg on the sidelines of the UN General Assembly session. The audience had a number of investment bankers and private equity players. A few speakers had already talked about FI when my turn came. I spoke about the efforts of the Indian government and the banking sector to bring about effective FI by leveraging the India stack and the JAM trinity. All were most impressed. But when I asked why the valuation of the banks undertaking these activities were being discounted as a result of such initiatives, there was no answer. Some muttered that shareholder/investor returns had to be thought of – and therein lies the crux of the matter. All of us are looking for short-term gains and results, ignoring the long-term benefits. And unless that mindset changes, the division between the haves and have-nots will continue to widen.

It was probably as a result of such exposure that I started appearing on *Forbes'* list of the Most Powerful Women in the World. I entered it at the thirty-sixth position in 2014 (my first full year in office) and ended at the twenty-fifth position in 2016 (my last full year as chairman of SBI). The first time it happened, I was in London when the list got published. A friend called up and asked me to check it out. I was tickled pink, as I was in London and the Queen was just ahead of me. I was quite delighted and messaged Pritimoy, who promptly replied: 'She will be on that list for life, whereas you will be off it in three years as soon as you retire.' That brought me back to reality super quick. My family, as always, helped me stay grounded. I also appeared on *Forbes'* 2016 Most Powerful Women in Finance at the fifth position, and in *Fortune's* 2016 list of Top 50 Globally Most Powerful Women in Business and among the top five in the Asia-Pacific Region. What pleased me even more, though, was being listed as one of the Top 100 Thinkers in 2014 by *Foreign Policy* (one of the two Indians featured that year) and twenty-sixth in *Fortune's* 2017 World's 50 Greatest Leaders (the only Indian featured in the list that year). All of these made me realize one thing – that it was important to use my voice to give expression to the thousands of voiceless women and, hopefully, this is something that I will effectively achieve one day.

## Did I Make a Difference as a Leader?

This is a question I have often asked myself. For one, I did ensure that women would cease feeling frozen (quite literally) in the boardroom. For as long as I could remember, I was always uncomfortably cold in the boardroom, where the temperature was set at a point where men in suits and ties felt comfortable. But for women clad in saris it was deeply uncomfortable, and I refused to give up wearing the lovingly hand-crafted saris that I wore to work. I became so used to cupping the hot cup of tea to thaw my cold hands that it's become a habit, and I can barely drink tea in any other manner now. So on becoming chairman, I thought I needed to assert myself on behalf of the women in the boardroom and requested my male colleagues to leave their coats and ties behind in their rooms. Those who didn't perforce had to do so during the meeting, as the air conditioning provided an ambient temperature that was suitable for those used to the Indian weather.

On a more serious note, while I strictly promoted on merit, I ensured that the unconscious bias that many had against women was kept firmly at bay and the boardroom soon wore a more diverse look. Not a single one of the women I promoted faltered at their responsibilities, amply proving how deserving they were as candidates. One of those, as I mentioned earlier, is today the CFO of the World Bank and another just received the Best Banker Award this year as the MD of another bank. All of this further attests the potential of women. While I tried to ensure this at every level, I don't believe that I was entirely successful. Nor could I put in place a formal mentoring programme for women, though informally many did find mentors.

For example, the year before I retired, I found that not a single woman appeared on the list of India-based officials who were being posted abroad. When I asked Siddharth Sengupta, DMD, he said that very few women had applied for these positions in the first place. This got me seriously worried and I amended his KRAs to include mentoring women and enthusing them to take up these challenges, so that in the coming years at least one third of the list would comprise women candidates. The next set of promotions happened after my retirement, but Siddharth rang me up to confirm that he had fulfilled his KRA and that more than one third of that year's list were women.

I also recommended to the board a two-year sabbatical for women employees for child and elderly care, resulting in a lot of headwind, including someone suggesting that I was perpetuating stereotypes. I considered the observation, but determined that given the realities of the situation, I could only term this as 'affirmative action'. When I took stock two years later, I had probably saved the careers of 600-plus women. I especially remember one of them. She came up to me and, clasping my hands, thanked me. When I looked at her questioningly, she explained, 'My mother-in-law was very unwell and I couldn't bring myself to leave her with an attendant. Earlier I would have had no other option other than to put in my papers. But I availed a year's sabbatical now. Unfortunately, my mother-in-law passed away within three months and I have rejoined work. My twenty-year-long career would have been lost, but for this facility that the bank gave me.' I later extended this to single men as well, as they had the same issues. The other women-centric initiatives I put in place were introducing free cervical cancer vaccines, creating joint living spaces for the female staff serving in rural areas and ensuring that we appointed either a gynaecologist or paediatrician at each of the LHOs so that women could get medical support in their offices.

Another area where I used all my persuasive powers was to convince the government to give two Saturdays off each month, while making the other two full working days. This was already being negotiated as part of the Eleventh Bipartite Settlement. It did not change the hours worked by any employee, but reduced stress hugely. My thoughts were for those colleagues who worked in rural areas, where the family couldn't accompany them. They would visit their families over the weekend, but many could spend only a few hours at home after completing the half-day they needed to work each Saturday. I was also thinking of the women who would be working right through each of their Sundays, catching up on domestic chores and returning to work on Monday mornings, more exhausted than rested. For all such people, two weeks with two days off would be a big boon. So I pleaded with the government to allow this as part of the bipartite industry-wide settlement. The secretary, DFS agreed and this was implemented.

I often feel that I could have done much more, but I can only hope that I at least smoothened the path a little for those who would come after me.

## My Untiring Cheerleaders

Through all of this, how was my family faring? Sukrita had completed her class twelve through NIOS in 2013. We were wondering what to do next when colleagues in Bengaluru, who had helped out with her education for so long, suggested that we try Sikkim Manipal Open University. I took her over to Bengaluru, and they felt that given her comfort with a computer, she would be able to complete her bachelor's degree in business administration, as the exams were online and there was sufficient study material on the site to help her get through. We thought it was a great solution and admitted her to the course. I had been able to help her up to the completion of her school studies, but now, with the chairman's responsibilities, I was finding it increasingly difficult. My whole day at the office was spent in either internal or customer meetings. I would be in the office by 10 a.m. and could only return home by 9–9.30 p.m. We would finish dinner by half past ten and then after a half-hour break, I would need to get back to the two large briefcases (they were small suitcases, actually) full of files that accompanied me home every day.

I think we are the only company in the world that had weekly meetings of the executive committee of the board, the quorum for which, besides full-time directors, required a minimum of two independent directors. As we were never sure who could attend, we invited all, so most days it appeared like a full board meeting. In spite of the high frequency, we often had in excess of twenty-five agenda items to go through each week. All these papers, and the very many files besides, had to be read and disposed of. In the four years that I was chairman, I rarely went to sleep before 1 a.m. and always got up at 6.30 a.m. And this was only if I didn't have an early flight to catch, which was often – in which case, I would be up at 4 a.m. I could see that I was not devoting enough hours for Sukrita's studies as I had done earlier. I had also admitted her to a school that taught students like her life skills and some work skills. She was learning how to work in an office on account of her comfort with a desktop. Most of her classmates had borderline issues, so she could vibe well with them. She was also the only girl in her class, and so was a little spoilt by the attention that her classmates heaped on her.

Her days were quite full. She would attend school from 8.30 a.m. to 3.00 p.m. On her return, she would take a quick nap before her tutor arrived around 5 p.m. She was free after 7 p.m., but she refused to study on her own, and so the time thereafter was spent with the TV and her mobile phone. No amount of exhortations to study a little more seemed to work.

On top of that, I had to travel quite a bit. One of the longest trips I took as chairman was for ten days. I was getting ready in front of the mirror when she came into my room and watched me intently as I dressed. Seeing her watching me closely, I tried to gauge whether she was upset. When I couldn't make out what she was thinking, I asked whether she could manage without me. With a serious, adult look on her face, she retorted, 'I have been managing since I was five, and you are asking me now?' The retort brought a smile to my lips – my little one was growing up – but also a wave of guilt washed over me as I questioned my image in the mirror as to whether I was doing the right thing. And then Pritimoy stepped in to help. He decided to retire and move permanently to Mumbai.

While I was hugely relieved that I would no longer have to leave Sukrita and her caretaker by themselves in the huge chairman's bungalow with its drawing room, piano room, dining room, billiards room and bedrooms, each the size of a small Mumbai apartment, I was also apprehensive about how Pritimoy would adjust to retirement and how he would connect with Sukrita. Luckily, he adjusted very well. He had always been happy with his mobile phone and his laptop and his unending desire to learn about the advances in IT, and this kept him well occupied. He wrote an occasional poem of which I was always the first reader, and he took my inputs with good grace.

During earlier times, when Sukrita was in school, he had been unable to connect with her in the area of studies. He just lost his patience. He couldn't understand why she couldn't follow what he was saying. Having taught IITians, the gap was too wide. But this time, things seemed to get better. Father and daughter sat down with their iPads, quizzing each other. They developed their own way of learning by competing – for the subjects were new for Pritimoy too. On my birthday in 2017, I got the best gift of my life. At midnight, father and daughter crept up behind me and placed a printout on the file I was perusing. It was her college result, declaring the completion of her bachelor's degree!

## Four Years Pass in a Flash

It was 6 October 2017, my last day in office. I took a minute to look around my room – the place where I had spent the maximum number of waking hours over the last four years. I had shifted my desk to face the windows – the sky and the sea, and, dead in the centre of my vision, the RBI building. Every time I looked up from my desk, there it was, reminding me of the duties I needed to perform. I hoped I had done it well. I went into the boardroom one last time. I looked at the seat I used to occupy as a DMD and then as an MD. Did I ever think then that I would sit at the head of the table? I remembered the day I first took the chairman's seat. I had been a little surprised that it hadn't felt very different. Except that I had felt the weight of expectations – my own expectations from myself. Had I done justice to those? Maybe the rows of portraits of past chairmen that hung on the walls could give me a truthful answer. I looked at them, sombrely, looking on in their blue, grey and black suits. I had deliberately worn a flame-red sari for my portrait. It now hung at the end of the row. Did it look out of place there? But the people in the other pictures were smiling, so maybe I hadn't done too badly and just maybe they didn't mind my company after all.

I thought back to what had been my most difficult job in my years as chairman, and I realized it was changing people's perception. I hoped that I had succeeded, at least partly, to make a difference to our stakeholders and mainly our customers' perception, and show them that we were a giant in our industry. I wanted to showcase the potential and resilience of this iconic institution, and its ability to evolve. And lastly, I wanted to prove that a woman could do this job just as well as a man. I hoped I had created awareness of the need for a strong technology backbone and an awareness of never undertaking anything before fully understanding the risks involved. I also hoped I had changed our employees' mindset to fearlessly experiment, even if it meant to fail. That way they could learn from the process. I wanted all the bank's employees to keep the customers firmly at the centre of all our strategies and activities so as to continuously address their pains and needs, to shift the focus to outside-in rather than the other way around and to collaborate rather than work in silos; to work with various stakeholders in the ecosystem and uphold our values of trust and integrity. I aimed to create a safe and nurturing atmosphere that would make our employees eager to come to work and to constantly innovate, innovate, innovate. I firmly believed it was the only way for any organization to survive in this uncertain and swiftly evolving environment, and I hoped I had been able to set an agenda on those lines for the days to come.

In a way, I had scaled my personal mountain, but, in my mind's eye, as I looked out at the horizon and saw the various peaks, big and small, that stretched out before me, I knew that there were other challenges that I would face, other obstacles I would have to overcome. I prayed that the grace I have always received would continue to surround me as I walked away from this great institution into an unknown future.

# Acknowledgements

This missive is incomplete without my expressing my gratitude to all those who made this book possible.

The first part, I dedicate to my parents, Prodyut and Kalyani, my aunt, Parbati, my siblings, Aditi and Amit, and my countless childhood, school and college friends.

My middle years were made wonderful by my spouse, Pritimoy, and my daughter Sukrita. I must also thank my support system of friends, who gave me their unflinching support and encouragement without which this journey would have been cut short much earlier.

The last part of this book I would like to dedicate to my colleagues from my earliest assignment to the last – much of what I received credit for were the fruits of their hard work, dedication and enthusiastic participation.

I am also especially thankful to my colleagues and friends Manjira Sen, Atul Kumar, Indrajit Gupta, Deepak Thakkar, Sunil Srivastava, Mrityunjay Mahapatra and Indrani Sengupta. They willingly spent time going through the text, giving me valuable inputs, pointing out over-long pieces and reminding me of some notable incidents that I had forgotten about. I also need to thank my colleagues Anuradha Rao, Padmaja Chunduru, Geeta Narsimhan and Aveek Ray for their contribution and for jogging my memory about some conversations and events that I have included in the book.

There are so many people who aided my journey, be it our caretakers, Buddhi Ma in Kharagpur or Sulekha, who is still with us. Friends such as Jayanti and Raj Chatterjee, Shree Atul Kumar and umpteen others who supplemented my role as a mother. I must also mention all of my daughter's teachers – I owe them all.

Lastly, I want to thank all my teachers in school and college. At first, I felt that the fact I had studied English Literature had absolutely no bearing on my banking career. It was much later that I realized that it laid the foundation of my communication skills, which, over time, I found invaluable in my contribution to my workplace. I must specially mention Rev. Fr. John Moore and Fr. Tom Keogh, the principal and vice principal of my school, who believed that I had a flair for writing. I hope they take this book as a homage to their belief in me.

Of course, I must give thanks to Sachin Sharma of HarperCollins India who believed I could write this book, and never lost faith in the face of all my doubts.

As they say, 'It takes a village' – and it is true! I have missed many names here, but they all hold a special place in my heart and have my eternal gratitude.

# About the Author

**Arundhati Bhattacharya** is best known as the first woman to chair the State Bank of India (SBI), a 210-year-old institution, India's largest bank and a Fortune 500 company.

She was born in Kolkata, and grew up in the steel cities of Bhilai and Bokaro. Youngest of three siblings, she studied at the Bhilai Project School and then at St. Xavier's School at Bokaro Steel City. She completed her graduation with honours in English literature from Lady Brabourne College at Kolkata and obtained her postgraduate degree from Jadavpur University, also in Kolkata.

Under her leadership SBI metamorphosed into a customer-centric, digitally advanced bank while continuing to play a pivotal role in national development.

During her career Arundhati has displayed a deep understanding of and insights into financial services, particularly of the banking industry and related areas of digital banking.

Under her leadership SBI was adjudged as one of three best places to work in India, by a global job site based on 15 million reviews surveyed on the basis of overall employees' experience.

During her tenure as chairman of SBI, she introduced an industry-first practice of a two-year sabbatical leave for female employees, for the care of children or the aged.

She has earned many awards and recognitions including being ranked twenty-fifth in the list of most powerful women in the world and fifth most powerful woman in finance by *Forbes.* She was included in the Top 100 Global Thinkers in 2014 by *Foreign Policy* magazine. She also featured in the *Fortune* List of Top 50 Globally Most Powerful Women in Business and was ranked amongst the top five in the Asia Pacific region. Further, she was ranked twenty-sixth in the fourth edition of *Fortune's* 50 Greatest Leaders, becoming the only Indian corporate leader to be featured in the list.

On retirement in October 2017, the government nominated Arundhati to a few select committees such as the Lokpal Search Committee, Padma Awardees Selection Committee, National Coal Index Committee and SEBI's Mutual Fund Advisory Committee.

After completing the one-year gardening leave as per government policy, she became an independent board member in six companies, some of which are the largest in India. She was also a part-time consultant in five renowned companies, including AZB & Partners, Warburg PIncus, Chrys Capital, Bain Consultancy and was on the International Advisory Committee of Standard Chartered Bank.

Arundhati has also been associated with various institutions and initiatives for empowering the challenged and differently abled with the aim of integrating them in our society.

Currently she is the chairperson and CEO of Salesforce India, a cloud based SaaS company, listed in the USA and headquartered in San Francisco.